On Audrey Hepburn

On Audrey Hepburn

An Opinionated Guide

STEVEN COHAN

OXFORD
UNIVERSITY PRESS

Oxford University Press is a department of the University of Oxford. It furthers
the University's objective of excellence in research, scholarship, and education
by publishing worldwide. Oxford is a registered trade mark of Oxford University
Press in the UK and certain other countries.

Published in the United States of America by Oxford University Press
198 Madison Avenue, New York, NY 10016, United States of America.

© Oxford University Press 2024

All rights reserved. No part of this publication may be reproduced, stored in
a retrieval system, or transmitted, in any form or by any means, without the
prior permission in writing of Oxford University Press, or as expressly permitted
by law, by license, or under terms agreed with the appropriate reproduction
rights organization. Inquiries concerning reproduction outside the scope of the
above should be sent to the Rights Department, Oxford University Press, at the
address above.

You must not circulate this work in any other form
and you must impose this same condition on any acquirer.

CIP data is on file at the Library of Congress

ISBN 978–0–19–766828–3

DOI: 10.1093/oso/9780197668283.001.0001

Printed by Sheridan Books, Inc., United States of America

Contents

Acknowledgments	vii
Introduction	1
1. The Life	20
2. The Career	28
3. The Audrey Films	58
4. Fashion	90
5. Thrillers	119
6. The Actress	150
Conclusion	190
Notes	201
Works Cited	203
Index	207

Acknowledgments

I want to thank Will Scheibel for carefully reading the manuscript and offering insightful suggestions that made it better, and Karen McNally for our indispensable conversations about Audrey Hepburn, other actresses, and stardom. Both are very good friends, too. I should also take this moment to thank the anonymous readers for Oxford University Press of my proposal and manuscript for their valuable feedback. I also wish to thank my fellow panelists—Julie Grossman, Kristen Hatch, and David Greven—for their helpful responses at the Society of Cinema and Media Studies conference where I presented on Audrey Hepburn's performance in *The Nun's Story*, and David Lugowski in particular for our conversation about Barthes and the Garbo piece during and after the panel. Roger Hallas and Matt Fee were especially interested in and supportive of my work on Hepburn. Let me thank, too, a number of other people for their friendship and conversations about Hepburn, stardom, or film along the way: Andrea Scheibel, Mike Goode, Jolynn Parker, Karen Hall, Vanessa Watts, Matt Zych, T. J. West, Ina Hark, Paula Masood, Sean Griffin, Adrienne McLean, Alan Nadel, Harry Benshoff, Merrill Schleier, Desirée Garcia, Barbara Klinger, and Pamela Wojcik. My sister and her family—Shari, Roman, and Alex—deserve my heartfelt thanks too. A very special thanks to Linda Shires for listening to me talk movies and books all these many years—and for being a great friend. Let me take a moment as well to thank the staff of Interlibrary Loans at Syracuse University's Bird Library for helping me locate articles on Hepburn, and to express my appreciation to Eric Hoyt and his collegues for the invaluable Media History Digital Library, a treasure trove of fan magazines and trade papers along with other industry-related materials, which aided my research. I owe thanks to my editor, Norm Hirschy, for his advice and support, and for the kind and attentive people at the press who have shepherded my book to publication.

I was lucky to grow up in a family immersed in movie culture. When I was young, my parents, who have both passed, went to the movies almost every Saturday evening (when they weren't playing cards), and I usually went to see the same films the next day in the afternoon. We watched movies on TV all the time—the early show, the late show, the Sunday night movie, the Monday night movie, you name it. My grandmother took me to movies downtown, and she dated a projectionist for several years, so once or twice as a youngster I got to watch a film from the projection booth at the Rhodes Theatre on the South Side of Chicago. Movie magazines were always in our house; we moved to Los Angeles when I was fourteen, and I added *Variety* to the pile, which my mom eagerly read after I had finished each week's issue. I therefore dedicate this book to my late parents, Albert and Lillian Cohan, and the pleasure they took in moviegoing, which they instilled in me as I grew up.

Introduction

Why write a book on Audrey Hepburn? And an opinionated one at that? I don't think people's memories have served her well. Today, many fans recall Hepburn for her distinctive and regal look, especially as it resonated from her close identification with Parisian couture. This recollection views Hepburn primarily as a fashion icon and an inspiration for an elegant style. I believe that this memory now overshadows her career as an actress. It discounts the energy and dynamism she projected on-screen, just as it downplays the contradictions embedded in her Cinderella movies, gamine persona, and untypical body (by Hollywood standards of her era). It ignores how, as opposed to the many photographs of her, fashion operated in her films to signify motion and transformation, not stasis. And that memory looks past the historical context and hence importance of her emergence as a new young female star in the 1950s.

So for starters, let me confess that, as an avid moviegoer first during my adolescence and then as a high school student when Hepburn was a big star, I was always fascinated by the sound of her *voice*. At the time I didn't know what intrigued me exactly. There was a musical lilt to her speech, and I found her melodic voice enchanting in its suggestion of youthful innocence and wonder, but also in its implications of cultural difference and unconventionality. Hepburn did not speak with the mid-Atlantic accent common to most Hollywood stars of her era. Yet she didn't really sound very European, although she often played a character who was not or not quite American. Many of her films are either partly or entirely set in Paris, so Hepburn was closely identified with the City of Light, too, which further distanced her from other new English-speaking Hollywood stars of the 1950s. As Donald Spoto comments in his biography of Hepburn, "No other voice could be mistaken for hers" (2006: 22).

Of course, I now know that Hepburn's voice betrayed a slight accent because English was not her only language. Audrey Kathleen van Heemstras Ruston was born in Brussels on May 4, 1929, to Ella van Heemstras, a Dutch baroness, and James Ruston, a Bohemian-born ne'er-do-well and adventurer with a British father. The couple had met in the Dutch East Indies. Because Audrey's father was a British subject, she was born a British citizen. Ruston claimed to work in finance but could not hold down a steady job. During the first years of Audrey's life the family moved back and forth between London and cities in the Netherlands and Brussels. According to one biographer, Audrey's mother hyphenated "Hepburn" (the maiden name of Ruston's maternal grandmother) to her married surname to sound more aristocratic (Paris 1996: 6). According to another biographer, Audrey's father legally added it to his surname after the end of World War II to sound more "posh" (Spoto 2006: 10). Both accounts are probably true. Ruston had deserted the family in 1935 when Audrey was six, and her mother eventually obtained a divorce. Afterward, Audrey went to boarding school in England, then with her mother to the family estate in the Netherlands a short time before the Nazi occupation of the Low Countries. Before and during the war, her father was an active supporter of fascism in Britain and was interred for several years on the Isle of Man; her mother likewise had initially been swayed by the fascist cause but, seeing the devastation caused by the Nazis in her homeland, turned against their regime and worked with the Dutch resistance. After the war's end, Audrey returned to England with a scholarship to pursue a career in dance under the tutelage of Marie Rambert. At this time she dropped "Ruston" from her hyphenated surname and was henceforth known as "Audrey Hepburn."

Audrey was schooled in Britain in her early years, and the lasting evidence of her instruction there in English is the way she pronounced *ar* and *er* as "ah." During the Nazi occupation, however, Audrey was told to speak only Dutch to avoid being identified as British. Later, as an adult she also spoke flawless French and Italian. She herself stated that she had "no mother tongue" because her "ear has never been accustomed to one intonation," which she thought was the reason why some critics complained of her "curious speech" (quoted in Spoto 2006: 21). Furthermore, although Hepburn was Belgian born and spent her teen years in Holland, she held a British passport and was called a British actress in obituaries and encyclopedias; and although she made many films in France and lived in Rome during her second marriage, her longtime homes were in Switzerland.

Nonetheless, all this biographical information does not dampen *my* memory of the enchanting effect of her voice.

Audrey Hepburn's voice, I think, was a central component of her appeal as a movie star, although by now this element has usually been forgotten. But not always. Andrew Niccol's *S1m0ne* (2002) is a Hollywood satire in which Viktor Taransky (Al Pacino), frustrated by the diva behavior of a female star whose whims take precedence over his artistic ambitions, uses a software program, Simulation One, to fashion a simulated star composed of bits and pieces of actual stars. Fine-tuning his creation, "Simone," by tweaking her voice, he tells the image on his computer screen, "There's a little something I want to add to your repertoire. Remember that thing that Audrey Hepburn does in *Breakfast at Tiffany's*? Give me Audrey." "That thing" is the distinctive way that Hepburn asks George Peppard in this 1961 film, "How do I *look*?" She inflects her query as if it were a musical lyric, stressing the last word to end the question on a high note. In fact, the characteristic rhythm of her diction typically stressed the end of a sentence when she wished to emphasize it, with her voice going up on the accented last word or two.

I am no physiologist, but I know that vocalization is not an inert phenomenon. A voice is formed by the brain through its coordination of the motion of the tongue and the mouth as the body engages the larynx and vocal cords, and it also requires breath support from the respiratory system, expanding and contracting the chest as the windpipe takes in air and lets it out. Moreover, to utter a sentence creates a rhythm that gives phrasing its cadence, which, in addition to the specific sounds formed, is what makes a person's voice unique. If Marilyn Monroe had been cast as Holly Golightly, as was Truman Capote's own choice for the film adaptation of his novella, she would have asked, "How do I look?" more breathlessly, giving the question a different "little something" through her delivery.

Physiologically speaking, too, vocalization is a form of *motion* even if the actor otherwise remains still. Whether recorded on set or looped in afterward, speech creates an illusion of the actor's embodiment, giving the filmed two-dimensional image a virtual sense of three-dimensional visual and sonic depth. Her distinctive voice is why Hepburn's performance, while nuanced in her book scenes, makes her numbers in *My Fair Lady* (1964) fall flat; they ring falsely to my ears whenever she opens her mouth and out pours Marni Nixon's soprano. True, Hepburn does an impressive job of miming the lyrics, but all the expressiveness in her numbers comes from her face and body, not her voice, which seems disaggregated from her movement. Since Nixon's voice is higher and lighter than Hepburn's mezzo, and the dubber does not match the accents Hepburn uses to convey Eliza's transformation from a "gutter snipe" into a "proper lady," whenever Eliza begins to sing it sounds like Hepburn has swallowed a songbird.

Speech and the sound of her voice are essential to Hepburn's acting in her best and lackluster films alike, underlying her charismatic presence on-screen. On film, moreover, an actor's face is rarely static even though she may not be speaking; more so than the voice, the face is the screen star's valuable and indispensable instrument. When discussing *The Nun's Story* (1959) with its director,

Fred Zinnemann, Arthur Nolletti Jr. observed, "Audrey Hepburn's face is so expressive that you can read what she's thinking" (Nolletti 1994: 23). Along with her voice, Hepburn's face was not only expressive, as I discuss in later chapters, but distinctive, unlike the more common Anglo-American features of other young actresses to emerge at the same time. She had a relatively square head, a long nose with a bump, hazel eyes shaped like almonds, bushy brows, a dazzling, wide smile, and a long, swanlike neck. However, as Gary Cooper says in *Love in the Afternoon* (1957) after Hepburn's character, Ariane, lists those same odd features for him, "Yet it all hangs together."

Indeed, it does! George Cukor, Hepburn's director on *My Fair Lady*, has observed about movie stars, "It's a mysterious question, what makes them photogenic. I think it's very often the flesh quality. They're made so the light can come into their eyes and the face moves well. It's a very mysterious thing" (Basinger and Wasson 2022: 377). People have always mentioned, for instance, how Marilyn Monroe's flesh seemed to glow on celluloid. In Hepburn's case, it was not only the flesh quality but also the particular bone structure of her face that made her so photogenic on-screen; this was especially the case when she smiled widely, as she frequently did in her romantic comedies, and her face had lost some of the youthful roundness one can still see signs of at times in *Roman Holiday* (1953).

Along with her melodic voice, her having an unusual face that was both photogenic *and* deeply expressive was another source of Hepburn's on-screen charisma. She came to the Hollywood studio system when it was still functioning as it had since the advent of sound, though signs of its dismantling were already evident, and she was one of the last female stars with a distinctive face that was not traditionally pretty but whose beauty was singular: think Barbara Stanwyck, Joan Crawford, Bette Davis, Claudette Colbert, Marlene Dietrich, Katharine Hepburn, and others of an earlier era with unique faces that caught light and shadows so brilliantly, especially on black-and-white film. Yet Audrey Hepburn's face, like her thin body, slightly accented and musical speech, and her screen persona, was very much of her own time.

When *Roman Holiday* opened, Hearst gossip columnist Louella Parsons titled her review for *Cosmopolitan*, "Audrey Hepburn— Greatest Since Garbo?" In Parsons's commentary about Hepburn's debut, which kept her "spellbound," that was a rhetorical question (1953: 10). Parsons was not alone in thinking of the two stars together. As it happened, in the mid-1950s and on the other side of the Atlantic in France, Roland Barthes wrote in "Garbo's Face," one of his monthly magazine columns, that Audrey Hepburn's face is "an Event," unlike Greta Garbo's face, which he stated is "an Idea." For whereas he saw the Swedish star's face as being archetypal and ephemeral, Hepburn's face, he wrote in closing his piece, "is individualized not only by its specific thematics (woman-as-child, woman-as-cat), but also by her person, by a virtually unique specification of the face." Barthes concluded, "As a language, Garbo's singularity was of a conceptual order," whereas Hepburn's was "of a substantial order" (2012: 74–75).

Barthes's short essay, reprinted in his book *Mythologies*, is by now canonical among theorists of film and popular culture, so it is worth musing upon. Did he mean that Hepburn's face therefore signified with less resonance or value than Garbo's or that it signified differently? Probably, since his piece celebrates how Garbo's face "represents that fragile moment when cinema is about to extract an existential beauty from an essential beauty," and she becomes "a lyric expression of Woman" (74), Barthes meant the former meaning. Even so, his comparison refers to different standards of film stardom at the historical juncture when each woman became a big star. Despite the relative ease with which she transitioned to talkies, Garbo's face crystalized as a "concept," as "an Idea," in the silent era when female stars were viewed as (and fashioned by their studios to signify) ephemeral, larger-than-life goddesses. Hepburn's "virtually unique specification of the face, which has nothing essential left in it" (75), may therefore have seemed to Barthes to be more "individualized" and "specific" because she was filmed and photographed to appear "substantial," which is to say, mortal and earthbound, emphasized all the more by her slim frame and gamine ("woman-as-child, woman-as-cat") screen persona.

Garbo's face, according to Barthes, is a mask that occludes interiority, producing "a sort of Platonic ideal of the human creature" (74), whereas Hepburn's face expresses interiority, as Nolletti appreciated in his comment about her subtle, nuanced performance in *The Nun's Story*. Barthes's brief comments about Hepburn, in fact, allude to the historical specificity of her rapid rise to stardom in 1953. Noa Steimatsky explains that what concerned Barthes in "Garbo's Face" was the postwar shift "from the classical stars' ultra-face to a low-mythological order of accessible interiority," which coincided "with cinema's representation of the historical emancipation of women." Standing for the polar opposite of Garbo in Barthes's piece, Hepburn is the "modernized, secularized, particularized" star of postwar Hollywood who, in contrast with the Swedish diva, is "no longer a forbidding, hieratic image." For Barthes, in short, "the Idea" is "mythological," and "the Event" is "history" (Steimatsky 2017: 128–29).

But as Steimatsky asks, albeit rhetorically, by the early 1950s wasn't Garbo herself already "history" (2017: 129)? When Barthes wrote his piece, Garbo had been living in relative seclusion in Manhattan for many years, whereas Hepburn had recently had her star-making roles in *Roman Holiday* and *Sabrina* (1954). As Barthes recognized about Garbo, "The Essence has gradually dimmed, progressively veiled by dark glasses, hooded capes, and various exiles; but it has never altered" (74). Yet doesn't it follow from that perspective that, as it "dimmed," her "Essence" *did* alter insofar as Garbo's mythological face became more of a *historical* "Idea"? After all, her reclusive post-stardom life made Garbo the Goddess an absence, a memory, despite an occasional showing of one of her films in a Parisian repertory cinema. By contrast, at that very moment, Hepburn was very much "an Event," a palpable presence in cinemas and the European and American press. If Garbo was the historical past at this time, Hepburn was the historical present, and her bursting into stardom in 1953 had very much to do with postwar tastes.

Events imply the movement of people in time, and motion—of her face, her body, her voice—was still another basis of Hepburn's charisma on-screen, just as it was central to her performances, as this book will discuss at various points. But Hepburn as pure image was equally important, too, of course. Her relation to haute couture fashion gave her entire body its value as "an Event" but also as "an Idea" in its own right—the idea of a glamorous style in the 1950s that combined clothes, a thin body, and an elegant deportment. During her lifetime Hepburn was already considered a fashion icon, and this status has only intensified through time. Her glamorous image was due to a longtime collaboration on- and off-screen with designer Hubert de Givenchy, which began with her second Hollywood film, *Sabrina*. Discussions of *Sabrina* usually note the odd circumstance that Edith Head, who ran the costume department at Paramount, received the sole screen credit and the Oscar for Hepburn's clothes in the film (accepting the award, she thanked the presenters off-mic and strolled offstage), although the three outfits designed by Givenchy were what immediately stood out at the time of the film's release. Thereafter, Givenchy would design clothes for Hepburn on many of her films, such as *Funny Face* (1957), *Love in the Afternoon*, *Breakfast at Tiffany's*, *Charade* (1963), *Paris When It Sizzles* (1964), and *How to Steal a Million* (1966).

To be sure, fashion had already been firmly associated with female stars from earlier periods, when they were glamorously dressed by studio designers like Adrian at MGM and Travis Banton at Paramount. Nor was Hepburn the only star in the 1950s known for her spectacular clothes. Grace Kelly in *Rear Window* (1954) and *To Catch a Thief* (1955) and Doris Day in *Pillow Talk* (1959) and *Midnight Lace* (1960), to name two, also sported one fashionable outfit after another on-screen. But in contrast with those two stars, haute couture has adhered to Hepburn as her primary attraction. I therefore do not mean to disregard the role fashion played for her stardom. Hepburn's ultra-thin body stood out in contrast to the voluptuousness of the other major English-speaking female movie stars who came to prominence in the 1950s, notably Marilyn Monroe and Elizabeth Taylor. While Hepburn's costuming may have emphasized her femininity, her very slender figure, five feet seven height, flat chest, and pixie haircut connoted a boyish or androgynous body. Her gamine appearance would have been perfectly suitable for a live-action version of *Peter Pan* or a remake of the other Hepburn's *Sylvia Scarlett* (1935). Indeed, George Cukor had wanted to direct Audrey as the Boy Who Wouldn't Grow Up, but the project never came to pass. At one point, after making *War and Peace* (1956) she may have had discussions to play Napoleon's son in *L'Aiglon* for William Wyler, and that project never happened either (Jones 1956: 106).

Hepburn's unusual features were inconsistent with the bosomy look of other new and popular actresses from Europe like Brigitte Bardot, Sophia Loren, and Gina Lollobrigida, or of the various Monroe and Taylor imitators from Britain and America whose flash burned brightly for a moment before flickering out, but that made Hepburn's introduction to audiences in *Roman Holiday* all the more exciting as a revelation. Additionally, as Gaylyn Studlar reports, the French fashion industry "did not depend on an American model. It made the physical ideal of the French mannequin—long, slender neck; slim-waisted body; and long legs—the increasingly desired physical type for fashionable clothes" (2013: 211). Hepburn's uncommon body suited that French standard; this was another reason she was always not quite American even when playing someone from the United States. As Studlar observes, Hepburn's distinctive look was quickly commodified. "Throughout 1955 numerous models resembling Hepburn could be seen in fashion features and advertisements in *Vogue* displaying dark, cropped hair, swan-like necks, thick eyebrows, thin bodies, and wide-eyed youthfulness" (210).

Of course, not everyone admired Hepburn's unorthodox body. I recall a high school friend's mother muttering, when this star's name came up in conversation, that Hepburn was "*painfully* thin," a phrase my friend would repeat many times, usually with irony. Because of her association with high fashion, it is no exaggeration to say that Hepburn's body influenced the ultra-skinny look and gamine qualities of 1960s supermodels Twiggy and Jean Shrimpton (aka "The Shrimp"). Nor do I think it is much of a stretch to call Hepburn's body a very "mid-century modern" one. Like that European style of furniture and architecture, which became popular in the 1950s and is a definitive postwar style, her figure was angular, oddly shaped, organic in its association with naturalness, not very cushioned due to its thinness, and a flat surface. One scholar, in fact, has shown the extent to which *Funny Face*, like the fashion magazine *Harper's Bazaar* that it affectionately riffed on, was influential in "the incorporation of modern European design in the context of post-war American consumer culture" (Sellers 1995: 13).

At the same time, while the fashions "embodied minimalism as much as luxury," Hepburn's bony frame was "more suggestive of a European sensibility honed by the years of want" during World War II (Handyside 2003: 288). Speculation persists in biographies and other accounts of her life as to the cause of her extreme thinness. Was she anorexic or bulimic? Hepburn resumed ballet classes with rigor and dedication after moving to London with her mother in 1948 but had begun serious training too late because of the war; in addition, she was too tall to achieve the prima ballerina career she aspired to since at that time male dancers were not as tall as they are today. Yet she still may have fallen victim to the dancer's disease. Or was there a physical problem, a hindering of her bodily development or possibly a permanent disturbance to her digestive system, due to her adolescence in Arnhem under the Nazi Occupation of the Netherlands, when she often went without food or ate bread made from peas or tulip bulb flour to stave off her hunger? (Like other Dutch children, she also carried messages for the resistance hidden in her shoes.) Hepburn supposedly had a hefty appetite, a fact that *Charade* humorously refers to—she loved sweets, and according to her son she ate pasta every day (Ferrer 2003: 33)—yet she sustained her weight of 110 pounds for most of her entire adult life (Spoto 2006: 35). While there was no evidence of an eating disorder, she did smoke up to three packs of cigarettes a day—possibly to suppress her great appetite?

Regardless of the cause, her body was a subversive image in the light of fifties America's obsession with both the good health of its younger population and the big breasts and pointy bras of mature women and teenage girls. In this sense Hepburn was not only admired as a fashion icon but at the time also signified defiance of the traditional objectification of the female body on-screen and enabled alternate modes of watching the conservative Cinderella narrative that was the template for the films with which she is most identified and which many fans consider to be her very best: *Roman Holiday*, *Sabrina*, *Funny Face*, *Breakfast at Tiffany's*, and *My Fair Lady*—what I call in chapter 3 "the Audrey films."

This is not to say that Hepburn's screen persona was not conflicted and rife with contradictions. These may have already been evident in how I have been discussing her. Hepburn played girlish yet womanly; androgynous or boyish yet feminine; innocent yet sophisticated; playful yet elegant; independent yet controlled; sexually precocious yet virginal; American yet European; aristocratic yet ordinary. These contradictions cohered through her liminality; she was neither one side of the polarity nor the other, but suspended between them in a moment of transformation. Her youth was further problematized because of the many older male costars in her films, as I also discuss in chapter 3. Although cast as romantic leads opposite her, Humphrey Bogart, Henry Fonda, Fred Astaire, Gary Cooper, Cary Grant, and Rex Harrison were old enough to be her father. Fashion may therefore have enabled an alternate mode of addressing a feminine audience, as Rachel Mosely argues (2002a: 57–59) and as I discuss in chapter 4, but it also worked in part to congeal and smooth over ruptures in the narratives that the contradictions in Hepburn's star persona otherwise exposed.

The emphasis on fashion in her films and from many photographic spreads in magazines has encouraged some people to assume Hepburn was just a mannequin for the camera. Alternatively, others have dismissed Hepburn as simply a "personality" on-screen, an attractive, charming, and engaging star who behaved and capitalized on her obvious charisma. As a writer in *Photoplay* commented in a feature article on Hepburn, "Her simplicity of manner, poise, and gentle warmth shine through the screen because they are her own inbred personal qualities" (Jones 1956: 104).

That Hepburn still seems a transcendent personality on-screen has allowed many fans and pop journalists to feel they know her personally from her films and to seek parallels between what happens to her on-screen characters and in her own off-screen life—for instance, in the accounts of her experiences of hardship and deprivation during the Nazi occupation of Holland, or her deep sadness and profound sense of loss as a child when her father disappeared and her subsequent attraction to older, dominating, paternalistic men like her first husband, Mel Ferrer. Along with "fashionable" and "glamorous," in writings about her the adjectives applied to Hepburn tend to be ones like "kind," "gracious," "vulnerable," and, given her biography, "traumatized." From reading biographies of her one can add to this list "humble," "beloved," "private," "disciplined," and "insecure." By the same token, Hepburn's charm and charisma, the product of her labor as an actress, were exemplified by her wide, open-mouthed, radiant smile—a frequent facial gesture in her films that connoted not only joy or bliss but also a sense of mischief or wonder—which could also be misconstrued as a substitute for "real" acting.

In 2010, for instance, the *New York Post* quoted Emma Thompson's claim that Hepburn "can't really act." To be sure, at the time Thompson was celebrating her own star on the Hollywood Walk of Fame and promoting a possible remake of *My Fair Lady*. "I thought that there needs to be a new version," Thompson stated. "I'm not hugely fond of the film. I find Audrey Hepburn fantastically twee," by which she meant "whimsey without wit. It's mimsy-mumsy sweetness without any kind of bite" (Post Staff Report 2010). Gamely (and gamine-ly) performing "girlishness" opposite older men may be why Hepburn seems "twee" to those, like Thompson, who believe she "can't really act."

Back in the fifties, some reviewers were already complaining that Hepburn was not much of an actress, just a fashion plate. Dwight MacDonald, for example claimed, "She is not an actress, she is a model, with her stiff meager body and her blank face full of bone structure," and he went on to say, "She has the model's narcissism, not the actress's introversion" (quoted in Paris 1996: 162). Stanley Donen, who directed three of her best films, remembered that "Audrey was always more about fashion than movies or acting" (quoted in Paris 1996: 132). And in his book on *Breakfast at Tiffany's* and its influence on the sexually free single girl of the 1960s, Sam Wasson contends about *The Nun's Story* that Hepburn's performance, while "her greatest" up until that time, was "one built largely in the editing room. Of course Audrey gave him his material," Wasson claims, "but it was [Fred] Zinnemann who created her character's elaborate texture of thought and feeling" (2010: 153). Earlier in his book Wasson even attributes to Hepburn herself this belief that her performance owed much "to Zinnemann's clever cutting. . . . That wasn't acting, it was a magic trick" (103), she is supposed to have thought. Wasson then claims that Hepburn *had* to act in *Breakfast at Tiffany's*, because the script required more of her than her previous films, so she actively worked in partnership with director Blake Edwards to craft her performance. Even though Wasson fails to appreciate

Hepburn's nuanced acting in *The Nun's Story*, which I shall discuss in the sixth chapter, he may be making that bold assessment for a rhetorical purpose—though I have to take it at face value. Yet I also have to add that her Holly Golightly is indeed wonderful, a compelling and nuanced but very different kind of performance than when she plays Sister Luke.

Today's fans and some writers respond to Hepburn similarly, appreciating her as a fashion icon and personality, not as a great actress; they seldom comment on her line delivery or comic timing or dramatic intensity. On Facebook, since I follow many Classic Hollywood groups, a post was once suggested for me by the site's algorithm, an image of Hepburn from *My Fair Lady* with this caption: "The classic elegance of Audrey Hepburn is timeless. She never stops inspiring us with her grace and charm!" In many ways, that statement of her "timeless" yet "classic elegance" sums up what Hepburn means in popular culture today as a frozen image from the past, ironically so since in Barthes's terms, she has ceased to be "an Event." Rather, I like to think he would call this view of her an "ersatz Idea."

Hepburn thus survives today in a multitude of photographs. She was frequently photographed and highly photogenic, whether in candid shots or staged settings. Years after her death, the publisher of *Life* brought out a book of photographs taken by Bob Willoughby, who met Hepburn in 1953 and remained friends with her until her death. With photos of her at home as well as at work, this volume is a visual record of her family life, her career, her retirement, and her later role as a humanitarian and official ambassador of the United Nations Children's Fund (UNICEF), beginning in 1988 and lasting through her final trip to the Sudan, when she began to show symptoms of the cancer that ended her life in early 1993 (Willoughby 2008). Another book on her partnership with Givenchy lavishly illustrates with black-and-white or color photographs the outfits that the designer created for each of their films together (de La Hoz 2016).

Whereas Monroe's posthumous stardom has been defined by the uncertain circumstances of her death and Taylor's by her unflagging AIDS activism, and although, after retiring permanently from films and until her death, Hepburn traveled widely and tirelessly to raise funds and publicize child hunger and disease around the world for UNICEF, her stardom is still mostly defined by imagery from her two most famous films: Holly Golightly in a "little black dress," streaked hair piled high in a beehive on her head, and holding a long cigarette holder in a gloved hand; or Eliza Doolittle in her black and white wide-brimmed hat and matching gown, the elegant ensemble worn at Ascot—the very costume she wears in the photo suggested to me by Facebook, as mentioned above. Such imagery from *Breakfast at Tiffany's* and *My Fair Lady*, respectively, freezes Hepburn's stardom and disaggregates it from the oftentimes contradictory texture of her films and ignores their vitality, just as those images make one forget her skill as a performer.

Since her death, moreover, Hepburn has been turned into a guru of feminine style and behavior, as many relatively recent books have depicted, reproducing photos, quotations from her films or interviews, and biographical anecdotes: Pamela Clarke Keogh's *Audrey Style* (1999), Melissa Hellostern's *How to Be Lovely: The Audrey Hepburn Way of Life* (2005), Pamela Keogh's *What Would Audrey Do?* (2008), Jordan Christie's *How to Be a Hepburn in a Hilton World: The Art of Living with Grace and Style* (2009), Cindy de la Hoz's *So Audrey: 59 Ways to Put a Little Hepburn in Your Step* (2011), Margaret Cardillo and Julia Denos's *Just Being Audrey* (2011), Katrina Hughes-Eperson's *How to Audrey: Hepburn Lessons in Love and Life* (2012), and Hardie Grant's *Pocket Audrey Hepburn Wisdom* (2020). From a Cologne bookshop, friends gifted me a photo book with a bilingual text in German and English (though printed in Italy), Klaus-Jergen Seinbech's *Adieu Audrey* (2018). In *Audrey Hepburn: International Cover Girl* (2009), Scott Brizel recounts her life and filmography through the scores of international magazine covers, all reprinted in a handsome, hefty tome.

Additionally, her older son, Sean Ferrer, wrote a memoir, *Audrey Hepburn: An Elegant Spirit* (2005), and with his daughter, Katherine, a children's book, *Little Audrey's Daydream: The Life of Audrey Hepburn* (2020); and her younger son, Luca Dotti, published two books of photographs and memories, *Audrey in Rome* (2013) and *Audrey at Home: Memories of My Mother's Kitchen* (2015). Within the fashion industry, "That's so Audrey!" is a common catchphrase indicating approval of a style recalling the star's.

Related to this phenomenon is the repurposing of Hepburn's image in commercials and on TV series. In 2006 The Gap featured a promotion abstracting her solo dance from *Funny Face* (the one in which she wears a black sweater and tight trousers, a costume that I discuss in chapter 4) to promote its new skinny black pants line; and in 2014 Dove candy sold chocolates by drawing on *Roman Holiday*, filming an actress who resembled Hepburn in Princess Ann's outfit but whose face was then enhanced with CGI to look eerily like (but not exactly like, at least to my eyes) the star. The season 1 finale of HBO's *Big Little Lies* (2017–19) took place at a fundraiser where the women dressed in costumes inspired by a Hepburn movie, mostly from *Breakfast at Tiffany's* but with a few from *My Fair Lady* too. And with the casting of (somewhat) look-alike Lily Collins in the lead and the camera's attention in every episode to her clothes, some styled on moments in Hepburn's films, the Netflix series *Emily in Paris* (2020–present) has the star in mind as an ongoing point of reference. (And if you want an example of "twee," it is not Hepburn but Lily Collins as Emily.)

Hepburn's star wattage, then, is complex for being riddled with contradictions but also because of the multiple ways her image has been used, commodified, and viewed. In chapters to follow, I shall negotiate my way through this apparent web of meanings to document my own responses to her films, her screen persona, and her performances. Specifically, I want to appreciate anew her skill as a movie star who could act, so I wish to examine how she achieves a performance by using her voice, face, body, movement, props, and Givenchy.

So consider this: at the height of her career Hepburn worked primarily with Academy Award-winning directors, men well accustomed to using movie stars to their full advantage *as* actors; this fact about Hepburn's career matters greatly but is usually forgotten or glossed over. Hepburn made three films for three-time Academy Award winner William Wyler (*Roman Holiday, The Children's Hour* [1961], *How to Steal a Million*), two for six-time Academy Award winner Billy Wilder (*Sabrina, Love in the Afternoon*), three for Honorary Academy Award winner Stanley Donen (*Funny Face, Charade, Two for the Road* [1967]), and one each for four-time Academy Award winner Fred Zinnemann (*The Nun's Story*), two-time Academy Award winner John Huston (*The Unforgiven* [1960]), one-time Academy Award winner George Cukor (*My Fair Lady*), and Honorary Academy Award winner King Vidor (*War and Peace*, which costarred her first husband, Mel Ferrer). Hepburn also acted for other directors, too, of course. She made two films with Terence Young, who had directed three early James Bond flicks among many other films (*Wait Until Dark* [1967] and *Bloodline* [1979]), and one film with Blake Edwards (*Breakfast at Tiffany's*), Richard Quine (*Paris When It Sizzles*), Richard Lester (*Robin and Marian* [1976]), and Peter Bogdanovitch (*They All Laughed* [1981]). Additionally, Anatole Litvak and Kirk Browning directed her and Mel Ferrer in a TV production of *Mayerling* (1957), and Ferrer directed her in *Green Mansions* (1959) and produced *Wait Until Dark*. Not all of these films came off as planned, but what is amazing to me is that so many of them did, especially those made before her first retirement from acting.

Nor was Hepburn confined to romantic comedies and musicals, although she made several and they were her signature genres. She also made dramas, period pieces, thrillers, a heist comedy, a road movie, a western, and a colonial adventure. For that matter, as well as gaining a Tony for Lead Actress in *Ondine*, Hepburn won the Academy Award for Best Actress for her first Hollywood film, *Roman Holiday*, and was nominated four times subsequently (for *Sabrina*, *The Nun's Story*, *Breakfast at Tiffany's*, and *Wait Until Dark*). And it is worth pointing out that Hepburn was the fifth person to attain EGOT status (a winner of an Emmy, a Grammy, an Oscar, and a Tony), and the first to do so posthumously. Across the pond, she won three BAFTA Awards from five nominations as well as a career achievement award in 1992, shortly before her death.

Throughout this book I focus on what is remembered about Hepburn as an icon and what has been forgotten or ignored about her. My approach takes as its premise that the filmography, more than the biography or the present-day reception, is central to understanding Hepburn's significance as a major star of the postwar era. I concentrate on her screen persona, looking at the narrative patterns of her best-known films to show how the persona was established, reiterated, modified, and altered as she aged; and I progressively add to these discussions commentary on how her performances, her skill as a movie actress, created rich characters such as Princess Ann, Sabrina Fairchild, Jo Stockton, Sister Luke, Holly Golightly, Regina Lampert, Eliza Doolittle, Joanna Wallace, Susy Hendrix, and Maid Marian.

First, to get you oriented before looking closely at her films, chapter 1 delineates a year-by-year checklist of the major events in the life of Audrey Hepburn, and the second chapter follows with a narrative account of her career that adds additional information about the films. After that, I have chapters on what I call "the Audrey films," which follow a Cinderella template (chapter 3), on the transformative function of fashion in her films (chapter 4), on the thrillers (chapter 5), and on her dramatic performances (chapter 6). But be forewarned: with my own longtime interest in narrative, I will be looking closely at many of Hepburn's films, so if you aren't familiar with some titles there will be many spoilerish details in what follows. I also do not discuss her films chronologically; nor do I give the same amount of attention to each film. I devote most of this book to the Hepburn films that interest me and those that I like very much, so a few I discuss only in passing. After all, this book is meant to be an *opinionated* guide!

1
The Life

1926. Ella van Heemstras and James Ruston marry in the Dutch West Indies. It is Ella's second marriage; she has two sons from her first.

1929. Audrey Kathleen van Heemstras Ruston is born in Brussels, Belgium, on May 4. Six weeks later baby Audrey "dies." Developing a bad case of whooping cough, she stops breathing and turns blue in the face. Her mother, a devout Christian Scientist, refrains from calling in a doctor; instead, she slaps her baby so hard on the buttocks and so repeatedly that young Audrey begins to breathe again. As a child, Hepburn loves to hear this story of her "death" repeated to her.

1935. Audrey's father leaves for Britain, never to return to his family. Ella moves with her children to the family estate in Arnhem, Netherlands.

1937. Ella sends Audrey to boarding school in Kent, England, where the child begins to take some dance lessons and discovers a passion for ballet. Supposedly the school's location will enable Ruston to visit his daughter, but he seldom does.

1938. Audrey's parents officially divorce.

1939. As World War II begins in Europe, young Audrey returns to Arnhem, where she continues to study dance until the invasion of the Netherlands by Germany.

1940–45. The Germans occupy the Netherlands. Arnhem is badly damaged after D-Day in 1944, and the Dutch famine occurs in winter of that same year when the Germans blockade food and fuel supplies from entering the country.

1945. At the conclusion of the war Ella moves her family to Amsterdam, where Audrey continues her ballet training.

1948. Audrey has her first film role as a stewardess in *Dutch in Seven Lessons*, a travel film promoting the Netherlands; she appears for several minutes in mostly silent footage with voice-over narration. Later that same year Ella and Audrey move to London, where Audrey has a scholarship to study at Ballet Rambert. Although she and Ella were close—and the baroness scrubbed floors and did other menial jobs to obtain room and board for the two of them—Ella was an emotionally distanced mother; she loved her daughter and took great pride in her daughter's success but could not convey her feelings to Audrey, who always said what she got from her mother was a strong sense of discipline. While taking ballet classes, Audrey works in the chorus of *High Button Shoes* in the West End. She now begins using "Hepburn" as her surname.

1949. Forsaking her dream of becoming a prima ballerina, Audrey appears in the chorus of a revue, *Sauce Tartare*, in the West End.

1950. Audrey appears in another West End revue, *Sauce Piquante*, and moonlights in a nightclub revue, *Summer Nights*. She has bit parts in several British feature films: *One Wild Oat*, *Young Wives Tale*, *Laughter in Paradise*, and *Lavender Hill Mob* (all released in 1951).

1951. A big year for Audrey. She has her first part of substance in *Secret People* (released in 1952). At a cocktail party in April she meets James Hanson, a wealthy industrialist, and they begin a love affair. She gets cast in the bilingual production *Nous irons à Monte Carlo / Monte Carlo Baby* (1952/1953) and is the only performer to act in both the French and English versions. While Audrey is filming on location in Monte Carlo, Colette sees her and declares that she is her Gigi. In September Audrey screen-tests in London for *Roman Holiday* and is cast as the female lead. She signs a seven-picture contract with Paramount that allows her time away to do stage and TV work; the studio can also loan her out to another company as part of that number. In November *Gigi*, the non-musical stage adaptation of Collette's novella, opens on Broadway at the Hudson Theatre and Audrey receives great acclaim.

1952. Audrey is engaged to James Hanson. She travels to Rome to make *Roman Holiday* with William Wyler directing, which is shot entirely in the city. Hanson tries to bully Paramount into rushing the film's completion so he and Audrey can marry and honeymoon before she has to return to the United States for the national tour of *Gigi*, but to no avail. Back in the States, Audrey decides to end the engagement, claiming that her career will prevent them from being together in the way a married couple needs to be.

1953. *Roman Holiday* opens in the summer, is a great success, and a star is born. Before then, Audrey completes the national tour of *Gigi*. In July she travels to Paris to select a designer wardrobe for her upcoming film, *Sabrina*, and meets Hubert de Givenchy in his salon; they begin what will become a lifetime collaboration and close friendship. *Sabrina* begins shooting in September under Billy Wilder's direction with locations in New York and on Long Island. During the production Audrey has an affair with married costar William Holden. At a party hosted by Gregory Peck, her costar in *Roman Holiday*, she meets Mel Ferrer.

1954. In February Audrey returns to Broadway in *Ondine* opposite Ferrer. On March 25 Audrey wins the Academy Award for Best Actress in *Roman Holiday*, and a few weeks later she wins the Tony for Best Lead Actress in a Play for *Ondine*. In September *Sabrina* opens and is another hit. On September 25 she marries Ferrer in Switzerland.

1955. Audrey receives her second Best Actress nomination from the Motion Picture Academy for *Sabrina*. In March, she has a miscarriage. She signs on to play Natasha opposite her husband's Prince Andrei in *War and Peace*, which is mostly filmed in Rome with King Vidor directing. Beginning in July, it is a long shoot and a long picture.

1956. *War and Peace* opens in the fall to mixed reviews, but Audrey is generally praised and Vidor receives a Best Director nomination from the Motion Picture Academy. In April she begins filming *Funny Face* in Hollywood for director Stanley Donen, with the company traveling to Paris in the summer for location scenes. In late September, filming begins on Billy Wilder's *Love in the Afternoon* in Paris.

1957. On February 4, Audrey and Ferrer star in *Mayerling* on NBC's *Producers' Showcase*. *Funny Face* opens at Eastertime to critical approval and very good business, and *Love in the Afternoon* in the summer to a more muted reception.

1958. In January Audrey travels to Rome (for interiors) and the Congo (for a month of filming at the story's actual location) to make *The Nun's Story* for Fred Zinnemann. Afterward, in July Ferrer directs her in *Green Mansions* at MGM's studio in Culver City.

1959. In January, Audrey begins *The Unforgiven*, which is shooting in Mexico. On January 28, Audrey, who is pregnant, falls off a horse and severely injures her back. The shoot is suspended while she recovers, and she is cared for by Marie Louise ("Lou") Habets, the real-life inspiration for Hepburn's character in *The Nun's Story*. Mostly healed but needing to wear a brace, Audrey returns to the Mexican location to complete *The Unforgiven* on March 5. In May she goes into labor but the child is stillborn. In late summer the Red Cross locates Audrey's father in Dublin and she visits him; the reunion is cordial but strained, yet afterward she will send him a monthly stipend and correspond infrequently with his new wife. *Green Mansions* opens at Eastertime and *The Nun's Story* in the summer. The latter is one of the year's most popular films, and Audrey gets what are probably the best reviews of her career so far. *Green Mansions*, on other hand, is a box-office and critical dud.

1960. Audrey is Oscar nominated again, this time for *The Nun's Story*. *The Unforgiven* opens in the spring. On July 17 her desire for motherhood is finally realized when Sean Hepburn Ferrer is born, and the child renews the Ferrers' marriage for a while. Givenchy designs Sean's christening outfit. In October, filming begins on *Breakfast at Tiffany's* under Blake Edwards's direction, first in New York for location filming and then on the Paramount lot in Los Angeles, where Ferrer arrives with baby Sean and a nanny.

1961. Filming begins on *The Children's Hour* in May with William Wyler directing. *Breakfast at Tiffany's* opens in the fall and is a hit. *The Children's Hour* begins an Oscar-qualifying run in Los Angeles in late December, though it will not open nationally until March 1962.

1962. Audrey receives another Oscar nomination, this time for *Breakfast at Tiffany's*. She is signed to play Eliza Doolittle in the screen version of *My Fair Lady* at a salary of $1 million plus incidentals, reportedly the highest payment to an actor at this time. Beginning in July, she makes *Paris When It Sizzles* on location with William Holden, but release of this film, directed by Richard Quine, is delayed for a year and a half. The shoot is complicated by Holden's alcoholism. Almost immediately upon the completion of that film, in mid-October, filming begins on *Charade*, also shot in Paris, with Stanley Donen at the helm and Cary Grant as her costar.

1963. In May Audrey begins voice and dialect coaching in preparation for the start of *My Fair Lady*. She assumes she will sing the score and records her songs but is ultimately dubbed by Marni Nixon. When Audrey learns she will definitely have a voice double, she uncharacteristically gets angry and walks off the set; returning the next day, she apologizes to everyone. In the meantime, *Charade* opens at Christmastime and is a big hit.

1964. *Paris When It Sizzles* finally opens in the early spring but pales beside the popularity of *Charade*. *My Fair Lady*, directed by George Cukor, premieres in the fall to mostly ecstatic reviews despite some backlash in the press over Audrey's dubbed vocals.

1965. Audrey presents the Best Actor Oscar to costar Rex Harrison. Julie Andrews, Broadway's Eliza Doolittle, wins the award for Best Actress in *Mary Poppins*. Audrey herself was not nominated. In August filming in Paris begins on *How to Steal a Million*, her third film for William Wyler. In late December she has another miscarriage.

1966. *How to Steal a Million* opens during the summer. While filming *Two for the Road*, which started filming in France in May and is her third film for Stanley Donen, Audrey has an affair with Albert Finney, her costar in the film.

1967. In January, filming begins on *Wait Until Dark*, which Mel produces for Audrey with Terence Young directing. The Ferrers announce their divorce in September. Audrey has two pictures released this year, *Two for the Road* in early summer and *Wait Until Dark* at Christmas.

1968. Audrey receives her fifth and last Oscar nomination for *Wait Until Dark*. Saddened by the breakdown of her marriage to Ferrer, Audrey moves to Rome, although she keeps her beloved estate in Switzerland, which will remain her home and sanctuary until her death. In April she accepts a lifetime Tony Award. Back in Europe, on a yacht party in May she meets Dr. Andrea Dotti, a psychiatrist, who is nine years younger; they eventually begin a discreet affair. In December the Ferrers' divorce is finalized with Audrey having custody of Sean.

1969. On January 12 Audrey marries Dotti.

1970. Audrey's second child, Luca Dotti, is born on February 8 at her home in Switzerland. Audrey retires from the screen to raise her two sons.

1975. Audrey returns to the screen in *Robin and Marian*, which is filmed in Spain. She receives a salary of $1 million. Her costar is Sean Connery and the director, Richard Lester.

1976. *Robin and Marian* opens in the spring.

1978. In November, filming begins on *Bloodline* (aka *Sidney Sheldon's Bloodline*), directed by Terence Young. Unhappy in her marriage, mainly because of Dotti's philandering and infidelities, Audrey has a fling with costar Ben Gazzara.

1979. *Bloodline* opens in the summer to poor business.

1980. Audrey files for divorce. Audrey meets Robert Wolders, and their friendship blossoms into the intimate relationship that she will consider to be the happiest of her life. He will remain her companion until her death. In April filming begins on *They All Laughed* in New York City under Peter Bogdanovich's direction. In October Audrey learns of her father's terminal illness and with Wolders goes to visit Ruston, who dies shortly afterward.

1981. *They All Laughed* opens in early winter, its release having been postponed by over a year due to the murder of Dorothy Stratten, who costars in the picture.

1984. Audrey's mother dies on August 2 in California, where she had lived during her last years.

1987. Audrey's TV movie *Love Among the Thieves*, directed by Roger Young, airs February 23 on ABC.

1988. Audrey begins her role as Special Ambassador for the United Nations Children's Fund (UNICEF), which will only conclude with her death. She will do benefits, testify before Congress, and travel with photographers to areas suffering from famine, disease, and other natural disasters in Asia, South and Central America, and Africa.

1989. Wanting to work with director Steven Spielberg, Audrey takes a brief role as Hap, an angel, in *Always*, her final film, which is a Christmas release.

1990. Audrey begins work on the Public Broadcasting Network television series *Gardens of the World with Audrey Hepburn*.

1990–91. Audrey and composer Michael Tilson Thomas develop *From the Diary of Anne Frank*, a concert in which she reads selections from the diary set to his music, and it tours as a benefit for UNICEF in several US cities and London. During this period, Audrey also records her voice-over narration for *Gardens of the World with Audrey Hepburn*.

1991. A star-studded "Gala Tribute to Audrey Hepburn" is held at Lincoln Center. Audrey promotes the *Gardens of the World* series and PBS broadcasts a one-hour introductory special about the series.

1992. Audrey is awarded the Presidential Medal of Freedom by President George H. W. Bush and a Lifetime Achievement Award by BAFTA. She records the album *Audrey Hepburn's Enchanted Tales*. Suffering extreme stomach pains, Audrey undergoes surgery in Los Angeles. The prognosis is terminal, and she returns to Switzerland for her last Christmas with her family and Wolders.

1993. Audrey Hepburn dies of abdominal cancer on January 20 at her home in Switzerland. The first of the six episodes of *Gardens of the World with Audrey Hepburn* premieres on the local PBS channel in Los Angeles on January 21 and is broadcast over the entire network a few days later on January 24. Later this year, the Motion Picture Academy posthumously awards Audrey the Jean Hersholt Award for her humanitarian work. Still later, she receives a posthumous Emmy for Outstanding Individual Achievement—Informational Program for the PBS series *Gardens of the World with Audrey Hepburn*. She is also given a posthumous Life Achievement Award by the Screen Actors Guild. Sean Ferrer creates the Audrey Hepburn Children's Fund in memory of his mother.

1994. Audrey receives a posthumous Grammy for Best Spoken Word Album for Children for *Audrey Hepburn's Enchanted Tales*.

1996. Two additional episodes of *Gardens of the World with Audrey Hepburn* air.

1999. In a CBS Special, "AFI's 100 Years . . . 100 Stars," Audrey places third among the fifty women listed, after Katharine Hepburn and Bette Davis and before Ingrid Bergman and Greta Garbo.

2
The Career

Although the previous chapter outlined the major personal and professional events in Audrey Hepburn's life, it is worth looking more closely at her career as a whole before beginning a discussion in depth of the films, her screen persona, and her acting. The career falls into three phases: first, her initial small roles in British productions in the early 1950s; second, her major Hollywood years from 1953 to 1967; third, her sporadic "return" in middle age after leaving films to raise her second son, Luca, and spend more time with her first-born, Sean.

To start with, I was surprised to learn that dancing was Hepburn's true love, not acting, which she initially fell into just to make a living. She took private ballet lessons as a youngster and during the Nazi occupation continued to study the best she could, wearing handmade toe shoes with little foot support; she even crudely choreographed recitals as entertainment for family, friends, and neighbors in a room concealed by blackout curtains and without much illumination or music so as not to attract German soldiers. She only stopped dancing when she succumbed to malnutrition because of the scarcity of food during the Dutch famine of 1944. Once in London after the war, when her teacher Marie Rambert regretfully stated that a solo ballet career was not in her future, Audrey earned wages dancing onstage in the chorus of musical revues. While doing that, she moonlighted in a cabaret and worked as a photographic model. Despite her aristocratic background, or so *Modern Screen* informed readers in a 1954 feature article, "Audrey didn't act like a princess or a *prima ballerina*. She acted as a chorus girl" (Baskette 1954: 93). That same year, though, *Top Secret*, a racy scandal magazine, published photographs of Hepburn in scanty costumes as a member of the chorus line in those revues, claiming that "her press agents and studio bosses are trying to suppress [these pictures]. Read and decide for yourself how angelic she really is!" (Taylor 1954: 6). From the beginning and over the years, the verdict from friends and coworkers alike was that Audrey Hepburn was in fact pretty "angelic" because of her warmth, generosity, loyalty, and modesty.

Hepburn's "star is born" moment, moreover, did not first happen on film but on the New York stage. Anita Loos had adapted *Gigi*, a novella by the French writer Collette, and producers had yet to cast the title character. Catching sight of Hepburn on location in Monaco for her part in *Nous irons à Monte Carlo*, Collette instantly decided that the young actress was the embodiment of Gigi, a teenager being trained by her grandmother and aunt to be a courtesan but who ends up marrying a rich suiter for love. Although she confessed to having no stage training or much experience but was a dancer, Hepburn was cast in the play. It opened on Broadway in November 1951 to mixed reviews, but she received raves for her charismatic presence onstage, resulting in her being given star billing on the Fulton Theatre marquee after the premiere. Hepburn was subsequently offered the lead role when MGM decided to musicalize *Gigi* later in the decade, but she declined.

Before rehearsals began for *Gigi*, Paramount was still searching for the female lead opposite Gregory Peck in *Roman Holiday*. In London, a studio executive saw some footage of Hepburn and urged Paramount and director William Wyler to give her a screen test. In addition to her performing a scene from the script, they let the camera continue afterward without telling her in order to see what she was like in impromptu conversation. Wyler liked what he saw, and she was signed for the film, but its start date had to be pushed back to summer because of her commitment to *Gigi*. Hepburn traveled almost immediately to Rome for *Roman Holiday* after the play closed, and once the shoot completed, she as quickly returned to the States to tour in the play, a condition of its early closure in New York so that she could do the film.

When *Roman Holiday* premiered in London on September 21, 1953, and then in New York City at Radio City Music Hall on September 27, Audrey Hepburn seemed to have emerged on-screen as a full-fledged movie star and overnight sensation. In fact, though, *Roman Holiday* was not her first film, as the chronology in the previous chapter already indicated. In addition to the Monte Carlo film, and while still in Holland before her move to London, Hepburn first appeared in a travelogue meant to promote Dutch tourism. In London she then worked as a bit player in several British pictures while dancing on stage in the revues. She had signed with Associated British Pictures Corporation (ABPC), but the company loaned her out more than it used her in its own productions. When Paramount signed Hepburn for seven pictures, the American studio at first had to share her with ABPC since the latter company refused to sell her contract outright to the Gower Street lot, though she never again worked for that British company.

In most of her early films you pretty much missed her if you happened to blink. At this time her persona on screen (as that *Top Secret* article implied about her days in the chorus) was a sort of flirtatious coquette with a wide-eyed demeanor, such as a hotel receptionist in *One Wild Oat* (1951), a kittenish cigarette girl in *Laughter in Paradise* (1951), and Conchita, apparently a lover of Alec Guinness's character, in Ealing Studios' well-received *Lavender Hill Mob* (1951). In that last film she received no billing in the opening titles but was included in the cast list at the end. She has only one scene early in the film when Guinness gives her some money and she nuzzles his cheek in thanks. *Laughter in Paradise* premiered a few weeks before the Guinness comedy and gave Hepburn an "introducing" credit along with Veronica Hurst, who has a more sizable role in the film (but have you ever heard of her?).

Hepburn did get one substantial part, the second female lead, as a ballet dancer in *Secret People* (1952), again on loan from ABPC to

Ealing Studios. This film was directed by Thorold Dickinson, who would subsequently direct the screen test for Paramount that earned her the role in *Roman Holiday*. Unlike her other early films or her part in the revues, Hepburn's performance in *Secret People* gives one a better sense of the raw, unpolished "Audrey Hepburn" before she became a Hollywood star. This film is a political thriller reminiscent of Joseph Conrad's novels. Valentina Cortese and Hepburn play sisters who are refugees from an unnamed European country overtaken by a dictator. The two are sent to London by their father, who is ultimately killed in his native country by the dictator. Maria (Cortese), the elder of the two young women, reunites with a former lover, now part of a terrorist cell, who gets her mixed up in an assassination plot when the dictator visits London. The plot goes awry, a young servant is killed instead, Maria feels guilty and confesses her part in the accidental killing, and after much *mishigas* as the police use her to track the conspirators, she is given a new identity. Throughout all this, the younger sister, Nora (Hepburn), lives only for her dancing, and she has several ballet numbers, although they are truncated. In a sense, this character allowed Hepburn to live out her now-forsaken dream of becoming a soloist on the ballet stage.

As for her acting in *Secret People*, until her final scene—when she gets to emote after finding out her sister is alive, realizes that she herself has also been exploited by the anarchists, and then watches one of them kill Maria—mostly Hepburn just has to look young and enthusiastic and dance. She twirls a lot en pointe, and one can see her muscular legs. Her face looks somewhat fuller than we are accustomed to, the roundness suggesting her youth. As in her other British films, her voice seems higher than we are used to, which may be a result of the recording or duplicating mechanisms of the time and place, but it is also the case that her voice would continually get deeper as she aged, became more confident on-screen, and continued to smoke a lot.

Roman Holiday introduced Hepburn to a mass audience globally, ensuring a popularity in North America, Europe, and Asia (Japan especially, where she still has a big fan base today) that would eventually make her one of the highest-paid and beloved movie stars in the 1950s and 1960s. It is not clear who suggested that she receive equal billing with costar Gregory Peck, already an established star. One story has it that Peck wanted her to get the credit after watching her performance during the early days of the shoot; another account says it was the studio and Wyler who made the decision after viewing dailies or a rough cut, which required renegotiation of Peck's contract. In the end, Peck was first "presented" and then Hepburn was "introduced," with both performers receiving comparable type in the main titles on-screen and both given star billing in the posters and newspaper ads. The decision to put her on the same level as Peck was on the mark since Hepburn would go on to win the Academy Award, the Golden Globe, the New York Film Critics Circle Award, and the British Academy Film Award for her first leading role in a major Hollywood motion picture. The trade journal *Motion Picture Herald* named her "the Number One Star of Tomorrow" after polling circuit and independent exhibitors (Remer 1954: 14). And the *Independent Film Journal*, in a special feature, "Top Exhibitoratings [sic] of 1953–54," ranked Hepburn third of the "Ten Top Money Actresses" for that period behind Marilyn Monroe and Ava Gardner ("Ten Top" 1954: 38–39) and first for "top dramatic performance" ("Top Dramatic" 1954: 45).

Roman Holiday was the first American film shot entirely in Rome. The delightful and imaginative story was written by the blacklisted writer Dalton Trumbo, who could not get screen acknowledgment in 1953 because of the era's repressive political climate. Instead, his friend Ian McLellan Hunter, who cowrote the Oscar-nominated screenplay with John Dighton and Trumbo (whose name was erased on this as well), received credit for the original story as a "front." Trumbo's story nonetheless won the Academy Award, which was given to Hunter. (In 1954, when nominations were announced, the Academy still had separate classifications for original story and for a finished screenplay, and *Roman Holiday* was nominated in both categories, though it only won for story.) The Academy finally awarded Trumbo the prize posthumously in 1993, and his name was restored to the film's opening credits for both the story and, along with Hunter and Dighton, for the screenplay. *Roman Holiday* was a major critical as well as popular success, receiving ten Oscar nominations overall, a rarity for a romantic comedy.

Roman Holiday opened just a few months after the coronation of Queen Elizabeth II and while gossip swirled about the love life of Princess Margaret, the new queen's younger sister, so it benefited from widespread interest in the British royal family. As Princess Ann, whose character evokes those two royals, Hepburn is positively charming, perfectly natural, and her performance seems utterly spontaneous as the day becomes more rambunctious, unpredictable, and carnivalesque. *Roman Holiday*, furthermore, crystallized the European associations that would remain attached to Hepburn's star image even those few times when she plays American. Given her biography as well as the nationality of many of her characters, Hepburn would always represent the Europe rescued from the Nazis by the United States and its allies. Her second film, *Sabrina* (1954), reiterated this European affiliation through the titular character's time in Paris at a culinary school, from which she returns to the United States as a fashionable French sophisticate dressed by Givenchy.

Sabrina was another enormous hit, confirming Hepburn's star power and establishing a gamine persona that appeared to reflect her off-screen personality: youthful, charming, sincere, authentic, intelligent, fashionable, whimsical, irresistible—yet dependent on the patronage and affection of an older man, a half-lover and half-father figure. A recurring comment in biographies and articles by her directors, costars, and others was that everyone who met Hepburn fell a little bit in love with her. Perhaps everyone but Humphrey Bogart; on the set of *Sabrina* he was impatient with her need often to do additional takes, he fought with William Holden and insulted Billy Wilder, and away from the set he felt cut off from the camaraderie

Hepburn shared with their costar and director. Wilder and his wife became lifelong friends with Hepburn. And Holden? Unhappily married, he fell madly in love with her, and she returned the feeling; they began an affair, which she ended upon learning that he had had a vasectomy and could not give her the children she craved.

After making *Sabrina*, Hepburn returned to the Broadway stage one more time in the play *Ondine* opposite Mel Ferrer, whom she had met and dated before starting the Billy Wilder comedy and whom she would soon marry. Shortly after getting the Oscar for *Roman Holiday*, Hepburn won a Tony for her performance of the title character in *Ondine* despite the poor reviews and backstage troubles, as Ferrer repeatedly interfered with Alfred Lunt's direction, putting Hepburn in the middle of that power struggle. Ferrer was a dozen years older and had already been married three times (twice to the same woman), with four children from those unions. Fan magazine articles reported the opposition of Hepburn's mother to the engagement because of Ferrer's age and prior marriages (Cronin 1955; Johnson 1955). As Hepburn and Ferrer became a public couple, gossip that he was "a modern-day Svengali, completely dominating Audrey and controlling her every word and move," began to spread, gossip that she took pains to discount (Jones 1956: 53). "'Audrey,' [Ferrer] announced, 'must be protected from people as if she were royalty'" (Cronin 1955: 70). Speculation about his possible jealousy also spread, for it was already evident that her stardom outshone his by several hundred light years. "Mel's intentions were certainly benevolent," one of Hepburn's biographers concludes. "But remarkably often, her cause coincided with his own best advantage. It seemed never to have occurred to him that their deepest aspirations were, in the final analysis, incompatible" (Spoto 2006: 133). The marriage helped to perpetuate Hepburn's star image as a girl dependent on the love and guidance of an older man as well as confirming her distance from Hollywood. She and Ferrer soon settled in Switzerland, and she reportedly followed his advice on what films to accept and to decline.

Ferrer costarred with his wife in her next film, *War and Peace* (1956), which Dino DeLaurentis produced for Paramount with King Vidor directing. The film was made when almost every studio in Hollywood had one or two big-budget spectaculars in production; indeed, Warners' *Giant*, United Artists' *Around the World in Eighty Days*, and Paramount's *The Ten Commandments* were all released in the fall of 1956 within weeks of *War and Peace*'s opening. Unlike those blockbusters, *War and Peace*, based on the classic Tolstoy novel, was a multinational production of the sort that would become more common in the 1960s: Swedish actresses Anita Ekberg and May Britt, along with many Italians in small roles, were dubbed, although the two women would each go on to have a subsequent career in Hollywood films with their own accented voices; playing a Russian peasant, John Mills speaks with a cockney accent; Italians, such as Vittorio Gassman and Milly Vitale, play Russians; Henry Fonda is miscast and way too old for the lead character of Pierre; and filming began with a script that was not finished and had been cobbled together from numerous revisions by many hands, including director King Vidor's (half a dozen names are ultimately attached to the screenplay, with four more people uncredited). The result is a big, splashy epic with no discernible rhythm to it overall, as battle scenes on the western front of Russia depicting Napoleon's attempts to invade and conquer the vast nation alternate with domestic scenes of life in Moscow or the countryside, first during a brokered peace and then during the resumption of war, when the French emperor temporarily occupies the Russian capital. To be frank, though Vidor's direction was Oscar-nominated, the three-and-a-half-hour length seems to me three times as long, as the film slogs from one set-piece scene to the next.

As an indication of Hepburn's superstardom just three years after being cast in *Roman Holiday*, and thanks to her agent, Kurt Frings, Hepburn received $350,000 plus a weekly expense allowance for *War and Peace*, the most an actress had yet to earn for a single film (and thirty times the $11,900—before fees for her agent, manager, lawyer, and taxes—that was her payment for *Sabrina*); her husband, on the other hand, got $100,000 (Spoto 2006: 133). Given the gamine, charming, and mischievous characters she played in her first two Hollywood films, Hepburn was perfectly cast as Natasha, the impetuous and charismatic girl who matures during the course of *War and Peace*, and she received generally good reviews. Ferrer, who is usually cold, impersonal, and distant on film, gives a fine, subdued performance suitable to his character, Prince Andrei. But much as the twenty-seven-year-old Hepburn plays a character who is a very young teen as Tolstoy's novel begins, the fifty-year-old Fonda is playing one who is thirty years younger at the start. Though older than her character, Hepburn still convincingly radiates impulsive girlishness, but Fonda, otherwise a fine actor, mostly seems tired and bored, not to say middle-aged, as Pierre (he reportedly took the job for the money after other actors had declined the part). By comparison, Hepburn's acting shows nuance as Natasha progresses from her infatuation with and engagement to Andrei, flirtation with and seduction by Anatole (Vittorio Gassman), redemption through nursing the fatally wounded Andrei, and ultimately her maturation with Pierre at the end. However, many of Natasha's scenes in Moscow happen apart from Andrei's and Pierre's domestic scenes there or in the country, with their comrades, or at war, an effect of the film's fidelity to Tolstoy's sprawling scope and his narrative.

After *War and Peace*, the Ferrers appeared together in a television production of the warhorse melodrama *Mayerling*. This is the much-filmed true story of the suicides of the Crown Prince Rudolf of Austria-Hungary (Ferrer) and his teenage mistress, the Baroness Marie Vetsera (Hepburn). Forced to give her up by his father, the emperor Franz Joseph, the already married Rudolf travels with the unsuspecting Maria to a hunting lodge in Mayerling, where he shoots her and then himself. As the young baroness, Hepburn has one note to play: sweet and innocent. She is essentially passive and reactive to Ferrer's older prince, which makes sense since

Mayerling is basically Rudolf's story. Still, even in what amounts to a secondary role opposite her husband, Hepburn gives what may be her worst, or at least her most colorless, performance. Ferrer dominates the production with a loud and sometimes manic performance but loses sympathy due to his character's self-indulgence and self-entitlement, which are his two notes to play. The production itself is sumptuous and was telecast in color on February 24, 1957, as part of NBC's monthly *Producers' Showcase* series of ninety-minute specials; an edited version was released theatrically in Europe. According to the IMDb, this was Ferrer's TV debut but not Hepburn's. While appearing in *Gigi*, in 1951 on a CBS morning show she had previously re-enacted a wartime Christmas when her starving family received a gift of potatoes from the Dutch resistance; and in 1952 she had appeared in a thirty-minute CBS drama. (I have not been able to see the latter.)

Hepburn's next two films were shot back to back while her husband was on location making films in France and Spain. She first made *Funny Face* (1957) with Fred Astaire for director Stanley Donen, with whom she would work again two more times in the 1960s. *Funny Face* is the best MGM musical that MGM never made, a marvelous concoction of song and dance that premiered in theaters just as the cycle of original film musicals meant as standard movie fare was nearing its end, to be succeeded by the big-budget, "event" roadshow attractions of the 1960s.

The project actually began at MGM before ending up at Paramount. *Funny Face* was originally a Broadway musical in 1927 with a score by George and Ira Gershwin, a very different plot, and starring Astaire, who at that time was famously teamed with his sister Adele before she retired and he moved to Hollywood, where he headlined a cycle of hit RKO musicals opposite Ginger Rogers. After his contract with RKO ended, Astaire worked independently of a single studio, though he appeared somewhat regularly for producer Arthur Freed at MGM, making several profitable musicals for that studio such as *Easter Parade* (1948) and *The Band Wagon*

(1953). MGM had the script of an unproduced play by Leonard Gershe, now intended as an Astaire musical with some songs from the stage *Funny Face* that were licensed from Warners, which held the rights to the Gershwins' catalog, and some new tunes by Freed's right-hand man, Roger Edens, who had guided Gershe on a rewrite more suitable for the screen. Edens intended to produce as well, and he wanted Hepburn for the female lead since the role in this new musical was tailor-made for her. Paramount, however, refused to loan its new star to Metro, which ended up selling the entire package—Astaire, the script by Gershe, the score with the old and new songs, and the services of producer Edens and director Stanley Donen—to Paramount in exchange for an eventual loan of Hepburn, which would in turn count toward her contractual commitment to do seven pictures for Paramount.

This musical, Hepburn claimed when her *Funny Face* costar received the AFI Lifetime Achievement Award in 1981, allowed her to experience "the thrill that all women at some point in their lives have dreamed of—to dance just once with Fred Astaire" (Pasetta 1981). In her preface to a biography of Donen, Hepburn recalled being so anxious about being introduced to the famous dancer that she threw up her breakfast beforehand, and she also remembered that she nervously stepped on his feet during their first rehearsal (Hepburn 1996: xii). Nevertheless, in her solos and duets with Astaire and costar Kay Thompson, Hepburn put her dance training to good use, although the choreography of her numbers with Astaire seems tailored to her ballet training. She also is not dubbed in her four songs, which Edens arranged to suit her mezzo voice.

Additionally, *Funny Face* was notable for the many fabulous Givenchy outfits that Hepburn wears as a fashion model and for Richard Avedon's contributions to the visual design of the fashion shoot montage, the main titles, and the photograph of Hepburn's face used in the darkroom sequence. Billed in the credits as a "special visual consultant," Avedon was a famous photographer for whom Hepburn had already posed and would continue to do so many times in the future, and he inspired Astaire's character, "Dick Avery," much as Avedon's first wife, Doe Avedon, who had reluctantly become a top fashion model before turning to acting, was a model for Hepburn's "Jo Stockton." And although Astaire had been a major and influential star of musicals since the mid-1930s and usually received first billing, Hepburn's name appeared before his in *Funny Face*, indicating how, in only her fourth film, she, more than he, was the major selling point. And bankable she was, for *Funny Face* received sterling reviews and did well at the box office. It was Hepburn's second film to play Radio City Music Hall, then the most prestigious and famous movie palace in New York City.

Most of *Funny Face* was shot in Hollywood, but the production did memorable location shooting in Paris. *Love in the Afternoon* (1957), Hepburn's next film, was filmed entirely in Paris. This romantic comedy reunited Hepburn with director Billy Wilder in an homage to his mentor, the famed director Ernst Lubitsch. Wilder had signed Hepburn for this film before *War and Peace* was released and had wanted but failed to get Cary Grant as her costar, as he had similarly failed to secure Grant for the role Bogart played in *Sabrina*. Unfortunately, Wilder settled on Gary Cooper, whose age and wrinkled look only emphasized his costar's youth all the more. According to the negative reviews and the poor reception at the box office, the age difference posed a problem for audiences, and *Love in the Afternoon* was Hepburn's first box-office failure in the United States. "It was a flop," Wilder stated. "Why? Because I got Coop the week he suddenly got old" (Sikov 1998: 397). However, as likely, the slow pace (it runs two hours, ten minutes) and continental flavor à la Lubitsch were not in sync with the era's more ribald if still "tasteful" tastes, at least in America in the late 1950s, where Wilder's sex farce with Marilyn Monroe, *The Seven Year Itch* (1955), had been a big hit, and the Doris Day–Rock Hudson sex comedy *Pillow Talk* (1959) and Wilder's own *Some Like It Hot* (1959), also with Monroe, were on the horizon. By contrast, released by foreign distributors, *Love in the Afternoon* was more successful in Europe (Chandler 2002: 192), continuing Hepburn's global popularity.

After *Funny Face* and *Love in the Afternoon*, and following her husband's advice, Hepburn's next projects began to expand her range as an actress. In 1958 she traveled to Rome and the Congo to play Sister Luke in *The Nun's Story* (1959), based on a bestselling novel by Kathryn Hulme. While preparing for *The Nun's Story* Hepburn became close friends with Hulme and her life partner, Marie Louise ("Lou") Habets, the real-life Sister Luke of the book. Upon completing *The Nun's Story*, Hepburn began *Green Mansions* (1959), which her husband was directing for MGM. This project was the loan of Hepburn to Metro as part of Paramount's purchase of the *Funny Face* package two years earlier.

Release dates for these two films flip-flopped their production, with *Green Mansions* premiering in 1959 at Radio City Music Hall for Easter and *The Nun's Story* opening there the following June. The two films met different fates, critically and at the box office. *Green Mansions*, in a word, bombed. As director, Ferrer could not overcome the negative factors of his production: visually, the artificial sets at MGM contrast with the establishing location shots and South American vistas that he was able to capture before filming began at the studio in Culver City; the weak script suffers from Anglo colonial stereotypes of the native people; as Nuflo, the grandfather figure to Hepburn's character, Lee J. Cobb hams it up, further emphasizing the colonial treatment of the jungle people; and Hepburn and Anthony Perkins lack chemistry as a romantic pair. As Rima, the mysterious bird girl, Hepburn, who wears a long wig and shift for a costume, gives a bland performance, possibly as a result of her husband's direction. Throughout, her voice is low and soft-spoken, and she speaks in a monotonous cadence, all presumably to underscore Rima's mysteriousness, the sense that she is not of this world. Ferrer and Hepburn build Rima's character mainly through the star's association with being natural. "She is like all the beautiful things in these woods," Perkins states of her in the film. In fact, publicity about the production featured the fawn that went to live with the Ferrers to be made comfortable on set as Rima's companion; one photograph showed Hepburn and the tiny animal grocery shopping together.

By contrast, *The Nun's Story* was a big hit, receiving eight Oscar nominations; as well as her own nominations for an Oscar and Golden Globe, Hepburn won the Best Actress prize from the New York Film Critics Circle and BAFTA. For this film Hepburn received $250,000 plus 10 percent of the gross receipts, and given its hefty box-office take, her agent had made a wise deal with Warner Bros. Aside from Fred Zinnemann's expert direction, an intelligent screenplay by Robert Anderson, and Hepburn's intense performance as Sister Luke née Gabrielle van der Mal, *The Nun's Story* was notable for its strong cast in support of the star: Peter Finch is Dr. Fortunati, Sister Luke's colleague in the Congo; Edith Evans, Peggy Ashcroft, Ruth White, Beatrice Straight, Mildred Dunnock, Patricia Collinge, and Barbara O'Neil play various nuns during Sister Luke's career; Dean Jagger is Gabrielle's father, Dr. van der Mal; and in her first film role, Colleen Dewhurst is the insane patient who attacks Sister Luke in the mental hospital. Not surprisingly, perhaps, because of the acting challenge that her character posed, *The Nun's Story* would prove to be Hepburn's favorite film (though she also had a fondness for *Funny Face*). She reportedly did well with the rigorous location shooting in the Congo and developed a good rapport with Zinnemann, with whom she became a lifelong friend. According to biographer Donald Spoto, moreover, while preparing for the role Hepburn, whose marriage with Ferrer was crumbling, had an affair with Anderson, who was still mourning the death of his wife. The relationship cooled afterward, and some fifteen years later the writer published a novel, *After*, based on their affair (2006: 166–69).

In 1959 Hepburn was planning to star in an Alfred Hitchcock thriller, *No Bail for the Judge*, opposite Laurence Oliver as her father, a judge wrongly accused of murder, and Laurence Harvey as the barrister defending him. However, her dissatisfaction with the script due to its violence and her becoming pregnant again, along with the disinterest of the two British actors when she pulled out, not to mention Paramount's inability to secure permission for shooting in London's courts, were all factors that caused the project's cancellation.[1] Hitchcock made *Psycho* (1960) instead.

Hepburn's next three films further expanded her repertoire of roles, though not with the same results for each. She played a Native American girl adopted by a white family in *The Unforgiven* (1960), a western with Burt Lancaster, Audie Murphy, and Lillian Gish under John Huston's direction. Hepburn's character, the girl Rachel Zachery, is to my eyes somewhat similar to Rima, mainly because the part is underwritten; and, along with the miscegenation of their coupling, there is an incestuous sense to Rachel's burgeoning romance in the closing moments with her adopted brother, played by Lancaster. But while this relationship would have made for a more culturally profound as well as controversial theme in 1960, it barely registers in the film. There is not much chemistry between Hepburn and Lancaster to supply an underlying and ongoing sexual tension before the fadeout. He always seems like big bossy brother to her little sister.

The production was troubled and had a muted reception when released in the spring of 1960. Huston wanted to make a film that vilified racism and violence, but his intent was foiled by the producers, who wanted a more traditional western. Huston was contractually forced to make what he called, with reference to star and co-producer Lancaster, "a swashbuckler about a larger-than-life frontiersman" (Brizel 2009: 145). Huston would later claim that he hated this film, which he considered his worst. And it was during this production that Hepburn fell off a horse and seriously injured her back. Production had to be halted while she recovered. Afterward, she did not like to remember *The Unforgiven* because of the riding accident and subsequent stillbirth of a child shortly after the shoot had completed.

Hepburn's next film would become the one for which she is most remembered today. In *Breakfast at Tiffany's* (1961) she plays Holly Golightly, a "lady of the evening," as the parlance back then used to put it, and for that reason Hepburn hesitated before accepting the part. But she did accept, encouraged to do so by her husband. Hepburn successfully pivots between her character's kooky innocence and sexual sophistication, often capturing both senses of this woman together; it is a winning and complex performance. Her co-star, George Peppard, is stolid but no match for Hepburn's charisma and charm; he seems to be with her just for the ride, for the plot to have a more conventional couple, which may well be the intended characterization since Holly is so vital, so full of life, and so unpredictable and unconventional.

Breakfast at Tiffany's was a moderate hit when it first opened, mainly due to Hepburn's star power, her Givenchy wardrobe, and the Henry Mancini–Johnny Mercer song, "Moon River," which Hepburn sings in the film without having her voice dubbed by someone else. Over time the film's popularity has increased fourfold, and Holly Golightly has become the star's signature role. Aside from the unfortunate and racist casting of Mickey Rooney as the angry upstairs neighbor, Mr. Yunioshi, which seriously mars the film at several points, director Blake Edwards pulls off a wacky depiction of the New York sophisticated cohort at the start of the sixties. His set piece is Holly's wild cocktail party, where she first appears draped in a white bedspread before changing into her black cocktail dress, as more and more guests crowd raucously and drunkenly into her tiny apartment until Mr. Yunioshi calls the police. In this expertly staged scene every visual joke is nailed. In terms of Edwards's career, the party sequence predicts the importance of perfectly timed slapstick in his subsequent comedies like the *Pink Panther* series.

Breakfast at Tiffany's opened at Radio City Music Hall in October 1961, and *The Children's Hour* (1961), which gave Hepburn a second opportunity to work with William Wyler, began an

Oscar-qualifying run in December at an LA area theater, although it did not open nationally until March of the following year. Based on Lillian Hellman's play about two private-school teachers wrongly accused by a vengeful student of being a lesbian couple, *The Children's Hour* was first filmed by Wyler in 1936. Only then, to avoid association with the drama for its homosexual topic, the title had to be changed to *These Three* and the lesbian rumor altered to a heterosexual triangle. Of the two women in *The Children's Hour*, Shirley MacLaine's Martha has more depth and conflict, and more to do acting-wise, than Hepburn's Karen, who in comparison gives a more emotionally controlled performance.

The Children's Hour got respectable reviews and did decently at the box office, but Hepburn's performance in it, while nuanced and subtle, was overshadowed at the Oscars by her unexpected finesse as a party girl in *Breakfast at Tiffany's*. Also overlooked was MacLaine. The only performer to get Academy recognition was Fay Bainter as the gossiping and self-righteous grandmother of the troublesome student.

Hepburn's next two projects were filmed in Paris. A backstudio picture about writing a screenplay, *Paris When It Sizzles* (1964) meanders, looking for a plot, though the plot *is* the meandering. The shoot was difficult. After watching the first rushes, Hepburn was dissatisfied with Claude Renoir's cinematography and had him replaced with Charles Lang Jr., who had had that role on *Sabrina* and would do so again on her next film, *Charade*. More significant—since gossip columns picked this up—were the many delays caused by costar William Holden's heavy drinking, exacerbated by Hepburn's refusal to pick up in private where they had left off a decade earlier. At one point, production was shut down while he went to rehab to dry out; at another point, he was hospitalized after crashing his new Ferrari into a wall. Hepburn reportedly hated the film when she saw it (Paris 1996: 183). Yet it was nonetheless "a joy to make," as she told her son Sean Ferrer, so she further advised him "not to correlate the experience of making a movie with its outcome" (Ferrer 2003: 163). When studio execs saw the finished product, they found it incomprehensible and temporarily shelved it until April 1964, eighteen months after production had been completed. For both Hepburn and Holden, *Paris When It Sizzles* concluded their Paramount contracts, freeing each to be independent of a studio in the future.

The day after filming concluded on *Paris When It Sizzles,* Hepburn began *Charade* (1963) for her *Funny Face* director, Stanley Donen. This thriller would not only be the first of her "woman in danger" movies but would also mark the adjustment of her "Audrey" persona to suit her real age: she was thirty-three when production began and her character is a widow. On the Criterion Blu-ray Peter Stone says that he wrote the script with Hepburn and Cary Grant specifically in mind for the two main characters, Regina Lampert and Peter Joshua, and Hepburn agreed to do it only if Grant were cast. Donen had it ready to go at Columbia until Grant pulled out of the project to do a Howard Hawks comedy and Hepburn therefore declined. After toying with other stars, Columbia put the film in turnaround. By then, Grant did not like the Hawks script and was back on board for *Charade* along with Hepburn, and Universal greenlit production.

Grant agreed to rejoin the project if a change was made in the screenplay. Feeling it would be untoward for him (at age fifty-eight) to make moves on the younger (by a quarter century) Hepburn, the star had Stone flip the couple's sexual dynamic so that *she* repeatedly tries to entice *him* with charm and innuendo. Regina also has a ravenous appetite when stressed, so we see her eating in many scenes. For audiences, the in-joke is that her character eats like a horse but never gains weight, forever looking like the ultrathin Audrey Hepburn, who herself reportedly had a good appetite, so the recurring joke appears to allude to the star with tongue in cheek. Stone says that this trope was in his original script and not something he added with reference to Hepburn once she was cast, but he also says he created the part of Regina Lampert for Hepburn to play: so the recurring joke was put in for the ultrathin Audrey Hepburn then, wasn't it?

Anyway, another joke in *Charade* refers to something that happened to the stars off-screen, and apparently this *was* intentionally worked into the final script as an in-joke for the two stars. When Hepburn and Grant met for the first time with Donen at a restaurant before filming began, she was so nervous that she knocked a bottle of red wine all over Grant's light-colored tan suit. The impeccably dressed Grant, a known clothes horse, then had to eat dinner in his visibly stained clothes. Ever the gentleman, to smooth over her embarrassment, the next day Grant sent Hepburn a tin of a caviar and a card telling her not to worry about the suit. Donen and Stone subsequently had art imitate life, for in the film, Hepburn accidentally knocks her ice cream cone on Grant's suit as they walk along the Seine (Hepburn 1996: xiii).

Charade was a huge hit nationally at Christmastime. With Hepburn and Grant in starring roles, it proved to be the most financially successful film of Donen's career. On the Blu-ray disc, he opines, I assume with tongue in cheek, "It's not a bad movie if you just look at their faces." Some reviewers, though, felt the series of gruesome deaths in *Charade* were inappropriate for Radio City Music Hall's big, tourist-heavy seasonal show, but the film had a hefty run at that massive movie palace nonetheless, even breaking the house record there during Christmas week. Nominated for best song, *Charade* was otherwise overlooked at the Oscars; however, Grant and Hepburn were both nominated for Golden Globes, and she won the BAFTA for Best British Actress of the year. Also notable about *Charade* were its several heavies: Walter Matthau, James Coburn, and George Kennedy would soon become well-known actors.

While making *Breakfast at Tiffany's*, Hepburn told a reporter that Eliza Doolittle in *My Fair Lady* was her dream role (Paris 1996: 175), and she was finally signed for this film in 1962 at a higher salary than any actress had received up until that time. Warner Bros paid $5.5 million for the film rights to the Broadway megahit and would pay another million plus incidentals to Hepburn, so before any footage was shot it was already proving to be an expensive project; the final cost would eventually be in the $17 million range. After unsuccessful (but publicized) attempts by Jack Warner to get stars for the two big male roles (Cary Grant as Henry Higgins, James Cagney as Eliza's father, Alfred Doolittle), Rex Harrison and Stanley Holloway were imported from the original Broadway cast. However, Julie Andrews, the stage Eliza, was never seriously considered, presumably because at this time she was not a big enough name beyond New York and London to anchor such an expensive production. Additionally, it was not uncommon practice then for Warners to buy a hot Broadway property, import most of the stage cast, but use a movie star as one of the leads, as the studio had previously done when Doris Day replaced Janis Paige to star opposite John Raitt in *The Pajama Game* (1957), Tab Hunter replaced Stephen Douglass to star opposite Gwen Verdon in *Damn Yankees* (1958), and Shirley Jones replaced Barbara Cook to star opposite Robert Preston in *The Music Man* (1962).

Hepburn took extensive vocal training before filming of *My Fair Lady* (1964) began on August 13, 1963. She prerecorded all of Eliza's songs to lip-sync to during filming. Lip-syncing was standard Hollywood protocol for musicals, with the audio and visual tracks of a number, each recorded and edited at different times during production, eventually united in what the industry referred to as "a married print," an expensive process usually reserved mainly for this genre. Rex Harrison balked at this practice because he could not match his lip movement while filming his talk-songs to a prerecording, so he recorded his numbers live with a tiny microphone hidden in his tie, with the full orchestral track added afterward. After a great deal of anguished discussion, music director André Previn, director George Cukor, and producer Jack Warner decided Hepburn's vocals were unusable and Marni Nixon was hired to dub Eliza's numbers in secret for the release print. When Hepburn found out that she would be dubbed, she was furious and angrily left the set, but returned the next day and apologized for her unusual outburst.

While Hepburn does an expert job of lip-syncing, Nixon's dubbing is forever problematic for *My Fair Lady* because her soprano does not appear to emanate from Hepburn's body; nor is Nixon's cockney accent in keeping with either the tone and depth of Hepburn's speaking voice or the star's more complex diction, whether screeching as the flower girl or speaking ever-so-correctly as a lady. On the release print one can still hear Hepburn's own voice in tiny, isolated sections of "Just You Wait," "The Rain in Spain," and "Show Me." Her complete prerecorded vocals for "Show Me," "I Could Have Danced All Night," "Wouldn't It Be Loverly?," and "Without You" are available on YouTube; and "Loverly" and "Show Me" with the addition of a full orchestra comprise extras on the Blu-ray edition of the film.

The problem Hepburn faced when singing was that Eliza's numbers were not arranged down from the stage version's high soprano to suit her lower mezzo range; although her voice is soft and only occasionally tinny, she holds the melody fine except in "I Could Have Danced All Night," where one can hear her struggling to reach the high notes. It is regrettable that Warners did not make an effort to use more from Hepburn's tracks in the release print. The studio might have edited a number's vocal track from Hepburn's different takes of a song, then amplified the volume of her soft voice so that it stood out more forcefully apart from the orchestra, and only inserted Nixon's soprano at moments where Hepburn's vocal grasp audibly (and harshly) exceeded her reach. Or it would have helped smooth over the dissonance between Hepburn's speech and the singing if the studio had used a singer whose soprano sounded like it could conceivably emanate from Hepburn, as happened when Nixon served as Deborah Kerr's voice double on *The King and I* (1956). For me, as I already complained in the introduction, the disconnect is always audible, which breaks the illusion of what I am watching.

Nixon's contract to overdub Hepburn's singing required complete secrecy, but word got out before the film's premiere, and the backlash to Hepburn's casting instead of Julie Andrews and her "incomplete" performance due to the dubbing, as Hedda Hopper complained in her gossip column, may have cost the star the Academy Award nominations that went to her costars, Holloway and Gladys Cooper, and the Oscar to Harrison (and, as it turned out, the Oscar to Andrews, the winner that year for her debut, *Mary Poppins*). *My Fair Lady* was an enormous hit, the year's top grosser, with very long runs as a roadshow attraction in big and small cities, and it received numerous accolades, including eight Academy Awards out of twelve nominations.

My Fair Lady played throughout 1965, and Hepburn's next film did not open until the following summer, when it again was a Radio City Musical Hall attraction, where it had a nice seven-week run. Originally titled "Venus Rising" during its production in Paris, *How to Steal a Million* (1966) reunited Hepburn with director William Wyler for a third time. It charmingly blends romance and comedy into its heist narrative; it's what my parents used to call a "cute" picture, highly enjoyable because of the clever script and great chemistry between Hepburn and Peter O'Toole. She plays Nicole Bonnet, whose father (Hugh Griffiths) descends from a line of art forgers; he himself is a master forger of post-impressionist painters and has a world-famous collection of those artists' works, all fakes. He has lent a fake Cellini sculpture of Venus, a small figurine actually carved by Nicole's grandfather many decades before, to a leading Parisian museum for an exhibit of local collectors. To prevent the fraud from being discovered by an art expert unexpectedly required by the museum for it to insure the sculpture, Nicole arranges with Simon Dermott (Peter O'Toole), a man she assumes is an art thief but who is really an expert in high-level museum security and art forgery, to steal the sculpture so it will escape examination and prevent her father from being exposed. Of course, in the process of successfully stealing the small statue, the couple fall in love. The film was moderately successful but did not break even given its expensive cost.

Two films starring Hepburn came out the following year, which would be her last ones for quite a while. The first, *Two for the Road* (1967), was filmed at various locations in the French countryside. This third time out with director Stanley Donen recounts the uncertain, often anguished or angry, yet always passionate marriage of a British couple, Joanna (Hepburn) and Mark Wallace (Albert Finney), as they take five road trips in France during a period of a dozen or so years. The film opens with the couple sullen and sniping at each other after Mark, by now a highly successful architect, has been summoned to meet with his patron and major client in France. Cued by Joanna's and Mark's voice-overs, the film then cuts to their accidental meeting over a decade earlier on a similar channel crossing; they unexpectedly end up hitchhiking together, fall in love, and decide to marry. Influenced by the period's European cinema, Frederic Raphael's intelligent screenplay is nonlinear, criss-crossing between the couple's multiple trips. Changes in Hepburn's costumes and hairstyles and in the automobiles as they become more upscale identify where we are in the film's intricate temporal structure.

At first Hepburn hesitated to take on the role, despite her favorite director's persistence. Ferrer also argued in favor of his wife's accepting Donen's offer, believing that the change of pace would benefit her career by expanding her persona, since she would be playing a mature, sexual woman who has a brief affair with the brother-in-law of her husband's major client. Actually, at one point before she has her affair, Finney's character hooks up with a woman for a one-nighter while on the road by himself, yet whereas her infidelity is made a plot point, his is treated as a mere dalliance. Joanna never discovers Mark's infidelity as far as we know, although she may suspect. When Mark finds his wife and her lover together at a cafe, she tells Mark she is leaving him but ultimately returns to her marriage shortly thereafter. On their final trip, the couple recommit again. "I love a happy ending," Joanna says, as he mutters, "Bitch," and she returns, "Bastard," which are the final lines of dialogue.

Two for the Road world-premiered in late April at Radio City Music Hall; it had a good but not smash four-week run before moving to an art cinema on the east side of Manhattan, where it found more of its intended audience. By comparison, the film was a big hit in Los Angeles; opening Memorial Day weekend exclusively at the Bruin Theatre in Westwood Village, the locale of UCLA on the affluent west side, the film stayed there for seventeen weeks. Though well received by critics and appreciated by older and college-age viewers, the film did not break even. All the same, Donen's biographer considers it "his best work. It is the picture that film students most request to speak to him about" (Silverman 1996: 299).

On a personal note, I was a freshman at UCLA when *Two for the Road* opened and saw it five times during its first-run engagement at the Bruin. (In college my friends and I used to see films we liked multiple times—this was before home video.) From a radio contest I entered because of my deep admiration for the film, I happened to win a pair of those huge sunglasses exactly like the ones Hepburn wears in the movie and the ads, but unfortunately, they were lost or broken a long time ago. Flash to the present day: I had not seen *Two for the Road* since then until I started writing this book and am happy to say it still holds up.

The years 1966–67 were a pivotal time for Hepburn. She was thirty-seven when making *Two for the Road*, and no longer the pixie Audrey of her past successes. While she convincingly plays a nineteen- or twenty-year-old virgin at the start of the story, *Two for the Road* gave her a rich, complex character who is sometimes emotionally effusive and very sexual, at other times bitter, brittle, and bitchy, and who matures through the course of the film. Hepburn was more than up to the challenge of the role; in fact, from the perspective of the wide emotional range required of her as Joanna, in my view it is her greatest performance. And as if art reflected life, her marriage to Mel Ferrer was failing; while making *Two for the Road* she had a not-quite-all-that-secret love affair with her costar, Albert Finney. Their relationship ended only when Ferrer threatened to divorce Hepburn and gain full custody of Sean. The Ferrers then temporarily reconciled.

In a final effort to save their marriage, Ferrer produced his wife's next film, *Wait Until Dark* (1967). This thriller, based on a stage play, has Hepburn terrorized by three men (Alan Arkin, Richard Crenna, Jack Weston) trying to locate a doll stuffed with heroin that was handed to her unknowing husband (Efrem Zimbalist Jr.) in JFK airport. The men are certain that Hepburn knows the whereabouts of the doll, and to persuade her to hand it over, they will make her believe that her husband is the chief suspect in a murder and the doll is the only thing that will keep the police from arresting him. The twist in this plot is that Hepburn's character, Susy Hendrix, is blind, initially an easy audience for this charade until things do not start to add up for her, and she figures out that she is being played by all three men—but not before she finds the doll in her apartment. The famous climax occurs in complete darkness after Alan Arkin has killed his two cohorts and comes to collect the doll and murder Hepburn, while she has eliminated all the lights inside her apartment and the outer hallway in order to create a more even playing field.

Wait Until Dark, with a late October opening at the Music Hall and national openings at Christmastime, was an enormous hit, and even today it ranks very high among fans of horror for its thrilling climax, which, when I rewatched it, *still* caused me to jump in surprise: after Hepburn stabs him with a kitchen knife, from the dark a dying Arkin lunges out on the floor and grabs her ankle. Under Terence Young's skillful direction, Arkin is chillingly effective as a maniacal sadist who gets a kick out of killing. Overlooked at the Oscars (whereas he was nominated the year before and the year after), Arkin has said he was not surprised to be ignored because you hardly get nominated for being mean to Audrey Hepburn. On a Blu-ray supplement, he confessed, "I hated terrorizing Audrey Hepburn. . . . Whatever her screen persona appears to be, that's what she was like." Hepburn gives a standout performance as Susy; she is understated at first, always convincing as a blind woman, and her intensity and fear build as the terror mounts.

Wait Until Dark was Hepburn's fifth and final Academy Award nomination for Best Actress. At the time some felt it was overdue consolation for being ignored for *My Fair Lady*, but I think it was a deserved recognition of her craft in playing to such powerful effect a deceived and terrorized character. Later, Hepburn said she would have preferred to have been nominated that year for *Two for the Road*, where her acting is more varied and reveals more depth (Paris 1996: 239). Interestingly, *Wait Until Dark* was also a reunion of sorts for Hepburn and director Young, for he had been a wounded Allied soldier whom, as a volunteer, she had helped to nurse in a Dutch hospital during the Battle of Arnhem in World War II.

Though *Two for the Road* and *Wait Until Dark* displayed her acting chops, Hepburn was absent from the screen for the next nine years. During this period, she and Ferrer finally ended their marriage, and soon afterward Hepburn met Andrea Dotti, who became her second husband. The couple had a child, Luca, and until her new husband's infidelities became intolerable, Hepburn enjoyed being momma to her two sons in Rome. She said afterward she had not intended to retire, but life and children apparently got in the way, and no film offers interested her enough to leave her family.

Then, after almost a decade away from the screen, Hepburn returned to acting in *Robin and Marian* (1976), a bittersweet meditation on growing old, when one's spirit and body lose their synchronicity. Reportedly, her sons persuaded her to accept the role of a mature Maid Marian, now a mother abbess, because her costar would be James Bond, aka Sean Connery, who plays the older, battle-scarred, arrogant Robin Hood returning to Sherwood Forest from the Crusades. With a distinguished cast alongside Hepburn and Connery—Robert Shaw as the Sheriff of Nottingham, Nicol Williamson as Little John, Richard Harris as Richard the Lionheart, and Denholm Elliott as Will Scarlett—Richard Lester directed the film on location in Spain (standing in for Merry Olde England). Lester had found his audience as director of two frantic comedies with the Beatles, *A Hard Day's Night* (1964) and *Help!* (1965), and he was known for his frenetic editing. He also shot his films quickly without many retakes or additional setups, a practice that made Hepburn uncomfortable during the shoot. Despite the literate screenplay by James Goldman, the theme of aging and mortality that dominates the storyline of Robin's reunion with Marian did not go over well with younger audiences.

Robin and Marian was the final Hepburn film to play Radio City Music Hall. When the film premiered there with "a nice $235,000 despite tame reviews," *Variety* went on to note in its weekly grosses report: "If only the Hepburn fans show up, it could run for the next 10 years" ("Early Easter" 1976: 18). The trade paper was probably being sarcastic with this remark, though no doubt even with the verbal side-eye, it was recognizing the immense appeal of Hepburn as a box-office draw, despite her having been off-screen for nearly a decade. That nine of the seventeen films she made up to this time were booked at this cavernous movie palace, which could pick and choose what it played because of its own prestige and draw to tourists, I think, was indicative of her enduring and widespread popularity.

Alas, *Robin and Marian* would also prove to be Hepburn's last good film. She returned to the screen three years later in *Bloodline* (1979), based on Sidney Sheldon's potboiler bestseller. Though she is the lead, surrounded by a solid international cast (James Mason, Ben Gazzara, Irene Pappas, Romy Schneider, Michelle Phillips, Omar Shariff, Beatrice Straight), and directed by her friend Terence Young, as soon as it opened "the Hepburn fans" failed to show up; this preposterous thriller failed loudly at the box office and critics panned it in scathing reviews.

Hepburn should have been luckier with her next film, *They All Laughed* (1981), a screwball romantic comedy directed and cowritten by Peter Bogdanovich, but this film ended up having trouble getting released. Hepburn had agreed to do it for personal reasons: her son Sean was given a supporting role as well as the position of Bogdanovich's assistant, enabling him to learn the business firsthand; and her costar was again Ben Gazzara, with whom she had had a romance while making *Bloodline*. Gazzara by now had found a new companion and Hepburn herself was getting to know Robert Wolders, a fellow native of the Netherlands who would become her final life partner in what she later stated was her most fulfilling relationship. As for Bogdanovich, he fell in love with an actor in the film, Dorothy Stratten. After *They All Laughed* completed shooting in 1980, Stratten was murdered by her possessive ex-lover, a horrible turn of events that cast an indelible stain on the film. The original distributor pulled out and the film was shelved for over a year, its limited release ultimately funded by Bogdanovich himself, but without success, plunging the director in debt.

A weightiness hangs over the film due to Stratten's murder but also because of an uneven screenplay, uncertain direction, and tonal inconsistency between the two major plots. In each, a husband has hired private detectives to follow his wife, and in each the detective falls for his quarry. Especially when viewed today, this plotting is plain creepy, since not much humor or romance genuinely resonates from the situation of men stalking women. As the detective pursuing Stratten, John Ritter acts as if he is still in a TV sitcom; his many pratfalls and stumbles, meant to level the stalking with physical humor, don't generate much laughter and quickly become tiresome. Gazzara typically seems like he is in a bad mood throughout, but I imagine he means to project a certain kind of virile masculinity. As important, Hepburn initially is shown from a distance through his POV shots as he follows her. She does not get a chance to speak until nearly an hour has passed. Playing a woman who knowingly embraces a transient affair with the man following her, Hepburn is radiant, looking more refreshed and beautiful than in *Robin and Marian* or *Bloodline*. In particular, her scenes with the boy playing her son display a warmth and affection that seems artless and natural.

Hepburn returned to acting again six years later with a movie made for television, *Love Among Thieves* (1987). Built around the chemistry of Hepburn and her costar, Robert Wagner, and rehashing some tropes from *Charade*, this film would have been sure-fire theatrical entertainment in the 1930s, but I imagine this kind of light romantic road movie would have still worked for older TV audiences in 1987. Hepburn plays a countess who has stolen three Fabergé eggs from a museum as ransom for her kidnapped fiancé. She and Wagner, who may or may not be an art thief or an Interpol agent, meet cute on a small airplane and end up on the road together as she travels to a backwater Latin American town to deliver the ransom. Despite its silly and unrealistic plotting, I find this screwball road movie more watchable than either *Bloodline* or *They All Laughed*.

Although she had already begun her humanitarian work as ambassador for UNICEF the year after *Love Among Thieves* aired on ABC, in a sort of coda to her film career, Hepburn agreed to a brief role as an angel in order to work with Steven Spielberg in *Always* (1989), his remake of *A Guy Named Joe* (1943). Wearing all white, she gives a haircut to recently deceased pilot Richard Dreyfus, as she tells him his job is to pay forward to another pilot with the inspiration that had once helped him. Hepburn's final television appearance was as the host of a PBS series on famous gardens of the world, which aired on the network shortly after her death and won her a posthumous Emmy Award.

In closing, I want to point out what has probably already been obvious to you, namely, that Hepburn's career as a major movie star pretty much occurred in a fourteen-year period from 1953 (*Roman Holiday*) to 1967 (*Wait Until Dark*) when she was in her twenties and thirties. That these are the films for which she is remembered, and that her appearance on screen changed very little during this period—for she could still convincingly play the same virginal girl in the first road trip of *Two for the Road* that she had played in *Roman Holiday*—accounts for her lasting impact as a screen icon. She not only seems charming and elegant but ageless as well. That is also to say that her status as a Hollywood legend owes much to the fact that the few films she made when she returned to acting in her late forties and early fifties were not big successes and have pretty much faded into obscurity. Though on YouTube there is footage of her in middle age at various tributes, award shows, and interviews, her youthful image from her famous films remains indelible as the Audrey Hepburn who still charms and fascinates, while the real woman's own mortality gets forgotten.

3
The Audrey Films

Audrey Hepburn's acting has not been fully appreciated because so many of her films from the 1950s and early 1960s, most made under her contract with Paramount, recount a romantic, fairy-tale-styled narrative with a Cinderella heroine: *Roman Holiday* (dir. William Wyler, writ. Dalton Trumbo, Ian McLellon Hunter, John Dighton, from a story by Trumbo), *Sabrina* (dir. Billy Wilder, writ. Wilder, Ernest Lehman, Samuel A. Taylor, from a play by Taylor), *Funny Face* (dir. Stanley Donen, writ. Leonard Gershe), *Love in the Afternoon* (dir. Billy Wilder, writ. Wilder, I. A. L. Diamond, from a novel by Claude Anet), *Breakfast at Tiffany's* (dir. Blake Edwards, writ. George Axelrod, from a novella by Truman Capote), *Paris When It Sizzles* (dir. Richard Quine, writ. George Axelrod, from a French film by Julien Duvivier and Henri Jeanson), and *My Fair Lady* (dir. George Cukor, writ. Alan Jay Lerner, from a play by George Bernard Shaw as adapted for the musical stage by Lerner). To appreciate this group of Audrey films as a cycle one has to look past the individual contributions of directors and screenwriters—for, as I have just shown, these films were made by different people and came from various sources—and appreciate how these were all crafted for the Hepburn persona, which is also to say that her persona centers these films and gives them their coherence as what I call "the Audrey film." From this perspective, Audrey Hepburn can be seen as the films' "auteur," not in the sense that she created them but, rather, with the understanding and appreciation that without her in the starring role their creation now seems inconceivable. It is also important to remember that while starring as what I also term "the Audrey figure" in this cycle, during this same period, Hepburn acted in other, generically different films as well: *War and Peace, Green Mansions, The Nun's Story, The Unforgiven, The Children's Hour,* and *Charade.*

Hepburn's own biography, as she went from an initial aristocratic upbringing to extreme and fierce hardship during World War II to glamorous movie stardom, was read as a Cinderella story in its own right. "Audrey Hepburn's happiness is contagious," wrote Pauline Swanson in *Photoplay* when Hepburn sat down for an interview after finishing *Sabrina.* "It springs from the heart of a girl who once knew life at its darkest" (1954: 58). This article devotes a good deal of space to describing the young star's traumatic experiences during the war, beginning with the moment when "Ten-year old Audrey lost the security of her protected childhood brutally fast," and it goes on to recount the grueling five years of poverty and privation, the constant hunger and bitter cold, along with the actual danger, during the Nazi occupation. "If we got through [it] with our lives, that was the only thing that mattered," Hepburn remembers. Swanson comments that the star "doesn't like to talk too much about it any more [sic] or even to think about it, but those years were crucial in forming the personality as well as the physical person of this stimulating newcomer to the screen" (102).

Sabrina, Billy Wilder's witty romantic comedy about class snobbery at both ends of the social spectrum, may be the quintessential Audrey film. It begins with Hepburn's voice-over: "Once upon a time, on the North Shore of Long Island, some thirty miles from New York, there lived a small girl on a large estate." That "small girl," Sabrina Fairchild (Hepburn), daughter of the estate's British chauffeur, is infatuated with the younger Larrabee son, David (William Holden), a twice-divorced playboy, who barely notices her. The night before she is to leave for culinary school in Paris and deeply unhappy because of David's indifference, Sabrina attempts suicide but is rescued by the older Larrabee son, Linus (Humphrey Bogart), a staid, conservative, Brooks Brothers type of CEO. An unhappy Sabrina goes to learn cooking in Paris, as shown in a montage of her disastrous attempts at perfecting recipes—until an older gentleman in her class, the eighty-year-old Baron, takes her in hand after she has forgotten to turn on the oven for her soufflé. He rightly attributes her many culinary failures to her being unhappily in love, introduces her to the delights of Paris, and helps her to become chic, sophisticated, and adorned in Parisian couture and with a stylish cropped haircut. After two years in Paris, Sabrina returns to the States.

When she arrives at the Glen Cove train station on Long Island, David, who happens to be driving by, at first doesn't recognize the newly cosmopolitan young woman but falls head over heels for her and offers her a ride; once he learns who she is, he invites her to a ball to be held that evening at the family mansion. Unfortunately, he is now engaged again, this time to a woman whose family's business the Larrabee Corporation needs for its new line of indestructible plastics. This merger and the marriage that will secure it do not seem to matter to David, who at the dance arranges a tryst in the indoor tennis court with Sabrina. However, knowing his brother's seductive tactics with women and determined to push through the merger, Linus slyly puts David out of commission and courts Sabrina in his younger brother's place—with the latter's consent since Linus convinces him the two brothers are allies in David's courtship of the chauffeur's daughter. As they dine out, go to the theater, go dancing in the evening and boating in the afternoon, Sabrina and Linus begin to have feelings for each other.

During all of this, Hepburn's face registers Sabrina's growing if uncertain attraction to Linus. In contrast with her vivaciousness and high spirits when she returns from Paris, Hepburn's animated expressions change to divulge the character's ambivalence about turning her heart from one brother to the other. As their night on the town begins with frozen daiquiris in Linus's office at the Larrabee Building in Manhattan, Sabrina is happy and playful until he feigns confessing that he is sick of business and, inspired by her descriptions of romantic Paris, plans to go there. Hepburn smiles widely to show surprise but also delight in his declaration. Still smiling, she says she is so very glad he is going. But the smile quickly fades, as she looks down at her drink and says to herself quietly, "Or am I?" In profile, a pensive Hepburn looks directly at Bogart without saying anything more.

Later, as the two dance cheek to cheek in a nightclub, in a close-up Hepburn's face silently registers Sabrina's growing puzzlement at her new feelings for the older brother. As they drive back to Long Island, Linus mutters, "suppose I might ask you to go with me," but quickly admits he is "talking nonsense." Sabrina closes her eyes and agrees sadly, "I suppose so." When they arrive at the Larrabee estate, David is waiting for them in the car park. As she watches Linus depart for the family mansion, Sabrina asks David to kiss her, then to kiss her again, and finally to hold her closely in his arms. A close-up shows Hepburn looking as if she is about to cry, reflecting not only her confusion about what she now feels for each brother but also that this uncertainty pains her.

Despite his own growing attraction to Sabrina, Linus still plans to trick her into returning to Paris alone, albeit with a first-class ticket on the *Liberté*, a hefty letter of credit, and an apartment in the city. Eventually, Sabrina finds two boat tickets and assumes that Linus intends for her to go with him, expressing her great joy at this discovery; but he guiltily tells her the truth, that he was only pretending in order to get her away from David so the merger could proceed, and that she will find his stateroom on the ship unoccupied. Sabrina takes a single ticket and unhappily departs, intending to return by herself to Paris. Of course, true to the fairy tale, "once upon a time" opening voice-over by Hepburn, it all ends happily: David realizes that he and Sabrina are not in love with each other; he commits to his engagement, the family business, and the merger; and he arranges for his brother, who he proves *is* in love with Sabrina, to join her on the ship.

The musical *Funny Face*, Hepburn's fourth film, is another Cinderella narrative. Hepburn plays Jo Stockton, an intellectual working in a Greenwich Village bookshop who becomes a fashion model, despite (or rather because of) what she considers to be her "funny face." Led by bullying editor Maggie Prescott (Kay Thompson), the crew of *Quality* magazine invade the bookshop for an impromptu fashion shoot. The next day, when he develops his pictures and enlarges her face from the background, Dick Avery (Fred Astaire) sees Jo's potential for modeling because of her unusual but captivating face. Though she initially considers fashion to be "silly dresses on silly women," Jo agrees to go to Paris to be photographed as the *Quality* woman in a line of couture by Duval (Robert Flemyng), a noted designer like Givenchy, because it will give her the opportunity to meet Professor Émile Flostre (Michel Auclair), whose theory of empathetical communication she endorses and whom she considers to be "the greatest living philosopher."

Hepburn's first song in *Funny Face* positions her as a Cinderella. When everyone from the magazine but Dick leaves, Jo finds the bookstore in chaos with piles of books scattered everywhere. Dick helps her replace the books to their proper shelves and asks her to define "empathy" for him. Then he kisses her, explaining, "I put myself in your place and felt you wanted to be kissed." Informing him that she does not stock what he is looking for, Jo sends him away, and alone, begins to sing "How Long Has This Been Going On?"

This well-known Gershwin standard is about the wonderment of unexpectedly falling in love. Even though some lyrics have been added in the film's version to emphasize that Dick's surprising kiss prompts the song, Hepburn's performance and director Stanley Donen's staging also make it a number about Jo's discovering glamour, which gives her the same wonderful sensations that a kiss does. The magazine people have accidentally left in the shop a hat worn in the photo shoot. The hat has a yellow crown and a wide orange brim surrounding it; two long, gauzy, chartreuse veils are attached to the sides of the brim. This boldly colored chapeau stands out from the dull, dark brown colors of the bookstore setting, and it serves as Hepburn's only prop as she performs the song. Jo sings, "How long has this been going on?" and smiles, contemplating the question. Putting on the hat, holding the end of a veil in each outstretched hand, and assuming a wondrous expression, she looks in a mirror at her reflection and sings that she knows how Columbus must have felt when he found another world. But when she immediately goes on to ask if she can trust how she feels—or "Is this my Achilles' heel?"—her face turns solemn as she muses about her vulnerability. When she subsequently again asks the question posed by the song's title, she smiles gently, this tentative expression again showing her introspection.

Then, in the dance break, Hepburn removes the hat from her head and excitedly runs around the shop and twirls, waving the hat back and forth, up and down, the two long veils swirling like colorful kites in the air. Putting the hat back on, her arms outstretched, she sings about being "in such a lovely state" with another big smile. But when the song concludes with her shaking her head as she quietly sings, in a new final line written for the film, "Can one kiss do all of this?"—reminding us that all along Jo has been singing about the sparks she felt from Dick's kiss—Hepburn's thoughtful expression shows not only that this question is still open-ended, but so is the antecedent of *this* in the song's title. Does the pronoun only refer to sexual feelings awakened by Dick's kiss, feelings Jo has repressed? Or can *this* also allude to her finding unexpected pleasure in the beauty of glamorous things, as symbolized by the vividly colored hat? The slight word is heavy with both meanings in this number, I think, making Dick's kiss and the appeal of fashion equivalent: both connote romance as opposed to philosophy for Jo. The number concludes with Hepburn lowering her head so that the wide brim of the hat covers her face. When she raises her head, she looks resigned to her situation. Once more staring at her reflection in the mirror, she frowns, tosses the hat onto a nearby sofa, and resumes cleaning up the bookshop.

The conflict left unresolved by the song rushes to the surface for Jo when she is in Paris, for she finds herself torn between, on one hand, the pleasure she experiences when modeling haute couture for Dick's camera, along with her growing romantic feelings for him, and, on the other hand, her commitment to empathicalism, since her meetings with Flostre and his acolytes in Paris distract her from her obligations to the fashion magazine, Maggie, and Duval. This results in several big quarrels with Dick, who she rightly feels belittles her intellect, and the couple's arguing triggers embarrassing pandemonium before a press conference begins at the salon to showcase Jo as the new *Quality* woman and almost cancels the next evening's fashion show that will display her in Duval's new line. However, Flostre turns out to be the womanizer Dick suspects he is, and by the end, the photographer and Jo happily reunite.

As it happens, though deriving from a George Bernard Shaw play and faithfully based on the musical adaptation by Alan Jay Lerner and Frederick Lowe for the Broadway stage, *My Fair Lady* tells the same story as *Sabrina* and *Funny Face*, especially when watched as an Audrey film—and why not? Hepburn *is* the star, though reportedly Rex Harrison thought it did not matter who played opposite him as Eliza Doolittle, Julie Andrews or Audrey Hepburn or whoever else might be in the running, for audiences came only to see him. Ha ha to that! Hepburn's Audrey persona was perfectly suited for Eliza, perhaps more perfectly than Andrews's would have been on film at that time, judging at least from *Mary Poppins* (1964) and *The Sound of Music* (1965), the two musicals that connected with audiences and made her a big movie star in her own right.

Eliza's numbers in *My Fair Lady* counterpoint Henry Higgins's. Whereas his solos express his misogyny ("An Ordinary Man," "Why Can't a Woman Be More Like a Man?") or his elitism ("Why Can't the English?"), hers express her anger at or frustration with him or with Freddy Eynsford-Hill (Jeremy Brett) as well as her independent spirit ("Just You Wait," "Show Me," "Without You") or her longing for a better life ("Wouldn't It Be Loverly?"). On stage, the contrast between Harrison's speak-singing and Andrews's glorious four-octave soprano voice brought their difference out. On film, Marni Nixon's dubbing of Eliza's numbers only makes me more aware of Hepburn's uninhibited, no-holds-barred performance. Even when taught to be refined and respectable, her Eliza is a young woman of loud, volatile emotions: at times angry, distressed, fearful, frustrated, unhappy, dreamy, all these feelings expressed by Hepburn's animated face and body. No twee is she!

Given her spirit and independence, I have to wonder why Eliza returns to Higgins in the film's final moments, especially since she departs the previous scene stating he will never see her again. And Henry's mother, Mrs. Higgins (Gladys Cooper), applauds Eliza's strength in this penultimate scene, exclaiming, "Bravo, Eliza!" If Henry has grown accustomed to her face, it is because she knows where everything in his house is and keeps it running and orderly, as he realizes when she leaves the morning after the Embassy Ball, presumably for good. Eliza's ultimate return to Higgins at the close of *My Fair Lady*, I think, seeks to disavow Mrs. Higgins's earlier accusation to her son about his and Colonel Pickering's (Wilfred Hyde-White) makeover of Eliza. After Eliza's disastrous attempt to act as a lady at the Ascot racetrack when she gets overexcited and curses, Mrs. Higgins calls the two men "a pretty pair of babies playing with your live doll." I am never quite convinced that Eliza ever ceases being Higgins's "live doll," however much he comes to appreciate her service in his household.

In sum, for all of the intelligence and independence Hepburn adds to her characters, *Sabrina*, *Funny Face*, and *My Fair Lady* exemplify the Audrey film's Cinderella plotting with its required happy ending. In each, a young girl—gangly and of serving-class people (Sabrina Fairchild in *Sabrina*); overly intellectual and indifferent to how she looks and dresses (Jo Stockton in *Funny Face*); dirty, uneducated, and selling flowers in Covent Garden (Eliza Doolittle in *My Fair Lady*)—elevates her social standing through the love and/or tutoring of an older man (Linus Larrabee in *Sabrina*, Dick Avery in

Funny Face, and Henry Higgins in *My Fair Lady*). Much as the fairy godmother turns Cinderella into a begowned and bejeweled princess, these three films reveal through a fashionable wardrobe the more elegant young woman initially hidden by the dowdy figure, a princess in her dress and comportment if not due to a royal birth. Each film gives Hepburn an older fairy godparent of sorts, too: the eighty-year-old Baron (Marcel Dalio), who introduces Sabrina to the sophisticated pleasures of Paris; Maggie Prescott, who takes Jo to Paris to model for her magazine; and Colonel Pickering, who teaches Eliza self-respect and treats her like a lady despite Higgins's misogyny and relentless bullying in *My Fair Lady*. Finally, in each film, the older man wins the Audrey figure away from the wooing of a younger seducer or suiter: David Larrabee in *Sabrina*; Professor Émile Flostre in *Funny Face*; and Freddy Eynsford-Hill, the upper-crust, swooning young gentleman who would have to live off Eliza's earnings in *My Fair Lady*.

However, what Sabrina's father says to Linus about his daughter's "in-between" or liminal social identity upon her return from Paris applies to the situation of the Hepburn character in an Audrey film, which gives her complexity and makes her a focal point of genuine interest and identification. "She's just a displaced person, I am afraid. She doesn't belong in a mansion. But she doesn't belong over a garage either." That is the idea also expressed in Jo's solo musical number in the Greenwich Village bookshop and by her conflict once in Paris when she finds herself torn between, on one hand, wanting to hang out in Left Bank cafes all day to converse "empathetically" with Flostre and his acolytes (for she does not speak French), and on the other, the fun she has when posing for Dick all over Paris and their growing mutual attraction. Liminality is also Eliza's quandary after the Embassy Ball: Where does she belong? She can't go back to Covent Garden but cannot imagine how or where to go forward. In order to close "happily ever after," the Cinderella plots give this liminal figure a clearer and more stable sense of belonging to a place: Sabrina and Linus sail to Paris, Jo will continue to model for Dick back in the States, and Eliza returns to Higgins's house. Presumably, these couples all marry, but if that happens, we don't see it occur. The closest we get to a marriage in these films is the end of *Funny Face*, but only because Jo still wears the wedding dress from the fashion show. The last number, which serves as the finale, "'S Wonderful, 'S Marvelous," concludes as Hepburn and Astaire float away into the distance while still dancing together on a raft.

Roman Holiday is another Cinderella fairy tale, but one told in reverse. Here the Audrey figure is a *real* princess! Hepburn plays Ann, a princess of an unnamed European country on a goodwill tour of the continent, where she visits London, Paris, and Amsterdam, during which she gives canned speeches at various state events, industrial buildings, and shipyards about Europe's economic future, predicting in a very indirect manner the formation of a nascent European common market. (Such a free trade zone for Western Europe did not actually emerge until the Treaty of Rome in 1957, and this common market would eventually form one basis of the present-day European Union.) Exhausted from her busy, repetitious schedule, upon arriving at her country's embassy in Rome, and following a boring formal reception for scores of dignitaries, Ann begins to protest hysterically until a doctor gives her a shot to calm her down and make her sleepy. Once her entourage departs from her chamber, the woozy princess gets dressed, sneaks out of the embassy building, climbs into the back of a laundry van leaving the gated grounds, and falls asleep there. Waking when the van stops on a busy Roman boulevard, a still-woozy Ann disembarks and, after stumbling around some pedestrians, goes to sleep on a bench, where an American reporter, Joe Bradley (Gregory Peck), finds her. He assumes she is drunk and tries to send her on her way in a taxi; from his behavior, we can infer he also thinks she may be a streetwalker.

Ann will not fully wake up, however, so Joe ends up taking her to his tiny flat to keep her safe. The next morning, the princess's entourage discovers she is missing, announces she has been taken ill, and cancels her scheduled press interviews. Joe himself has overslept and missed his own appointment with the princess; unaware of the cancellation, he tries to convince his angry editor that he did meet her, only to be found out. Upon discovering the real identity of the young woman whom he rescued, Joe convinces his editor that he can get an exclusive interview with the princess. So Joe and his photographer friend Irving (Eddie Albert) follow Ann on her Roman holiday as her companions, secretly interviewing and photographing her. (Irving has a camera hidden in a cigarette lighter.) At first, Ann wanders by herself and enjoys the Roman street life as well a newfound sense of freedom from royal duties, while Joe, never disclosing his real intent, follows her surreptitiously until the two meet up again, with Irving joining them in a series of amusing picaresque adventures arising from her encounter with the urban Roman locale, which places the princess in a liminal space for the first time in her life. For in Rome Ann gets to do things she has never done before. She wears men's pajamas, gets a haircut, buys gelato from a street vender, drives a motor scooter (and does it wildly), is arrested, goes dancing, participates in a mob fight on the dance barge when a cadre of security men try to take her back to the embassy, and dives into the Tiber alongside Joe to escape those men.

By the film's closing moments Ann and Joe have developed feelings for each other and they kiss, but she knows she must return to the embassy to resume her royal life. As for Joe, the next morning he tells his editor he has no story after all; and at the rescheduled press conference he and Irving give Ann an envelope with the many covertly taken photos of their day together as a souvenir of her Roman holiday. When asked for her most memorable stop on her European tour, Ann at first pauses but then with a smile, she states, "Rome," as her aides react uncomfortably to her break with protocol.

The reversal of Cinderella in *Roman Holiday* is explicitly signaled in the opening when, at the embassy reception in Rome, Ann loses a shoe (hidden inside the skirt of her long gown) while receiving the numerous guests, and she recovers it on her own, the assembled dignitaries none the wiser. Much later, indirectly acknowledging to Joe her inevitable departure, Ann refers to herself as a Cinderella who will leave at midnight and whose carriage will turn back into a pumpkin. At film's end, when the princess resumes her royal life and duties despite the potential for romance with Joe, she has been transformed by a new sense of empowerment resulting from her day's adventures.

Love in the Afternoon, Hepburn's reunion with Billy Wilder, varies the fairy-tale template somewhat but is still clearly another Audrey film. Hepburn plays Ariane, a young cello student in a music conservatory who is about ten years younger than Hepburn herself was at this point in time. Ariane is fascinated by the sordid cases that her father, a private investigator named Claude Chavasse (Maurice Chevalier), keeps in his files. Since his office is in their apartment, she also cannot help overhearing his conversations with clients (well, actually she eavesdrops) or peek at the photographs on her father's desk. The film implies that Ariane is a virgin, and the many accounts of promiscuity and adultery that she overhears and reads secretly in her parent's files inflame her curiosity about sex, fidelity and infidelity, and men. When she learns that one of her father's clients intends to shoot his wife's lover, the notorious middle-aged American playboy and frequent object of Chavasse's investigations, Frank Flanagan (Gary Cooper), Ariane decides to intervene to prevent that from happening.

Thus begin her afternoon flirtations with Flanagan, when Ariane poses as a woman of the world with a trail of former lovers left in her wake, as the playboy becomes besotted with her: fascinated, horny, and jealous all at once. *Love in the Afternoon* dramatizes Ariane's liminality as a sexual awakening through her pretending for Flanagan's benefit that she is his equal in having had numerous affairs. For even if we infer that Ariane sleeps with Flanagan following the discreet fadeouts required by the Production Code, she is still never the promiscuous girl she pretends to be. Before she enters Flanagan's hotel room for the first time, she stands outside on the balcony and peers inside; the close-up of Hepburn shows Ariane's utter astonishment at the lovemaking happening in the room. Indeed, throughout *Love in the Afternoon*, Hepburn's performance slightly heightens Ariane's posing as a sophisticated woman of the world—as when in a later scene, for instance, wearing a borrowed fur coat, she struts and sways into Flanagan's hotel room—to clarify that she is an innocent girl playacting at being a female Don Juan.

If her "love in the afternoon" reminds us of Cinderella at the ball insofar as Ariane is not only pretending to be someone she is not but also doing so in an environment safely disaggregated from her mundane home life, then we may also see her father as her fairy godparent. He indirectly gives her the opportunity to meet the roué Flanagan, and the files in her father's office form the basis of the stories she tells Flanagan about her many fictional love affairs. Moreover, when the jealous playboy hires Chavasse to investigate Ariane, her father is the means of ultimately getting the couple married, a highly unlikely turn of events given Flanagan's own sexual history. Yet the final scene—when Ariane says goodbye to Flanagan at the train station, the train starts to pull out, and he sweeps the girl in his arms and into the carriage, with Franz Waxman's romantic score playing on the soundtrack—is still one of the great rushes in my experience of film, even though at the same time I know better and otherwise find this film highly problematic because of the severe age difference in the casting of Hepburn and Cooper.

That said, in *Love in the Afternoon*, the Audrey figure is no passive shrinking violet but a young woman whose own desires move the plot from scene to scene and cause the complications that keep it going for over two hours. After all, Ariane first encounters Flanagan when she rescues him from the cuckolded husband who has murder in his eyes, and to get into the hotel room to warn the American playboy, she has to climb along the lodge from the balcony of the room next door. Ariane's home life, where her father shields her as best he can from the real sexual life of adults that he investigates for a living, stands in contrast to her afternoon dalliances with the playboy. In fact, she controls the terms of their meetings when Flanagan is in Paris; she will only meet him in the afternoon, never in the evening as he wants, and she will not disclose her name. To be sure, her stories give her a means of intriguing and seducing the playboy, since his history implies that he goes for women experienced in the art of love. But during their afternoon trysts, Ariane narrates a fantasy life for herself that allows her to experiment vicariously with her own sexuality as a grown woman, not as the young, virginal girl her father views at home. As for Flanagan, he is not an agent of the narrative but a passive receiver, acted upon by Ariane; her bogus past inflames his sexual attraction to "thin girl," so he calls her, as she recounts her affairs lover by lover, doling out new bits of information at each meeting. In this sense Hepburn is playing Scheherazade as well as Cinderella. And that the Audrey figure in *Love in the Afternoon* controls its narrative movement should alert us to how she does something similar in the other films in this cycle.

For example, to return to the other Billy Wilder romantic comedy with Hepburn, Sabrina's sexual curiosity motivates her infatuation with the handsome, virile David Larrabee, the well-known playboy. At first she is a voyeur of his exploits. The night before her scheduled departure for Paris, Sabrina observes the Larrabee ball from a tree; then, moving like a sleepwalker, she silently follows David to the indoor tennis court, where he plans to meet his new conquest, the giggling Gretchen. Standing outside in secret, Sabrina watches David seduce the young woman using his standard playbook of champagne and the melody of "Isn't It Romantic?" Much like Ariane's response to witnessing Flanagan's lovemaking when she stares into his hotel room from the balcony, in this film, too, Hepburn's face shows her youthful character's astonishment at the sexual byplay of the two adults; then she turns in profile and sobs, unable to act upon her own desire for David—and possibly frightened by it, too, given her amazed look. All that is left for the miserable and jealous Sabrina to do, she assumes, is to drown her sorrow in a cloud of carbon monoxide inside the vast Larrabee garage.

However, with her return from Paris, Sabrina gains the upper hand. Failing to recognize her and smitten by her new sophisticated beauty and charm, David keeps trying to guess her identity as he drives her home from the train station. Sabrina smiles, her mouth closed as if suppressing a laugh, because she enjoys fooling him. She controls the terms of the jest. When Sabrina tells him she won't reveal her name, she smiles with glee, saying she's having too much fun, as if playfully punishing him for not noticing her in the past. Even with Linus, while he schemes to have her transfer her affection from his brother to him, Sabrina upends his plans because he falls in love with her. The more Linus encourages her to tell him about Paris—with the aim of sending her back there by herself and out of David's life—the more her descriptions of the city's magic seduce him into wanting to go there with her. Indeed, while David initially would throw caution to the wind and risk being cut off from his allowance for marrying the chauffeur's daughter, Sabrina moves Linus to do just that, leveling the class divide (though obviously, he will still have his hand in the business and never want for money).

In the fairy-tale films starring Hepburn, this is all to say, the men are basically reactive to her. The Audrey figure and her desires drive the narrative, and the men react to *her*, to what *she* wants and does. Sabrina's infatuation with David threatens the family's plans for him and the merger; she is the obstacle to their impersonal corporate mentality and elitist class snobbery. And she knowingly moves in on David when she returns from Paris despite her awareness that he is already engaged to another woman. As the film's trailer exclaims after showing Holden and Bogart fighting in the boardroom toward the end, "And Sabrina's the cause of it all!" Intending to separate her from David, Linus becomes ensnared himself by her warmth and high spirits—and Hepburn's performance makes clear that, while increasingly torn between the two very different brothers, she *is* ensnaring both men with her newly acquired sophistication, youthful energy, delight in life, and sense of mischievous play.

Likewise, in *Roman Holiday*, Princess Ann leaves the embassy in secret, and she instigates her adventure in Rome. Joe soon recognizes her and accompanies her, hoping to get a blockbuster news story, but by the end, he decides not to write it out of respect for her position and reputation and because he develops feelings for her. Having failed to get his big story, Joe is still in debt to his editor, while Ann's holiday has given her a more independent spirit. In *Funny Face*, Jo agrees to go to Paris only so she can meet Flostre to discuss his theory of empathicalism, and, except for the montage of Dick photographing her wearing Duval's collection, her motive for going causes delays, disruptions, and embarrassment at the salon. And in *My Fair Lady*, Eliza seeks out the smug and condescending Higgins to learn how to speak like a lady in order to elevate her social standing so she can work in a respectable flower shop. No fool she, Eliza clearly recognizes and gets furious with his bullying; and when he takes full credit for *her* success in deceiving everyone at the Embassy Ball, she disturbs his equilibrium by leaving abruptly and taking refuge at his mother's.

At this point, though, I must finally address the elephant in the room. For the presence of the aged Cooper as the young Hepburn's love interest in *Love in the Afternoon* was not unique. During her most active period as a movie star, Audrey Hepburn *was* cast opposite much older men: Humphrey Bogart in *Sabrina* (thirty years difference), Fred Astaire in *Funny Face* (thirty years), Cooper in *Love in the Afternoon* (twenty-eight years), and Rex Harrison in *My Fair Lady* (twenty-one years). Additionally, she starred opposite Henry Fonda in *War and Peace* (twenty-six years difference) and Cary Grant in *Charade* (twenty-five years). Gregory Peck in *Roman Holiday* (thirteen years difference), William Holden in *Sabrina* and *Paris When It Sizzles* (eleven years), Mel Ferrer in *War and Peace* (twelve years), and Burt Lancaster in *The Unforgiven* (thirteen years) were somewhat younger, although still older men compared with the girlish youthfulness Hepburn projected on-screen. Peter Finch, her costar in *The Nun's Story*, was thirteen years older, but he was not really a romantic lead in the film. In fact, one can argue that the strongest emotional bond Hepburn's character has with a man in *The Nun's Story* is with her apparently widowed father, the famed surgeon played by Dean Jagger (twenty-six years her senior); it seems one-sided on his part, for he states several times how much he misses his daughter, who had assisted him in the hospital, and how lonely he is since she entered the convent (he has two other daughters and a son, by the way).

Although cast as romantic leads opposite Hepburn, some of these men, notably Fonda, Cooper, and Harrison, were not only old enough to be her father, but they *looked* it. With his Jiminy Cricket face that never seemed to change from his RKO musicals with Ginger Rogers in the 1930s, Fred Astaire always looked physically immortal because of his agile body and nimble, breathtaking, lighter-than-air footwork, still much in evidence in *Funny Face*. Cary Grant, whom Wilder had originally wanted for Bogart's and Cooper's roles, never seemed to age all that much either, at least not enough to lose his considerable sex appeal. In *Charade* he runs, jumps, climbs, and fights, demonstrating that he is still as limber as he was a few years earlier in *North by Northwest* (1959).

Why does *Sabrina* still work its fairy-tale magic today as it did in 1954, whereas *Love in the Afternoon* is more leaden and, frankly, a bit creepy when you think of it? Aside from the spell cast by Hepburn's contagious joyfulness over the entirety of *Sabrina*, the casting of Holden as the younger brother serves as a generational mediator between her and Bogart, who always had the face of an ageless character actor despite his status as a leading man since the 1940s, whereas the third person of the starry trio of *Love in the Afternoon*, Maurice Chevalier, is thirteen years older than Cooper yet on-screen the two men look the same age. That Ariane seeks a father replacement, that she replaces one patriarchal figure for another, is an inescapable conclusion from the casting, if not the script itself. By contrast, as Sabrina brings out Linus's romantic side, she makes him seem more like a reputable and more mature version of his rascally younger brother, the sexier and more classically handsome David. Also, despite his off-screen estrangement from his two costars and director, Bogart seems game to take on what for him was a new genre, light comedy, and to play against his tough-guy image, whereas Cooper seems tired and in need of a nap. In fact, while filming the scene where Ariane looks for the shoe Flanagan has hidden in order to prevent her from leaving his hotel room, Cooper kept falling asleep (Sikov 1998: 394)! In his off-screen life, too, Bogart's romance with and marriage to the much younger Lauren Bacall made him a more likely and attractive suitor for a younger woman like Hepburn on-screen, at least implicitly. Finally, Billy Wilder plays it safer with Bogart than he will later do with Cooper, though he took pains with lighting and camera angles to disguise the age of both men. When Linus first steps in for David on the tennis court, he kisses Sabrina in his brother's name, and Hepburn's face shows her surprise and puzzlement at how much Sabrina likes the kiss. But an hour later, in the final moment when Linus reunites with her on the ship, their clinch is shown in a medium long shot, placing the audience at a visual distance from this May-December couple.

With a few exceptions (Anthony Perkins in *Green Mansions* [three years younger], George Peppard in *Breakfast at Tiffany's*, and James Garner in *The Children's Hour* [both men one year older]), the uneven generational casting dominated Hepburn's filmography of the 1950s and early 1960s. Was this all that unusual for the period? Not really. It is a truism of 1950s Hollywood that as the big male stars of the 1930s and 1940s grew older, their female costars got younger (which is not say that it is any less true of many older male stars today). At the time, the on-screen courtship or seduction of young women by older men in Hollywood movies was taken for granted or accepted with a shrug. The only Hepburn film that may have failed at the box office because of the asymmetrical casting was *Love in the Afternoon*, due to how old Cooper looked alongside her, which some reviews noted. After making this film, he reportedly underwent a facelift—he thought he looked too old, too!

Furthermore, in 1955, as Hepburn was becoming wildly popular and an inspiration for models in the pages of *Vogue* and *Harper's Bazaar*, Vladimir Nabokov's *Lolita* was published, and the film version came out in 1962. Before then, recall, it was because of Hepburn's gamine yet nubile look that Collette personally selected her to play Gigi—the teenager being groomed as a courtesan for older men—in the non-musical adaptation on Broadway that opened in late 1951. Hepburn was the most famous and popular gamine star of the 1950s, but she was not the only such star to emerge then. In 1954 Sheilah Graham saw Hepburn as part of a trend, including her with all the other "gamine girls with the crazy cuts and the lean lines" who offered the antithesis of "the lush and lovely lasses," those sexy, bosomy women like Elizabeth Taylor, Jane Russell, Marilyn Monroe, and Ava Gardner (Graham 1954: 62). As young women, Leslie Caron, Shirley MacLaine, Debbie Reynolds, Jean Simmons, and Jean Seberg were all initially characterized with the same elfish, waifish, and mischievous qualities of a gamine as Hepburn, and they also were initially cast opposite older male stars. Alan Nadel comments that *Lolita* satirizes the postwar American male fantasy of romantic obsession with adolescent girls that, in turn, expresses a fear of mature women (2018: 75–87). This "Lolita syndrome" is especially evident in many films of the period, not the least those starring Hepburn, whom Nadel happens to discuss briefly in passing (he focuses mostly on films in which Reynolds and Caron play opposite older men).

Many of Hepburn's films may seem more unnerving to viewers today than in the past because of the drastic age difference in the romantic coupling of a young girl and an older man. The star casting and narrative closures can seem especially perverse for twenty-first-century viewers who balk at the subordination of her youthful, vital character to a much older male figure, a star like Gary Cooper in *Love in the Afternoon* who is visibly past his physical beauty and sexual prime yet in the film's diegesis still seems able to command his patriarchal authority over Hepburn, as when he pulls her into the train at the end. Her youthful energy and sexuality intrigue Cooper's character, but the conclusion's implication is that, while marriage to her will curtail his playboy ways, he will, in turn, tame her wild spirit and rebelliousness.

Admittedly, the Lolita fantasy resonant in so many of Hepburn's films from this era may have drawn some men into theaters alongside wives or girlfriends, who went if only for the fashion shows. Yet the youthfulness of Hepburn in contrast with that of her much older male costars may possibly suggest reasons other than sexual desire for her characters' attraction to these father figures. Does Hepburn's ultrathin, androgynous body, unlike that of the other gamine stars mentioned above, neuter the Audrey figure and, in desexualizing the age difference of the couple, make it more tolerable? Does it then go so far as to interrupt the Lolita fantasy, jamming the happy endings? Or is it possible that the Audrey figure welcomes the older man's tutelage, seeing him more as a teacher than a lover, even if that amounts to his domination of her? For that matter, rather than desiring the older man sexually or seeking his guidance and instruction, does she identify with him? Ariane is the most extreme case, perhaps, but can we not often see the Audrey figure fascinated by the older man's maturity as it implies a wealth of sexual experience as well as social authority that she herself lacks but fantasizes about? *Sabrina*, too, suggests this in the scene when the astonished Sabrina observes David and Gretchen's heterosexual byplay on the tennis court, her expression suggesting that she may be witnessing and understanding such sexy flirting for the first time. And can't all these questions arise in our minds simultaneously as Hepburn performs the Audrey figure on-screen? I do not mean to talk in circles about the age difference but am pointing out some competing impressions possibly arising from the May-December casting.

Breakfast at Tiffany's stands apart from the films I have been discussing insofar as Hepburn is cast opposite a male star who is her contemporary, and she plays a woman of her own age who is openly sexual and defiantly unconventional, quite a change from the rather chaste Cinderellas she had been playing. Nonetheless, *Breakfast at Tiffany's* should be viewed as an Audrey film, much as the Hepburn character, Holly Golightly, can be considered another Audrey figure, though one drawn in darker, more ambiguous, and contradictory shades. For *Breakfast at Tiffany's* turns the Audrey film inside out only to restore its shape in order to reach a conventional romantic conclusion.

In *Breakfast at Tiffany's*, Holly Golightly is living Ariane's fantasy of sexual experience and independence. Coming from the colorless rural Texas background and first marriage at age fourteen to a much older man (since annulled), Holly has reinvented herself as a stylish and sophisticated, yet kooky and unorthodox, woman of the world. She resists being possessed by anyone and won't even claim to own her pet cat or give him a name—or so she says, yet she does repeatedly call him "Cat." We get a glimpse of Eula Mae Golightly, the original Texan girl, when, forgoing her customary fashionable attire, in a sweatshirt and blue jeans, and with her hair wrapped in a towel, Holly sings "Moon River" while strumming a guitar on the fire escape of her apartment building. Holly is another liminal Audrey figure stuck in a perpetual state of midnight—the coach and footmen have not yet turned back into a pumpkin and mice, but she is no longer at the ball. For as she tells Paul Varjak (George Peppard) late in the film, she is not Holly nor is she Eula Mae; in fact, she exclaims, "I don't know who I am!" Neither waif nor sophisticate—or possibly both at the same time—she is suspended in a moment of transformation.

Holly's kooky personality, moreover, enables one to ignore or discount, if one wishes to, how she is really "a lady of the evening" wheedling fifty dollars for the powder room from rich gentlemen, her "dates," after which she departs without returning. An early scene following the credits has one such drunken man waiting outside her apartment building for her return (which implies he must have been there previously since he knows her address), where he pursues her into the vestibule and up the staircase to the second floor, shouts that she owes him for the fifty dollars he gave her for the powder room and another fifty for a taxi, as well as the nightclub check he covered for her and her friends, and loudly pounds on her door after she retreats inside her apartment. Is Holly a prefiguration of the sexually liberated single girl of the sixties (thank you, Helen Gurley Brown), as she thinks of herself (and as Sam Wasson argues), or is sex for her simply transactional, as her actions and the script's reiterated emphasis on her getting fifty dollars from a john keeps reminding us? Hepburn's performance keeps both interpretations in the air. Holly acknowledges several times how she earns her keep when she compares her fifty-dollar dates with the "rats," as she calls those men, to the financial/sexual arrangement Paul has with 2E (Patricia Neal), the older, married woman who is keeping him. Before Paul gets to witness the Eula Mae hidden behind the Holly persona, Holly has already seen Paul without *his* mask. From the fire escape outside his apartment (where she went to elude a persistent, drunken "rat" who is inside her apartment), she watches 2E leave money on the table and kiss Paul, who is naked and asleep.

Yet unlike Paul, doesn't Holly at least still seem virginal for all her sexual hustling? Some of this feeling may be due to how the screenplay has to treat Holly's occupation as a paid escort with discretion to satisfy Production Code requirements. Yet from Hepburn's performance, Holly often seems to me a girl playacting as an escort but at the same time one who is undeniably a "prick tease," as such young women at bars were called. Hepburn's Holly is innocent yet brazen, as when, entering Paul's bedroom from the fire escape and finding $300 on the table, she asks him if 2E pays him "by the week, the hour, or what?" When he seems offended by her question, she kneels by his bed and wants him to know, "I understand completely." Her response, which means to assure him that she was not putting him down and that the two are alike, shows her blunt candor. Her understanding of what transpired between Paul and 2E, though, also indicates that she appears to comprehend sexual relations primarily as economic transactions. Yet the seemingly worldly Holly then crawls into bed with the naked Paul, not for sex but for comfort, snuggling next to him as if he were her sibling; awakened by a nightmare that causes her to cry out, she rebuffs Paul's attempt to comfort her and leaves. The sophisticated Holly now seems more like a traumatized little girl lost.

Or is Holly really just a phony, as Holly's agent, sponsor, and fairy godparent, O. J. Berman (Martin Balsam), declares to Paul several times. In Berman's view she is not only a phony but, paradoxically, "a *real* phony," for "she honestly believes all this phony junk that she believes." That apparently excuses Holly's excessive behavior and her mistaking her own naiveté for kooky sophistication, as when she has no idea that she is carrying coded drug messages for the incarcerated Sally Tomato (Alan Reed).

Hepburn affects a somewhat flat American accent in her speech as Holly; listen to how she pronounces her vowels. As Holly, Hepburn's voice sounds familiar yet different from previous characters, for the actress exerts more emotional control over her speech so its volume seldom varies. She modulates her voice so that her diction is smooth, soft, and sweet, although the cadence of her speech still characteristically ends sentences on an upbeat, as I mentioned in my introduction. Moreover, one can hear faint traces of the Texan accent Holly has repressed in Hepburn's phrasing. Berman tells Paul that this diction was hard for Holly to achieve because she could not get rid of her thick rural accent until she took French lessons. The unnaturalness of Holly's speech, since she had to learn it like a foreign language, implies her inauthenticity, suggesting that she is always performing and wearing a Holly mask, as it were. So, is there a there there? One can't be sure, although the "Moon River" sequence attempts to strip away the glitz and glamour of Holly's made-up sophisticated identity.

Additionally, unlike in the other Audrey films, Holly's sexual behavior is not really aimed or directed at any one man romantically in the way Sabrina is infatuated with David or Ariane with Flanagan. True, Holly wishes to marry someone who is very, very wealthy regardless of his looks or her feelings for him, in large part to support her brother Fred when he gets out of the army. She has a fantasy of their raising horses together somewhere in Mexico. Trying to put away money for when Fred returns from the army, but unable to save more than "a couple hundred dollars at a time," Holly gets fifty dollars from each of her many dates, supplemented by the one hundred dollars a week she gets for visiting Sally Tomato in Sing Sing. Paul, on the other hand, finds himself attracted to Holly almost as soon as they meet, but she calls him "Fred," giving him her adored brother's name. She treats Paul as a surrogate sibling, not as a lover.

Paul's own sexuality is at first somewhat dubious, too, and not only because of the apparent ease with which he enjoys 2E's patronage. During the raucous party scene in Holly's apartment, while she herself makes a play for the wealthy nebbish, Rusty Trawler, Paul pulls José, the rich Brazilian visitor, toward the bathroom; and as Paul leads José through the tangled crowd of partygoers, they are filmed in a way that always gives me the impression the two men may be headed there for a quick sexual hookup. Given the Production Code, that is clearly never going to happen, of course. Yet the impression of queer behavior at the party lingers because, once inside the bathroom, Paul and José discover O. J. Berman in the shower making out with a female impersonator who gives the name "Irving" (and "girl in the shower" is, according to the IMDb, played by a man, Thayer Burton, whose two other roles were as a cashier in an episode of *Alfred Hitchcock Presents* and as "Betty Benson" in an episode of *Alcoa Premiere*). After Paul and José climb through the window, they shake hands and go their separate ways, almost as if they did hook up—and to my mind, that visual implication of Paul's possible queerness remains in the air for a while afterward, disavowed and displaced onto the sight of Berman and Irving kissing behind the shower curtain.

The film's tone changes and becomes more sentimental and conventional midway through. This happens starting with the sequence in which Holly and Paul spend a carefree day in Manhattan with each doing something they have never done before (drinking champagne before breakfast, walking on Fifth Avenue in daylight, buying something inexpensive at Tiffany's, going to the New York Public Library, stealing from a five-and-dime variety store). Their escapade ends with them kissing, which confirms their feelings for each other, but Holly resists their mutual attraction, aiming instead to marry José after learning that Rusty has himself wed an heiress because he is actually broke and in debt. On one hand, the next day Paul throws his fifty-dollar check at Holly when, stating her determination to marry wealth, she coolly rejects his declaration of love, and his gesture means to rub her prostitution into her face (but by extension, can we ever forget his with 2E?). On the other hand, their kooky daylight escapade, which depicts the two not only as harmless outlaws but also as a couple, already softens the more cynical temperature of the film with regard to transactional sex in order to prepare for the romantic conclusion in the rain.

To achieve this ending, though, Holly must accept her dependence on Paul, which in fairy-tale terms means she has to return to the cinders and her pumpkin and mice, thereby resolving what has been her liminality. As the film itself puts it, she must remove her own mask in order to see Paul as himself, not as one of the "rats" who gives her fifty dollars, nor as a substitute for her beloved brother. This may be why Fred has to die before Holly can begin to accept Paul's "ownership" of her (as he puts it) in the name of love. On his part, Paul essentially views Holly as a wounded bird. When he breaks up with 2E, he explains to his patron that he can help Holly. "She can't help anyone, not even herself." Later, as an inconsolable Holly sobs hysterically after learning of Fred's death, José asks Paul, "What can I do?" Paul replies, "Try to help her. I tried but it didn't do any good."

Holly has her darkest hour at this point; but afterward, she still expects to marry José, and in preparation for her departure to Brazil, both she and her apartment have been thoroughly domesticated, as evident in her knitting and its new, more conventional decor. Subsequently, when she is arrested as a confederate of Sally Tomato's drug ring, Holly again plays the kooky innocent who had no idea what those weather reports meant. But José's desertion of her the next morning returns her to Paul's care. He confesses his love again in the taxi as they leave the jail, and, when she still rejects him, insisting that she will never be owned by anyone, he declares that she *does* belong to him. "Okay," he chides her, "you're afraid to stick out your chin and say, 'Life's a fact, people fall in love, people do belong to each other, because that's the only chance anybody's got for real happiness.'"

After all is said and done, then, *Breakfast at Tiffany's* ends by confirming its inchoate fairy-tale template as an Audrey film. With the heavy rain washing away both her kooky facade and her resistance to Paul, who since their daylong escape in the city has wanted to save her and possess her in the name of "love," Holly finally submits to him. Her ceasing to be the liminal figure we have watched with pleasure during most of the film, however, limits what she can be in the future, because, as Paul claims, his love for her amounts to his ownership of her. Moreover, whereas Holly has just tossed Cat out of the taxi to assert both her defiance of Paul and her and Cat's mutual independence, she now races in the pouring rain to find the critter. As if Cat functions as the glass slipper that unites Cinderella with her prince, the animal signals her capitulation to Paul's entreaty to be loved and owned by him. Once she has the rain-soaked cat in her arms, she hugs and kisses both of them. Cue to "The End."

If, with its sex and the single girl, *Breakfast at Tiffany's* was very much of its moment in 1961, *Paris When It Sizzles* was probably before its time. The film recounts the effort of Richard Benson (William Holden)—an alcoholic Hollywood hack who has told his producer that he has over 130 pages of a screenplay finished but really has nothing to show but an intriguing title, "The Girl Who Stole the Eiffel Tower"—to write a script in two days with the assistance of his typist, muse, and eventual collaborator, Gabrielle Simpson (Hepburn). Richard and Gabrielle inspire the characters of Rick and Gaby, the main players in Richard's screenplay. But as they work on this script, they keep switching genres, as the pair (along with actual scriptwriter George Axelrod) keep tossing one more genre on the wall to see if that one will stick since everything else falls to the floor.

Nothing does stick *in* the film or *for* the film, mainly because the genre parodies are not very funny; whatever wit and fun there are in *Paris When It Sizzles* can be found in the repartee of Hepburn and Holden. For what really happens *as* the actual plot is that the two characters fall in love with each other. At the end of *Paris When It Sizzles* Richard knows his script is rubbish and that he loves Gabrielle (after having rejected her in the previous scene), and the couple go off into the night to write something good, using the solid characters of Rick and Gaby, although this will be a film we will never see. Or perhaps it is the one we have just watched—it is up to you to decide. The final shot is of the two stars moving in for their kiss, or as Richard had said to her in an opening scene and Gabrielle now repeats, "Two enormous, highly paid heads come together for that ultimately inevitable moment, the final, earth-moving, studio-rent-paying, theater-filling, popcorn-selling kiss." Aside from the on-screen heat between the two stars, most everything else in *Paris When It Sizzles* fizzles.

Today we may consider *Paris When It Sizzles* a "metafilm"; in the 1980s critics might have called it "postmodern." It is self-reflexive on many levels, and while I don't think it ultimately works, it is nonetheless interesting on those many levels. First, *Paris When It Sizzles* dramatizes the travails of writing an original screenplay, especially under pressure. Second, it reflects the bloated stakes of the film industry in the early sixties, especially as success seduces a hack writer like Richard into a life of leisure, luxury, and alcoholism. His heavy drinking and expensive tastes are omnipresent in his hotel suite: in the pitcher of Bloody Marys from which he repeatedly fills his glass and in his monogrammed suede shoes that are frequently visible in the frame. The film also self-reflexively registers the fact that millions of dollars can be wasted on a film (one like *Paris When It Sizzles*?) that finally just doesn't play. In the final act of Richard's screenplay, which he has sold to his producer (Noël Coward) on the sole basis of its snazzy title, Rick, the writer's fictional alter ego, has, with the help of Gabrielle's alter ego Gaby, stolen the negative and only workprint of a film also titled *The Girl Who Stole the Eiffel Tower*. Rick intends to extort a fortune from its producer (also Noël Coward) for the return of the twenty-eight canisters. However, knowing his film is a turkey—"The script is so ghastly," the producer tells Rick, that "it can never be released"— the producer promises he will give Rick the fortune if he does *not* return it! (a hint that execs at Paramount apparently heeded for eighteen months).

Third and more important for a discussion of Hepburn and the Audrey film, *Paris When It Sizzles* self-reflexively muses on the attractiveness of movie stardom. What pleasure there is to be found in this film comes from watching Hepburn and Holden, two top box-office stars of the era, reunited after *Sabrina* a decade earlier. The repeated dialogue about the import of two highly paid stars' heads meeting to kiss in a close-up tells us all we need to know; incoherent plotting aside, *Paris* means to sizzle by showing Holden and Hepburn getting all hot and bothered as Richard and Gabrielle work on the script together and fall for each other. This happens in the film-within-the-film as well. Only there, as Rick and Gaby move in and out of different genres, and the story becomes increasingly over the top and preposterous, Holden and Hepburn deliver their silly lines with a wink to the viewer. At times, Hepburn's performance even self-consciously evokes the behavior of figures in cartoons, as she acts wide-eyed and innocent, or devious and sexy, for the character of Gaby drastically changes and reverses course with respect to Rick, following Richard's dictum of "a switch on the switch on the switch" as the basis of a successful script.

Carried over to *Paris When It Sizzles*, too, is one's knowledge that Hepburn and Holden had an affair while making *Sabrina*, so one can watch wondering how much of this now is playacting or real, whether one-sided or two-sided. Likewise, one can wonder how much Richard's alcoholism, which is his primary character trait, refers to Holden's own heavy drinking, which caused delays and budget overruns for *Paris When It Sizzles*. (Holden recalled that Hepburn's disinterest in renewing a relationship beyond friendship intensified his already hard drinking habit.) In the penultimate scene, Richard puts Rick down as no more than a lazy hack yet is speaking of himself, and Gabrielle says of Gaby, though also of herself, "He may think he's all those things. But she knows he is not." Again, isn't it irresistible to speculate that perhaps this scene and the dialogue struck very close to home for both Hepburn and Holden?

Some of that curiosity may be beside the point, to be sure. What fascinates me most about *Paris When It Sizzles* is its self-reflexive treatment of Hepburn as the star of the Audrey film cycle. Perhaps that is not too surprising since George Axelrod had also scripted *Breakfast at Tiffany's*. Particularly telling to me is how he drenches the script with references to Hepburn's stardom. At one point Richard mutters, "Breakfast is at Tiffany's," and the ending as Richard and Gabrelle run off together is reminiscent of that film's conclusion and the earlier scene when Holly and Paul spend the day together doing things they never did before. At another time Richard explains to Gabrielle that *Frankenstein* and *My Fair Lady* have the same plot; each recounts how a man creates a new being and the only difference is that one ends tragically, the other happily. At the halfway point of *Paris When It Sizzles*, Richard puts on Fred Astaire's recording of "That Face." As the song plays, in extreme close-up Holden's hands isolate the famous features of Hepburn's face, her brows, her nose and cheeks, her smile. The couple then dance to the record, until Richard abruptly stops it, declaring that they are not writing a musical. The entire sequence evokes Astaire's singing and his dancing with Hepburn to the title song of *Funny Face* in the darkroom at *Quality* magazine's headquarters. Along with famous guest stars like Coward, Marlene Dietrich, and Tony Curtis, Hepburn's husband Mel Ferrer appears dressed as Dr. Jekyll and Mr. Hyde at the masquerade ball in the film-within-a-film.

The introduction of Gabrielle, moreover, cites the Audrey figure as the basis of her character. She enters like kooky Holly Golightly's cousin, also dressed by Givenchy (whose perfume Interdit, inspired by Hepburn, gets a film credit) and carrying a cage with a canary named Richelieu. When Richard engages her in conversation, she states that she came to Paris two years previously in order "to live," and spent the first six months "making a comprehensive study of depravity," which was difficult when one did not drink or smoke. (Nonetheless, she does both throughout the film.) The first scenes of the film-within-the-film, furthermore, evoke the Cinderella template of the Audrey film. On Bastille Day, the handsome stranger, who we soon learn is Rick, asks her to dance after she has been jilted by her friend, the method actor (Tony Curtis in an extended cameo). Late in the film-within-the-film, at the movie studio, Rick removes Gaby's wet shoes. And while *Paris When It Sizzles* makes Richard the nominal protagonist—he is, after all, struggling to write a script—everything he does and says always focuses on Gabrielle/Gaby. Gaby is at the center of the film he is writing in multiple genres, and his script expresses his fascination with Gabrielle; in short, the Audrey figure drives the writing process. When Richard begins to write, he borrows from what Gabrielle has told him about her desire to go to Paris "to live" and about her date for Bastille Day, which happens in both the film-within-the-film and later in the framing story, and at which Rick and Richard will each appear out of the blue to carry her away.

The self-reflexivity of *Paris When It Sizzles* queries whether there is life beyond or outside of the movies. The film itself and the film-within-a-film are mirror reflections of each other. Even at the very end, after searching for and finding Gabrielle on Bastille Day to say he loves her, Richard compares what he is doing to a scene he has previously written, and indeed this closing scene is set in the same outdoor cafe where the film-within-a-film began. In the world of *Paris When It Sizzles*, there is nothing external to film, which keeps referring back on itself and to itself in an endless loop of self-referentiality. And the ending pulls the rug out from under the entire film because Richard throws away the script, declaring to Gabriel that they will write a better one from scratch, using their alter ego characters of Rick and Gaby.

What this all means, I cannot help concluding, is that Gaby and Rick, Gabrielle and Richard, *and* Hepburn and Holden—these couples can only exist and fall in love *in a movie*. And when those "two enormously paid heads" kiss and fall into each other's arms, we fall in love with their larger-than-life images on the screen. The Audrey figure itself, this film goes even further to propose, likewise does not exist off-screen but is a creation of cinema, too. In saying that, I do not mean to discount Hepburn's charisma and talent as an actress playing "Audrey" here or in other films of the cycle, but it does help to expose the illusion at the heart of her magic, which is to say the craft of her acting. In *Paris When It Sizzles* Hepburn ably distinguishes through her performance the (relatively) realistic, wide-eyed, eager-to-learn-about-screenwriting character of Gabrielle—whose innocence was not shaken by her six months of "depravity" and who falls in love with the Richard hiding behind the cynical and drunk Hollywood sellout—from the artificial, mutating, devious, prostitute-with-a-heart-of-gold character of Gaby in the film-within-the-film, a figment of Richard's hack imagination. But the film's playful deconstruction of Hepburn's magic on-screen, I think, also announced the inevitable end of the Audrey film as a cycle.

Admittedly, *Paris When It Sizzles*, which was made before *Charade* in late 1962 but held back for release by Paramount until the spring of 1964, was not the final Audrey film produced. That honor belongs to *My Fair Lady*, which did not open as a roadshow attraction until October 1964 although Hepburn had signed her then-record million-dollar contract to star as Eliza in 1962. However, the commercial failure and aesthetic incoherence (for Paramount execs, reviewers, and audiences in 1964) of *Paris When It Sizzles*, I think, offered a tacit commentary on the Audrey film as it was self-reflexively deconstructing. While we would still get *My Fair Lady* later in 1964 to close out the cycle, that property was already somewhat antiquated and anachronistic, the film version's eventual huge box-office success and many Oscars notwithstanding. After all, on-screen *My Fair Lady* was a lavish and expensive but careful, respectful, and stage-bound replication of a 1956 stage musical, itself based on a much earlier play from 1913, Shaw's *Pygmalion*, that had been previously filmed in Britain with Leslie Howard and Wendy Hiller in 1938.

On film and on-stage, *My Fair Lady* is still very much a product of the mid-1950s; this is why it so neatly fit alongside *Sabrina* and *Funny Face* earlier in this chapter. As I have said, with her liminal screen persona firmly established for almost a decade, Jack Warner was probably right to cast Hepburn as Eliza Doolittle even though she could not reach the high notes that Julie Andrews effortlessly did on stage. Nonetheless, if *Paris When It Sizzles* sought to blow up the Audrey film, *My Fair Lady* would prove to be its swan song. After these two films, Hepburn would cease to play the girlish "Audrey": think *Charade*, *How to Steal a Million*, *Two for the Road*, and *Wait Until Dark*.

4
Fashion

Her indelible association with haute couture and designer Hubert de Givenchy since *Sabrina* has persuaded many admirers and critics alike to think of Audrey Hepburn simply as a model, a fashion plate. Obviously, Hepburn's influence as a fashion icon during the 1950s and 1960s was considerable; what she wore on-screen "trended," as we say today. Givenchy's contribution to Hepburn's screen performances, however, went beyond simply giving her a distinctive style, for on-screen his clothes allowed her to move in them freely and easily. As Fiona Handyside comments,

> In contrast to the sweetheart line promoted by popular culture as the look for women [in the early 1950s], which emphasizes the female "hourglass" figure and the relation between the presentation of the body in society and its biological function, Givenchy's clothes emphasized Hepburn's body as androgynous and modern. Furthermore, his clothes were not constructed using girdles and restrictive underwear. His was modern clothing emphasizing the freedom of the body to move. (2003: 298)

Hepburn's movement on-screen manifested how fashion liberates rather than confines or contains her characters. For as Rachel Mosely states, "Hepburn's difference was not simply located in her style and body shape, but also in her mobility and activity—she seemed freer and more independent" (2002b: 45).

Generally speaking, Givenchy's designs never tried to hide the star's uncommon features but highlighted them. Notice how frequently the cut and shape of the dresses showcase Hepburn's exposed back, and the many scoop collars do not hide her long neck though they sometimes cover the hollows of her collarbone (about which she was self-conscious). His dresses tend to have a cinched waist, too, sometimes emphasized with a bow or belt, so they do not conceal her middle. In the 1950s, Givenchy and Hepburn favored wide, flouncy ballerina skirts, and the cinched waists on these show off her thin torso all the more. In the 1960s, she wore many Givenchy suits and coats, which tended to be sheaths in their design with funnel collars and large, distinctive buttons. Hepburn typically accessorized dresses with earrings, seldom with necklaces, lockets, or chokers; sometimes she added gloves and a hat or cap. Because of her height (and, she thought, her big feet), she almost always wore kitten heels but occasionally substituted ballet slippers; and these shoes, in contrast with the period's widely popular stilettos, made for greater ease of movement, too.

Furthermore, the Audrey films discussed in the previous chapter visually record the transformation of Hepburn's characters *through* fashion. Such a transformation reiterates how their identities are in flux, for as Mosely points out, they are caught at the moment of "becoming a woman" (2002a: 37). The Audrey figure is both a girl and a woman, or possibly it might be more accurate to describe her as no longer a girl but not yet a woman—which is why in the previous chapter I emphasized how she is a liminal figure on-screen. Appreciating how fashion functions as a mode of transformation for Hepburn, particularly in the Audrey films, is a repeated theme in the many essays written by feminist academic-fan scholars ("aca-fans") for a collection edited by Jacqui Miller (2014) as well as in the comments voiced by the many British fans whom Mosley interviewed (2002a, 2002b, and 2005).

Fashion-as-transformation inscribes an alternate way to view an Audrey film, one that resists linear narrativity: it invites spectators to find pleasure in the film itself as pure spectacle and not as a narrative per se, and to value Hepburn's performance as an enactment of energy and vitality from a perspective that does not let her acting or her characters be bound solely to the plot's progress toward a conservative Hollywood ending in which she defers to her male costars. Transformation through fashion, in short, expresses another way of viewing Hepburn always being in motion.

The three Givenchy outfits in *Sabrina*, which began the designer's collaboration with Hepburn, announced how fashion would highlight the actress's dynamism and energy in two ways: first, fashion works as that transformative device or trope for her Cinderella characters, depicting their growth, spirit, and independence; and second, it does not restrict Hepburn's movement as an actress but assists and accentuates it. To be sure, a female character's transformation through fashionable clothing already had long-standing associations with Cinderella stories before Hepburn made movies, just as it was already a familiar trope for Hollywood, as for example, with Bette Davis's makeover in *Now Voyager* (1942). My goal with this chapter, then, is not to claim anything original to Hepburn, although it became her signature, but to look closely at how fashion served her on-screen.

But that is already to get ahead of myself. To return to Givenchy and *Sabrina*, the story goes that Billy Wilder and Paramount sent Hepburn to Paris to purchase several designer outfits for Sabrina's Parisian transformation into a chic, sophisticated young woman. The proviso was that, rather than Paramount itself contracting directly with a French designer for the wardrobe, Hepburn was given funds to buy the outfits herself so the studio could avoid paying duties and taxes at customs. This strategy also meant that Paramount would not be contractually obligated to give the designer a screen credit. At Audrey Wilder's suggestion, Hepburn intended to see Balenciaga, but, told he was too busy, she was referred to his young protégé, Monsieur de Givenchy. When the twenty-six-year-old Givenchy learned that a "Miss Hepburn" wanted to see him, he assumed his guest was Katharine Hepburn and was flattered. Appearing for her appointment at Givenchy's atelier in Paris, the skinny, unknown, and unrecognizable Audrey

Hepburn—*Roman Holiday* had yet to open anywhere—was so casually dressed she could have been mistaken for a mere tourist. As the designer himself recalled: "It was a very strange ensemble.... Capri pants, with ballerina shoes. A little white T-shirt and a gondolier hat—imagine this in Paris!—with a red ribbon across the top. And no makeup. She looked like a ballet dancer" (quoted in Buck 1989: 8).

Quickly realizing his mistake, Givenchy at first declined to meet with her, stating he had no time to fit her since he had his new collection to finish. Audrey persisted until, swayed by her charm and eccentric garb, he relented and let her look over the previous year's collection to see what she could use for *Sabrina*. Hepburn selected three outfits—a wool suit for Sabrina's return from Paris, a formal ballgown for the Larrabees' dance the evening of her return, and a cocktail dress for her date night in Manhattan with Linus Larrabee midway through the film—and she accessorized them with items she found in the salon according to her own taste. Givenchy saw that Hepburn's body perfectly suited his creations, even when they were pulled off the rack (so to speak). According to this oft-told tale, the two hit it off so well that afternoon that they went to dinner together that evening. Thus began their lifelong friendship.

At this point in the story, I have read conflicting versions of what happened next. One account says Hepburn brought the actual outfits back with her to Los Angeles. If Hepburn had the originals in hand, Edith Head, then in charge of Paramount's wardrobe department, would have probably altered the clothing on the star for a perfect fit. But another story says Hepburn only brought back the designs, from which Head reconstructed the clothing. Scott Brizel reports that Hepburn chose what she wanted from Givenchy's collection of the previous year, and the designer then gave her a sketchbook with the designs and samples of the materials to have the three outfits recreated at Paramount (2009: 45). If that were the case, then, possibly to assuage Head's ego, which was bruised at the thought that someone else would be responsible for Sabrina's

Parisian makeover, the studio exaggerated Head's contribution by allowing her to take sole credit for the entire wardrobe, a credit she did not dispute. Or did Givenchy follow Hepburn to Hollywood to supervise the fittings? In his memoir of his mother, Sean Ferrer includes a photo of Hepburn and Givenchy on the *Sabrina* set, dated November 3, 1953, which is when the film was still in production (though in this still, Hepburn is not in costume as they look over what appears to be a fashion magazine, which makes me wonder if the date is wrong) (2003: 156). Furthermore, even if Hepburn had transported the originals to the States, given the exigencies and mishaps of filmmaking, each outfit was no doubt duplicated in Hollywood, which would have taken place under Head's eye. The director's commentary on the Criterion Blu-ray of *Charade* informs us that Hepburn had three copies of everything by Givenchy that she wore in that film, so there is little reason to doubt this was not already standard protocol for costumes at Paramount, too.

The great buzz about the costumes once *Sabrina* opened dwelled on Givenchy's designs, yet, as I have noted, Head took sole credit on-screen for the film's costuming and won an Oscar for the clothes to boot. When Hepburn discovered that Givenchy did not receive a screen credit for *Sabrina*, she was miffed and promised that in the future she would insist on using him for her wardrobe whenever possible and with full acknowledgment, as would happen just a few years later on *Funny Face*. As important, Hepburn's choice of the three particular outfits was already telling of her own fashion sense, of her own understanding of how clothing supplemented her body by not overwhelming or attempting to hide her particular physical features. For instance, on the period film made after *Sabrina*, *War and Peace*, Hepburn refused to have altered a low-cut ballgown or have it adorned with a necklace simply because the neckline showed her upper ribs as well as her clavicle. The low neckline bothered cinematographer Jack Cardiff, but it was her body, she told him, and it had worked for her well so far in her career (Spoto 2006: 138). Knowing what best suited her physical features, Hepburn would prove to be Givenchy's partner on their future collaborations as well as his muse.

In the first scenes of Wilder's romantic comedy, Head's costuming for Hepburn as the teenage Sabrina emphasizes the character's youth and awkwardness. Hepburn wears a black tunic beneath a three-quarter-length jumper dress made of a geometric patterned fabric; her long hair is arranged in a thick ponytail and she has bangs. Sabrina's crush, David Larrabee, barely recognizes her when he finds her hidden up in a tree, from which she has been watching his family's grand party.

Sabrina does not change her style or girlish manner at cooking school in Paris until the eighty-year-old Baron takes her in hand, but not before first telling her, with reference to her single ponytail, that she must first stop looking like a horse. After two years in Paris, Sabrina graduates and returns home, having learned, as she writes her father, "how to live, how to be in the world and of the world, and not just to stand aside and watch." Closing her letter, she adds that, if he fails to recognize her, she will be "the most sophisticated woman at the Glen Cove station."

Accompanying a dissolve to a shot of a French poodle sitting by luggage, the melody of "La Vie en Rose," the tune Sabrina has heard playing on an accordion outside her window at night as she wrote to her father, morphs into a full orchestral soundtrack; the song now functions as a reminder of Paris for the scene of Sabrina's arrival at the train station. At first, director Billy Wilder delays showing either Hepburn's face in close-up or her full body in a long shot. Instead, slowly the camera travels upward from the poodle, also named David, first revealing half of a figure in a three-quarter-length dark gray skirt; then a gloved arm around the cinched waist of the matching suit jacket; then the torso with the other hand reaching upward; and finally, the newly fashionable and adult Sabrina. Hand on chin, she looks pensively and expectedly for her father.

Voila! At last we have been rewarded with the much-anticipated sight of Audrey Hepburn's face and her new, sophisticated look after her Parisian makeover. She wears hoop earrings, and a white turban, rakishly slanted on her head, conceals most of her fashionable (and trendsetting) pixie haircut; the hat stands out as a contrast with the dark suit and gloves. A subtle jump catches Hepburn in a medium shot as she turns to face the camera directly, yet her eyes glance to the left of the frame. The camera then pulls back until it reaches a long shot, as she looks around the station and begins to walk with the dog this way and that.

The slim silhouette of Givenchy's elegant, tailored wool suit accentuates Hepburn's thin figure without minimizing her height or the length of her neck. Moreover, it illuminates as an image Sabrina's transformation into a chic Parisian-styled young woman, yet, although the sequence begins with Hepburn essentially posing to show off the suit, the outfit does not constrict the actress's movement but frames it visually. And while the station platform may remind one of a fashion runway as Hepburn walks back and forth, she does not stroll as a model on the catwalk, for she looks up, she looks around, she looks down at the dog—until there is a cut to David driving and whistling the film's other repeated melody, "Isn't It Romantic?" Catching sight of Sabrina, he abruptly turns his convertible around in order to meet this attractive stranger, for he fails to recognize her. Sabrina thus has fun leading him on, confirming that, as she indicated to her father, her sophistication, the result of her two years in Paris, now gives her the upper hand in "life"—and in love. She no longer watches but acts. The chic wool suit, then, works as an objective correlative of Sabrina's newly found poise and confidence, implying her emotional maturity as well, and even—perhaps this may be a stretch, but it is nonetheless the effect of Hepburn's acting with her bemused smile and twinkling eyes—liberating her mischievous nature.

The second Givenchy design in *Sabrina* is a fitted white strapless sheath gown with a boned bodice and cinched waist; the dress is cut just above Hepburn's ankles and made from organdy material with a black-beaded, embroidered floral pattern. The outfit is accessorized simply. Hepburn wears white opera gloves and teardrop earrings, so her visible neck, collarbone, and shoulders become absorbed into the entire look of the gown. What gives the gown its wow factor is a long, wide, flowing overskirt or train in the same material as the sheath but lined with black taffeta; the overskirt trails on the floor behind Hepburn as she walks. The doubled skirt, with the narrow sheath enveloped on both sides and from behind by the expansive, ballooning overskirt, creates the impression that Sabrina floats in from the garden as she arrives at the Larrabees' dance and immediately attracts the gaze of all the young men there. The style of this ballgown colors Sabrina in a sense of enchantment, and Hepburn takes her cue from that for her performance in this scene as she enters the house to pair with David on the dance floor and accepts his invitation to a tryst on the indoor tennis court. Since she anticipates what he says, he wryly recognizes that she has witnessed his many past seductions, and Hepburn's wide smile again implies the mischief that is part of her sophistication and charm.

Despite the fitted sheath, the dress does not inhibit Hepburn's movement but illuminates it. When Sabrina goes to the tennis court expecting to meet David, Hepburn's face shows that she dreamily reflects upon how she finally gets to realize her adolescent infatuation; she is now in the very spot where, as a teenager, she had formerly watched the playboy take his dates from similar Larrabee dances to seduce them with champagne and the orchestra's playing of the song "Isn't It Romantic?" This implication is conveyed through mime as Hepburn dances to the music coming from the big house. Holding the sides of the overskirt with now gloveless hands, she sways slowly, the low angle of her head suggesting she is lost in thought; soon her pace accentuates, as she quickly twirls on the empty tennis court several times. She stops, looks to the left, and runs toward an observer's chair high above the court; climbing up the ladder, she sits down to wait for David, but instead Linus arrives in his brother's place. "It's all in the family," he says. He first tries to buy her off but without success, and instead the couple dance to "Isn't It Romantic?" and kiss. Once again, then, Hepburn incorporates the ballgown into her movement as she cues us to what Sabrina is thinking and feeling as she awaits David only to encounter Linus in his stead.

Hepburn's third Givenchy outfit in *Sabrina* not only became identified with her but also would eventually become a staple of women's wardrobes for decades afterward. Arriving at Linus's downtown office for their dinner date, Sabrina wears a black cocktail dress evocative of "the little black dress" that Coco Chanel had introduced in 1926 but which had fallen out of favor during the war. This dress features a wide ballerina skirt cut at mid-calf and is sleeveless, high in the front but without covering the neck and yet very low and V-shaped in back, the straps tied with small bows at each shoulder. According to Cindy de la Hoz, "This neckline became known as '*décolleté* Sabrina' and started a new trend for fashionable women to copy" (2016: 28). Hepburn wears diamond stud earrings, black opera gloves, and a beaded, black, fitted cap; the sparkling rhinestones on the cap, arranged in uneven geometric patterns, glitter in the light, and the shape of the hat's crown gives Hepburn's head a feline appearance (as Barthes noted, "woman as cat").

We first see Sabrina in this dress spinning in circles on a chair in Linus's office, as she pretends to be a CEO calling a meeting to order. She laughs, admitting, "The chairman is *so* dizzy," and slides onto the table, head and arms first. Taking a frozen daiquiri from Linus, she chats with him about his business enterprises as she strolls about the large room, playfully examining the ultramodern high-tech equipment in the office. The next scene shows the couple at dinner, where she tells him about romantic Paris; they go to the theater and dance in a nightclub afterward; finally, they drive back to Long Island. Their car ride rhymes with the earlier scene of David driving Sabrina home from the Glen Cove station. Repeating her mischievous smile, Sabrina does what she has wanted to do all evening: she turns down the brim of Linus's homburg hat, in effect suggesting he has to loosen up a bit. Then she becomes pensive, as she sings "La Vie en Rose," for now she begins to realize that Linus is displacing David in her affections. It is not for nothing that this long sequence began with a dissolve to Hepburn spinning rapidly, the quickness of her gyrations showing how giddy she is with happiness yet also because she is caught between her feelings for Linus and David. Throughout that scene in Linus's office, the ballerina shape of the skirt flows with Sabrina as she moves around the room, and the glittering reflections coming off her hat draw our attention to her and away from Linus.

All three sequences with her dressed by Givenchy display a radiant, smiling, joyous Audrey Hepburn, and this impression, I think, casts a spell over the entire film. These scenes invite viewers to focus on the actress's charisma and charm as their point of entry for watching *Sabrina*, thereby enabling them, if they wish, to look past her age difference from costar Humphrey Bogart and enjoy instead the pleasure of her performance. The Cinderella narrative of *Sabrina* then works simply as an excuse for watching Audrey Hepburn and identifying with Sabrina's energy, sophistication, and desiring and with how, as the trailer exclaims after a clip of William Holden goading Bogart to sock him, "Sabrina is the cause of it all."

Hepburn wears another Givenchy "little black dress" in *Love in the Afternoon* when Ariane leaves the music conservatory to warn Flanagan about the enraged, cuckolded husband determined to shoot him. This dress has a dropped waist, which lengthens the torso, and a flouncy three-quarter skirt; it also opens at the neck and throat, revealing her shoulder blades. To get into the playboy's hotel suite, Ariane has to climb along a high ledge and enter through a balcony door, and the dress does not encumber her effort but allows for it. Hepburn has many costume changes in the film, but this one for me is the most memorable; for in this dress, Ariane displays her audacious, curious, spirited personality, which is what attracts Flanagan when she unexpectedly appears in his room, substitutes for his paramour when the husband barges in with a gun, and agrees to meet the playboy again the next afternoon. Thereafter, the contrast between what Ariane wears at home or in the orchestra (like her single-breasted suit, white blouse with a Peter Pan collar, and pigtails) and what she wears during her many liaisons at the Ritz Hotel or at a picnic with Flanagan (her floral dress with a tight waist and shoulder-to-shoulder scooped neckline; her long dress with bows in back and a bateau neckline that follows the cut of the collarbone but is high in front and back; the full-length white fur coat she secretly borrows from her father's office; or a simple white blouse and multicolored striped cropped pants, with a sash tied around her waist for a belt, which allows her to show off the anklet that tantalizes and haunts the playboy as they picnic) indicate how fashion assists in actualizing her fantasy life.

Then in 1961 the black dress became forever part of Hepburn's star image. In *Breakfast at Tiffany's*, Hepburn wears a black cloque dress designed by Givenchy for Holly Golightly's two visits to Sally Tomato in Sing Sing prison and at her cocktail party. This "little black dress" is sleeveless, scooped out around her neck in front and back, and it has a bow at the waist and a large, fringed ruffle at the hem. For the party she adds a thickly beaded choker necklace with large matching earrings. Perhaps as famously, during the opening credits, Hepburn gets out of a taxicab at Tiffany's in the very early morning in another little black dress by Givenchy. This one is a full-length, sleeveless, black satin sheath, and she wears it with black opera gloves, dark glasses, five strands of pearls, a diamond mini-tiara, and diamond earrings. Advertising art for *Breakfast at Tiffany's* depicted Hepburn in either the cocktail dress or the evening gown, adding a foot-long cigarette holder, a slit skirt for the long gown to show her leg, and a cat stretched out on her shoulders. The art in the posters, by the way, gave Hepburn the ample hips she lacked in order to give her a more curvaceous figure.

Givenchy reportedly made two versions of the long black dress, one with a tighter, more confining skirt for looking at the display window of Tiffany's after Hepburn leaves the taxi and another one with a slit in the skirt for strolling around the storefront to peer in other display windows as she sips coffee and eats a pastry (Wasson 2010: 137). If this is the case, the switch from one version to the other is invisible. Cindy de la Hoz, however, claims that Paramount deemed the slit skirt too revealing and only approved the closed skirt, returning the one with the slit to Givenchy in Paris (2016: 93). I myself think that is probably what happened. If anything, and whether returned to the designer or not, the dress with the slit may have been used primarily as inspiration for the advertising artwork.

Hepburn wears the short black cocktail dress in sequences in which Holly has much to do. She hails a cab in the street in it; she goes to Sing Sing in it twice; she hosts her tumultuous, raucous, and packed cocktail party, first in a white bedspread but then in the black cocktail dress, after which she and Rusty Trawler leave to avoid the cops who have been summoned by the complaining upstairs neighbor, Mr. Yunioshi, because of the noise. The frequency with which we see Hepburn in this outfit, sometimes adorned by a wide-brimmed hat with a large, long ribbon that leaves a trail of motion in the air as she moves, establishes a motif that ultimately functions as a metonymy of Holly's chicness, that if she is a phony, she is "a *real* phony," as her mentor O. J. Berman explains to Paul. That is also to say that this little black dress works as an extension of Hepburn's screen presence in *Breakfast at Tiffany's*, not only to impart the famous image of her, on-screen and in the posters and advertising art, but as an important element in her performance of Holly Golightly as she tries to run from herself.

As for the formal black dress, during the credits of *Breakfast at Tiffany's*, as Hepburn leisurely strolls from one display window to another at the jewelry store, her full-length dress appears to slow down her movement, but she is never stationary in it for long; and after the credits conclude, we see her holding the long skirt of her sheath gown for easier and quicker movement as she briskly walks home, crosses the street, and runs up the front of the brownstone where her apartment is located. In short, the formal version of the "little black dress" shows off Hepburn's slim frame without inhibiting her movement at any point, since her slowness conveys not the confinement of the dress but Holly's quiet meditation as she stares at the storefront windows. (Remember that she later says that Tiffany's is her relief—or escape—from "the mean reds," which is how she internalizes her past in Texas as Eula Mae Golightly.) Yet even when breakfasting at Tiffany's, Hepburn is still in motion; peering at a window display, she is eating a pastry and sipping coffee. In this famous opening and subsequently throughout *Breakfast at Tiffany's*, the blond streaks in Hepburn's beehive hairdo, which sweeps up and over in a swirl at the back of her head, add additional hints of chromatic movement to her figure, whether she is relatively still or active, especially but not only in her close-ups, where the swirling blond streaks visibly seem to move through her dark hair.

Throughout *Breakfast at Tiffany's*, then, fashion empowers Holly to self-create her new identity as "Holly," freeing her from being "Eula Mae" in the patriarchal system of marriage in Texas to which her former husband, Doc Golightly, wants her to return—at least until the Hollywood ending, when Paul claims he owns her, and she finally submits to this form of Hollywood "romantic" love. From this perspective, fashion is liberating, a sign of Holly's sexual and economic independence. However, this should also lead us to realize that, by focusing on Hepburn's Givenchy couture as our pathway for appreciating her fashionable self-invention in *Breakfast at Tiffany's*, we may have to forget or consciously ignore that the price Holly pays for her independence, even if that means she is simply "a *real* phony," is her prostitution (the hundred dollars a week from Sally Tomato for sending coded messages, the fifty dollars from the many "rats" she dates).

Despite her indelible association with haute couture through Givenchy, off-screen Hepburn democratized French fashion insofar as her movies and her "look" inspired ready-to-wear knockoffs in American department stores, like "the little black dresses" worn in *Sabrina, Love in the Afternoon,* and *Breakfast at Tiffany's* and also worn at the start of the fashion photo shoot in *Funny Face* and in the nightclub scene and several scenes afterward in *Charade*. An article in *Photoplay*, timed to the wide release of *Breakfast at Tiffany's*, showed how a young woman—in this instance, starlet Deborah Walley, the movies' new Gidget—could "translate Audrey's chic, womanly look" through "fashion trickery that anyone can do," that is, with inexpensive, off-the-rack clothes and rhinestones (Saylor 1961: 68). Since then and in no small way due to Hepburn's influence, a basic black dress is considered essential for every woman's wardrobe regardless of the label or point of purchase. Furthermore, as the couturier himself recalled about the influence of Hepburn's fashionable look in *Sabrina*, "Everyone on the street was copying Audrey's [short] hair, the way she moved, the way she acted, the way she spoke. Everybody wanted to be like Audrey Hepburn" (quoted in Collins 1995: 294). One might say the same about the influence of *Breakfast at Tiffany's*, not only due to the pair of elegant little black dresses that she wears but also because of Hepburn's streaked hair and beehive hairdo, which was a new style and another trendsetter in the early 1960s.

Speaking of trendsetting, in yet another scene of *Sabrina*, Hepburn wears a black pantsuit with a slash neck top scooped out in the back and a cinched waist, and the trousers are hemmed above the ankle. Sabrina wears this casual outfit beneath a trench coat when she decides not to see Linus again out of fidelity to David, despite how her feelings for the younger man are waning, only to go up to Linus's office suite reluctantly. She removes the coat, fashions a towel around her waist in order to cook something when she finds two tickets on the *Liberté* for her and Linus to sail to Paris, and she becomes overwhelmed with excitement. Feeling guilty, Linus confesses his plan to break up her romance with David and tells her that the second stateroom would be empty; so she leaves, intending to return to Paris by herself.

Edith Head probably designed this costume for Hepburn in *Sabrina* and perhaps a similar one for the star in *Funny Face*, although for that one, I cannot be sure since Head gets credit for costume design, while Givenchy gets credit for Audrey Hepburn's wardrobe in Paris. However, according to Scott Brizel, Givenchy actually designed all the costumes for this picture, including Hepburn's beatnik outfits (2009: 98). In any event, three years after *Sabrina*, in *Funny Face* Hepburn wears a black wool sweater and tight black "stovepipe" pants for her character's bohemian uniform in the "Basal Metabolism" dance set in a Parisian cafe. (The trousers, by the way, were not designed by Givenchy or Head but purchased "off the rack" from Jax, a hip clothing boutique in Beverly Hills [Brizel 2009: 98].)

In this memorable dance, as the expression of Jo Stockton's excitement at being in Paris with fellow intellectuals and frustration with Dick Avery's cynicism about her companions in the cafe, Hepburn is an explosive fireball, all frenetic and exuberant yet stylized motion; it is her one dance in which she does not partner with Fred Astaire, whose choreography in their duets seems meant to compensate for her limited dance training beyond ballet.

"Dancing," Jo tells Dick Avery (and remember whom Hepburn is speaking to, the quintessential male dancer in American movies, Fred Astaire), "is nothing more than expression and release." Hence the number's title may be ironic. "Basal metabolism" refers to the number of calories needed for the body to perform its basic functions while at rest, like breathing, blood circulation, and so forth, where energy is used only for cellular activity. But the title may also be metaphoric. For dancing, Jo states, is both an emotional outlet ("expression") and motion ("release"), which the number defines as the basic functions contributing to her vitality, independence, intelligence, and youth.

At first the dancing seems slow, languid, random, and awkward, with Hepburn taking several angular poses that do not look like the choreography associated with Astaire, which will be on display in the very next dance number in *Funny Face*, "Let's Kiss and Make Up." Midway through "Basal Metabolism," a cut to Dick's point of

SOME IMAGES OF AUDREY HEPBURN ON-SCREEN

Figure 1 *Secret People* (1952), Audrey Hepburn's first major role in a motion picture

Figure 2 At the cafe with Gregory Peck in *Roman Holiday* (1953), Audrey Hepburn's breakout role in a Hollywood film

Figure 3a-c Audrey Hepburn wears Givenchy in *Sabrina* (1954)

Figure 4 Audrey Hepburn sings "How Long Has This Been Going On?" in *Funny Face* (1957)

Figure 5 Audrey Hepburn dances as Fred Astaire watches in *Funny Face*

Figure 6a–f The photo shoot in *Funny Face*

Figure **6a** In front of the Arc de Triomphe

Figure 6b Unexpectedly hooking a fish

Figure 6c Leaving the Paris Opera House in a huff

Figure 6d Standing atop the Daru Staircase in front of Winged Victory at the Louvre

Figure 6e Running down the Daru Staircase in the Louvre, Jo (Hepburn) shouts, "Take the picture!"

Figure 6f Still running down the Daru Staircase in the Louvre, Jo (Hepburn) again shouts, "Take the picture!"

Figure 7 Arielle (Hepburn) and Flanagan (Gary Cooper) meeting for a tryst in *Love in the Afternoon* (1957)

Figure 8 A new postulant, Gabrielle van der Mal (Hepburn), cannot control her curiosity during evening prayers in *The Nun's Story* (1959)

Figure 9a Sister Luke (Hepburn) is told to make "a sacrifice for God" by failing the examination in Tropical Medicine

Figure 9b At the exam, Sister Luke wrestles with her pride: Should she knowingly fail the exam to prove her humility as a good nun?

Figure 10a Who is the real Holly Golightly in *Breakfast at Tiffany's* (1961)? The kooky sophisticate dressed in Givenchy?

Figure 10b Or the waif from Texas who sings "Moon River" on the fire escape?

Figure 11 Hepburn, James Garner, Fay Bainter, and Shirley MacLaine in a powerful ensemble scene from *The Children's Hour* (1961)

Figure 12 William Holden and Audrey Hepburn dance to "That Face" in *Paris When It Sizzles* (filmed in 1962, released in 1964)

Figure 13a Cary Grant and Audrey Hepburn in *Charade* (1963)

Figure 13b Hepburn listens intently to Walter Matthau

Figure 14a Audrey Hepburn as Eliza Dolittle correctly says, "The rain in Spain stays mainly on the plain" in *My Fair Lady* (1964), but then we hear Marni Nixon's singing voice

Figure 14b At the Ascot races, one of Hepburn's most famous costumes

Figure 14c Eliza tells Henry Higgins she can live without him, though she will reverse course in the final moments of *My Fair Lady*

Figure 15 Audrey Hepburn and Peter O'Toole meet cute in *How to Steal a Million* (1966)

Figure 16a Tension flares between Joanna (Hepburn) and Mark (Albert Finney) during the red Triumph trip in *Two for the Road* (1967)

Figure 16b The young hitchhikers snuggle in a culvert during a rainstorm in *Two for the Road*

Figure 17a A close-up of Audrey Hepburn as Susy Hendrix in *Wait Until Dark* (1967)

Figure 17b After she has told him on the phone that she found the doll, Susy moans as she realizes that Mike has been deceiving her along with Roat and Carlino

Figure 18a In *Robin and Marian* (1976), Maid Marian (Hepburn) tells Robin Hood (Sean Connery) that she thinks he knocked a tooth loose when he rescued her from the Sheriff's men

Figure 18b Marian gives Robin the flask with poisoned wine

Figure 19 Hepburn and Robert Wagner at the end of *Love Among Thieves* (1987)

Figure 20 Hepburn's final appearance in *Gardens of the World*, an Emmy Award–winning PBS series that aired very soon after her death in 1993

view in the cafe, as he slaps his forehead in disbelief, indicates how ridiculous Jo appears in his eyes; we can infer he does not think she *is* dancing at all but is making a fool of herself. But her dancing here is simply meant to be a display of "expression and release," its idiom is something like the abstraction of modern dance, and it soon picks up speed with a more discernible choreographic pattern once two male dancers join Hepburn and their movement complements hers. This type of abstract choreography stands in contrast with Astaire's dancing in the next number, which has a clear and more linear narrative line. His tells a story, while hers is about the pleasure of a body freeing itself in motion through dance; the number's title thus asks us to think of this motion as a basic function of the body. The dance in this number therefore may, on one hand, be satirized as bogus high art (recall Astaire's POV shot), but, on the other, Hepburn herself is not to be laughed at, for her body is free and spirited and her face expresses great pleasure from her movement, so the dance celebrates her untamed, youthful energy, which offers a way to resist the judgment implied by Astaire's POV shot.

The image of Hepburn's dancing in the black pants outfit was prominently featured in the ads and posters for *Funny Face*, often with the slogan "Now Hepburn's Hep!" As Mosely has observed, "Hepburn's association with black clothing is perhaps a key way in which she has come to be understood as representing 'intellect,' despite the negotiations made in the narratives of her films" (2002a: 56). In the 1930s and 1940s, stars like Marlene Dietrich, Joan Crawford, and Katharine Hepburn were photographed in wide-legged trousers while working at the studio, disembarking a train, or strolling on a Manhattan street, but in the 1950s slacks on most women were still considered a bohemian or avant-garde fashion choice, as in cocktail pants at parties, or they were worn mainly for leisure or sports activities. Pants were also required of women by some occupations and by the military. By the late 1950s pedal pushers were becoming popular among teenage girls but were forbidden by high school dress codes. And many restaurants would not serve women wearing pants. Audrey's black pants in *Funny Face* inspired popular casual or everyday wear for young women and teenage girls while also attaching a sense of intelligence, bookishness, independence of mind and body, and overall nonconformity to her star image and presumably to those imitators of this look. This outfit has since become so iconic that, as I noted in the introduction, The Gap used a clip of Hepburn dancing in "Basal Metabolism" to promote its own skinny black pants revival in TV ads.

As it happened, one item of this costume, Hepburn's white socks, turned out to be somewhat controversial on the set. Otherwise clothed entirely in black, Hepburn protested that the socks broke up her silhouette and the line of her body as she danced; she wanted to wear only simple black ballet slippers. Director Stanley Donen, however, insisted that without the white socks, her feet would disappear, her intricate footwork would be lost, and she would fade into the smoky background of the nightclub. They argued back and forth until a tearful Hepburn ran to her dressing room. But she returned shortly afterward, wore the white socks, and filmed the dance. When she saw the rough cut of the number, she realized that Donen was right about the white socks and wrote a note telling him so (Spoto 2006: 141–42). Many years later, the white socks Hepburn wears in this dance sequence may have inspired Michael Jackson's trademark white socks in his music videos.

A musical gently satirizing while simultaneously celebrating *Vogue* and *Harper's Bazaar*, haute couture, photographer Richard Avedon, and French existentialism, *Funny Face* is now even more famous for the many striking outfits Givenchy designed for Hepburn once her character becomes a fashion model in Paris. In the middle of the film, Jo gets her makeover at Duval's atelier. Duval exclaims, "My friends, you saw in here a waif, a gamine, a lowly caterpillar. We opened the cocoon, but it is not a butterfly that emerges." "It's not?" Dick asks. "It is a bird of paradise," Duval replies. The room darkens, the curtains rise, and Jo appears, standing expressionless and statue-like at the top of the catwalk. She wears a champagne satin dress with long matching gloves; a short-sleeved pink top over the dress has a long train; and her hair is tightly pulled back, crowned by a beaded headdress. This gown is uncharacteristic of Givenchy and Hepburn both; the pink top covers her shoulders, chest, and most of her neck. She does not move except to blink; instead, the camera tracks in on Hepburn to feature her in a close-up. Only after shots of the appreciative audience (Dick, Maggie Prescott, Duval, various makeup artists, fitters, and other workers) does Stanley Donen's camera return to Hepburn in a long shot, as she slowly and with careful deliberation walks down the catwalk, with applause greeting her as she finishes. And only then does the star smile, but the long shot minimizes the impact of her relaxed expression until there is a medium close-up of her in profile as she speaks with the small group of people assembled in the salon.

Hepburn's appearance here is her most stationary—and she looks the stiffest and most uncomfortable—in the entire film, including other scenes at the salon, such as the meeting with the press (when Jo and Dick argue, knocking over the sprinklers and spraying themselves and the audience) and the fashion show itself (when Jo runs on and off to change while being anxious because Dick has apparently left Paris after quarreling with her at Flostre's flat). The Givenchy gown in the "big reveal" of Jo's makeover is the only outfit of hers in *Funny Face* that inhibits Hepburn's free and easy movement.

I therefore cannot help inferring from the design of this gown and Hepburn's stiffness as she poses on the catwalk a subtle critique of the fashion industry in its treatment of women as wooden mannequins. For this sequence stands in contrast with the montage that follows, which depicts Jo posing for a series of photographs for *Quality* magazine taken by Dick Avery at various landmarks in Paris. The montage is self-reflexively cinematic. At each stop, Dick supplies Jo with a narrative situation paired to the location and what she wears, until she takes over, imagining the stories herself. "You're not only a model, you're an actress," Dick tells Jo early in the shoot (when she poses as Anna Karenina at the train station and summons real tears for the effect), a statement that applies to Hepburn as well, in contrast to the genuine models (such as Suzy Parker, who would subsequently act in a few films, Dovima, and Sunny Hartnett) appearing in *Funny Face*.

The fashion shoot unites the bohemian Jo of "Basal Metabolism" with haute couture, which is to say that it adds fashion to the black pants outfit she wears in her solo dance number in the Parisian cafe. In most of the locations during the shoot, Jo does not remain still but moves. Now I well realize that *Funny Face*, like the other films discussed so far, is a *motion* picture, so Hepburn, no more than any other film performer, does not have to, she should not, remain motionless except in a tight close-up; but I do want to point out what she does when performing as a photographic model in the montage, which is revelatory of her relation to couture as a performer in her films more generally. For even when standing motionlessly as Anna Karenina or as the princess with her princely dove in front of a fountain, or bedecked with numerous bouquets at the flower market, Hepburn's face is not frozen, as it had been earlier on the catwalk at Duval's, for her expression responds to the narrative basis of the particular shot, and she is also moving as Dick sets up the photograph. Nor in the narrative are Jo's emotions stable during this montage, since the shoot records her growing ease and comfort in modeling for Dick and the development of her romantic feelings for him. The shoot ends with Jo unable to pose for her final photo in a wedding dress outside a rustic chapel because she feels the dress and situation are dishonest. Finally, she confesses that she loves Dick, they kiss, and he begins the number "He Loves and She Loves." The fashion shoot thus concludes with Hepburn and Astaire dancing together, with the dance now consummating the couple metaphorically.

The photo shoot montage reflects the wedding of fashion and motion for Hepburn. Outside the Tuileries, Jo, in a little black dress (much like the one the star will wear in her next film, *Love in the Afternoon*), clutches an assortment of colorful balloons as she runs in the rain; leaving the opera in a huff, she furiously turns on the staircase, and the thick skirt of her white dress spins out from under an emerald green cape; fishing from a riverboat on the Seine in a white pantsuit with a wide pink belt, she actually if unknowingly catches a fish, and, as she pulls her line out of the water, she is wide-eyed and open-mouthed at what she sees; and most strikingly, emerging from behind Winged Victory in the Louvre and wearing a sleeveless, vivid red gown with matching shoes, her white gloved hands holding a large red chiffon shawl overhead, she strides down the Daru Staircase and orders Dick to take the picture. He orders her to stop, but she shouts she doesn't feel like it and again shouts, "*Take the picture!*" What freezes each pose as a still photograph on film is Donen's tricky editing and processing work, as the on-screen image of Hepburn caught in motion changes into a still frame of high quality, then as a negative of the image, or colored tints are applied to the image, or color separations are shown in the image, or the image's shape changes dimensions. The visuals here, planned by Donen, Avedon, Leonard Gershe, and Roger Edens, simulate the process of manufacturing photographs for a fashion magazine, and such a process is another form of motion that visually energizes the still images of Hepburn.

Following the photo shoot montage and before the press preview that Jo and Dick ruin with their arguing about Flostre, *Funny Face* gives Hepburn a number with Kay Thompson that momentarily pulls the curtain away from the seeming natural relation of femininity and fashion to celebrate, in the way that Hollywood musicals celebrate, how easily both can be demystified. This number, "On How to Be Lovely," seems the antidote to the focus on fashion that otherwise dominates *Funny Face*. On the surface the song implies we ought not to take fashion—or the film itself—too seriously.

However, like so many other backstage musicals, *Funny Face* demystifies the show (here, a fashion show and not a play or revue) momentarily in this number, only to remystify it almost immediately afterward by elevating fashion back to its unchallenged and privileged position in the film.

Thompson's Maggie Prescott draws on the auras of *Harper's Bazaar's* then editor-in-chief Carmel Snow and the magazine's fashion editor at the same time, Diana Vreeland. Maggie is a fascinating figure in *Funny Face* for her difference from the ultrafeminine models she orders about as editor of *Quality* magazine. *Funny Face* begins with her number "Think Pink!" which satirizes the attention to ultrafemininity on the pages of *Vogue* and *Harper's Bazaar*. Evoking a somewhat butch personality with her deep throaty voice, masculine air, and no-nonsense attitude, Thompson remains dressed in a charcoal suit with white blouse and gloves while everyone else in the number—her various assistants and secretaries and the real-life models in the montage occurring in the number's middle—wears pink, just as half a dozen chorus boys paint the multiple doors of the set pink to revel in Maggie's theme for the next issue of her magazine. After the number's conclusion, an associate informs her that the whole country has gone pink, and he asks why she has not changed to that color. "Me?" Maggie replies incredulously, "I wouldn't be caught dead." Nonetheless, in the next scenes in the magazine's headquarters and then in the bookshop where Jo works, Maggie is wearing a cranberry suit with a pink blouse.

Now fast-forward about an hour into the film. Jo is nervous about answering questions from the press, so Maggie tells her it's very simple, as one woman to another knows. "But first we ought to look like one woman to another," she adds. Both women are wearing white blouses and black slacks, and Hepburn has on sensible oxfords—these are theatrical rehearsal clothes—so they drape a tablecloth around their waists and a napkin over their heads to simulate more feminine attire. Their duet, "On How to Be Lovely," mocks the supposed naturalism of female beauty, of the sort that fashion supposedly enhances, by showing how it is performative, and doubly so—the two characters sing about the application of loveliness as something a woman performs, equating her happiness or joy with her gaining beauty, while at the same time the two actresses are singing and dancing in gender-neutral clothing and performing stock gestures that signify "femininity." To view feminine loveliness as performative, according to this number, is to see it not as something static or innate but as a transformative activity, reiterating how fashion functions for Hepburn in the photo shoot, where Jo's femininity is similarly performative. Each new outfit gives her a new story for her to act out, so each outfit places her in a different theatricalized setting for her to perform "glamour" for Dick's camera.

Visually, then, *Sabrina*, *Funny Face*, *Love in the Afternoon*, and *Breakfast at Tiffany's* record the transformation of the Audrey figure from awkward girlishness to sophisticated womanliness through Givenchy fashion. The Audrey films as a cycle invest fashion with more weight, more significance than mere attire. For as Mosley notes, "Selfhood, in [Hepburn's] films, is articulated through dress" which "carries and expresses the weight of [her characters'] emotional development, and frequently, acts as protection" (2005: 109, 116). But that does not mean fashion functions as an armor so much as it visualizes a mode of self-expression, energy, motion, even empowerment, as I have been stating. This happens in *Roman Holiday* as well even though Hepburn has fewer costume changes and Givenchy was not involved in the production (nor was he yet an influence on Audrey's career). Princess Ann loosens her tightly buttoned blouse to make it look more like fashionable Roman street-clothing; she also gets a trendy cropped haircut and purchases open-toed shoes.

Compared with *Sabrina*, *Funny Face*, *Love in the Afternoon*, and *Breakfast at Tiffany's*, Givenchy's designs for Hepburn in the 1960s are, with some exceptions, not as extravagant, mainly because the films' narratives encourage a more ordinary look for her characters, so a distinctive color palette stands out to highlight costumes that could easily be high-priced streetwear. In *Paris When It Sizzles*, Gabrielle is a working woman who wears solid pastel-colored suits with sleeveless blouses or dresses, sometimes with the addition of a matching sweater. Only as the film-within-the-film gets more fantastic does the clothing style change for Hepburn, climaxing in the masquerade ball, when everyone, including Gaby, is in a costume, with hers being that of a medieval lady in pale silk brocade with a black velvet collar and a princess cone headdress with a long, trailing veil carried over her arm.

Furthermore, Givenchy's designs during this decade seem more reflective of fashion trends than instigators of them, as in the sleeveless shift dresses that Gabrielle wears, a style worn by Jacqueline Kennedy. Despite the influence of *Breakfast at Tiffany's*, which had popularized the little black dress for women everywhere, and while Hepburn herself remained a fashion icon and frequent image on magazine covers globally, in the 1960s Kennedy's greater impact on women's clothing was becoming undeniable, whether in terms of haute couture or off-the-rack dresses and coats. That influence was perhaps already evident in *Breakfast at Tiffany's* in Holly's daywear, such as the apricot-colored coat with a funnel collar and cinched waist, accessorized by a mink derby, which she wears in the montage with Paul as they go around Manhattan in the daytime. Hepburn's coat and hat in this sequence remind me of Kennedy's outerwear at her husband's inauguration on January 20, 1961—though admittedly, since shooting on *Tiffany's* had begun several months before then, both coats, while from different designers (Kennedy's was by Oleg Cassini), may have been inspired by the same new trends in fashion that year; moreover, Kennedy did wear Givenchy sometimes, and she was known to admire Hepburn. In any event, Kennedy's influence is apparent, I think, in the costumes Givenchy provided for *Charade*, which seem to have been inspired by the coats, hats, and dresses that she wore in public appearances during her husband's presidency.

A good deal of *Charade* takes place outside, so Hepburn's Regina Lampert wears several sheath coats with stand-up funnel collars, three-quarter sleeves, and large, interesting, decorative buttons. Her coats and dresses tend to be in bold, solid colors: red, gray, navy, black, and mustard, often accessorized with pearl earrings, silvery or black leather opera gloves, and pillbox or oversize cloche hats. One- or two-piece dresses are mostly collarless with a scooped neckline; the little black dress Hepburn wears lacks sleeves as well, and it has a matching boxy jacket, which was a popular style then. Hepburn has to move a lot in these clothes, from strolling with Cary Grant along the Seine or in a park, to running from him in the Paris Metro station when she suspects he may want to kill her.

Upon her return to the French capital after the opening scene set in Megève, where she wears black ski attire, Regina only has the clothes from her two Louis Vuitton suitcases (since her late husband sold the entire contents of their apartment while she was on holiday with her friend Sylvie), so we may be amazed at the number of outfits she apparently packed for her ski trip (by my count, three wool coats, one trench coat, the boxy jacket, six one- or two-piece dresses, four hats including the one with a veil worn at Charles Lampert's funeral, two pairs of long leather gloves, a silk scarf, a long dressing gown, shoes, boots, and house slippers), but—and kudos to the set dresser—because of their bold, solid colors, we can glimpse some of these clothes hanging in her hotel room wardrobe after she moves out of her now-empty apartment for greater safety. Hepburn's couture becomes the object of a visual joke in one scene, too. Distrustful of Grant's character, Peter Joshua, when she discovers he has lied to her, Regina follows him to the American Express office covertly; but since she is wearing a white trench coat over a white dress, with a white babushka on her head, she stands out in the street like a nightlight in a darkened room. Yet Peter is oblivious to her tailing him.

In *How to Steal a Million*, the Givenchy fashions take on more of a mod look, as in Hepburn's first scene when, dressed entirely in white and driving a small red convertible, she sports big sunglasses and a bullet hat. Her clothing in this film consists of many suits or two-piece dresses that have wing collars and waists cinched with thin belts; some of these have relatively short skirts and are accessorized with patterned leggings. Hepburn does wear a spectacular costume, but it is for comedic effect as it again foils her intent to be secretive. When Nicole Bonnet (Hepburn) meets Simon Dermott (Peter O'Toole) at the Ritz bar to arrange the theft of her father's counterfeit sculpture so it can't be examined by an art expert, Hepburn wears an elaborate ensemble: she is dressed all in black, with lace sleeves, bodice, and overskirt, and a lace mask that covers her brow and her eyes, which are highlighted with sparkling dark shadow.

Whereas Givenchy designed clothes for Hepburn that accentuated but flattered the idiosyncratic features of her body, Cecil Beaton, by contrast, tried to downplay them. His gowns for *My Fair Lady*, which are by now as famous as Givenchy's, hide Hepburn's long neck with high collars, as in the clothes she wears in Henry Higgins's house, or with tightly wound jewels, worn as adornment to amplify her sparkling Empire gown at the Embassy Ball. Admittedly, the colorful costumes were created with an eye toward the Edwardian period, yet many female extras in crowd scenes—for instance, some of the fashionable women leaving the opera in the opening, standing at the races at Ascot, or dancing at the Embassy Ball—wear gowns that show the neck, and some are cut to feature the bosom. Hepburn's gown at the ball would be as revealing, for it has an open neckline, except for the jewels wound around her throat from under her chin to just above the top of her sternum, though her shoulder blades are visible (and, if you look closely, her upper ribs are too).

Whether Hepburn is dressed as a flower seller, student of Higgins, or a lady, in *My Fair Lady* she is buttoned up to her neck. The only time we see her bony throat and long neck is when she removes the rented jewels after the ball and returns them to Higgins in a huff.

Her final outfit has a frilly, ruffled collar that fits tightly around her entire neck up to her chin; while the upper chest area appears visible due to a low neckline, it is covered with gauzy, opaque material of the same pink color as the dress. When I watch *My Fair Lady*, rather than distracting my eyes from Hepburn's long neck, the high collars and necklaces only place greater emphasis on it because they call attention to the effort at concealment.

As important, as Eliza moves from flower girl to lady, the clothing increasingly constricts Hepburn's movement. She is most active in Covent Garden when she dances in "Wouldn't It Be Loverly?" and less so when she does a modified tango to "The Rain in Spain." By the time Eliza enters the Embassy Ball, where she will get to waltz for a bit, the gown makes it seem like she is a mannequin on wheels. The visually elaborate gowns for Hepburn to wear at Ascot and at the ball eerily remind me of her stiff posing on the catwalk in *Funny Face* when Jo has her makeover. The intent may well be for the clothes to capture the reserve of the gentry class in Edwardian England, which seeks to stifle Eliza's energy as well as her outspokenness, but the confining clothing, in my view, also visually works against the vivacity of Hepburn's performance by attempting to tamp it down.

How to Steal a Million, released a year and a half after *My Fair Lady* but while that musical was still in some neighborhood theaters nationally, was the last major production that teamed Hepburn with Givenchy, though he would continue to dress her off-screen. Almost as if aware that the heist comedy would be more or less the end of the line, on-screen at least, for Hepburn and Givenchy for a long time, in *How to Steal a Million* Peter O'Toole delivers a much quoted in-joke. As part of the scheme to steal the sculpture, Nicole must pass as a washerwoman, and as she changes into a shapeless, nondescript uniform, O'Toole's character, Simon, mutters, "Well, it gives Givenchy a night off." The next year, when Hepburn and Stanley Donen teamed for a third time on *Two for the Road*, the director refused to hire Givenchy but in effect gave him "a night off."

Donen sought a look for Hepburn in *Two for the Road* that suggested the type of clothes one could buy off the rack at expensive stores without having to go to a French couturier. The credit on-screen may remind some of you of the names from department stores or boutiques of your youth. The card says: "Miss Hepburn's clothes by Ken Scott, Michele Rosier, Paco Rabanne, Mary Quant, Foale and Tuffin, and others." In addition, her wardrobe was "supervised by Clare Rendlesham." Whew! That's a lot of people but fitting since the film covers multiple time periods for Hepburn and costar Albert Finney, during which their characters, Joanna and Mark Wallace, go through changes in their income from poor hitchhikers to a wealthy bougie couple. Hepburn sports a variety of styles, from jeans and a red sweater to a black plastic pantsuit with a pink and black striped shirt; from a canary yellow dress to a cocktail minidress made of metal disks; from a pale pink blouse with shocking pink shorts to a shirt of peacock blue and chartreuse stripes over a lime green skirt.

To be sure, much of the action in the film occurs while Mark and Joanna are seated in cars, so there is not a lot of physical movement until they stop at a restaurant or hotel, their car catches fire (as happens at one point), they hitchhike, or are at a beach. At one point Joanna even changes outfits in the car while Mark drives! Like the many different automobiles that the two characters travel in and her different hairstyles, Hepburn's many costume changes serve to identify the continuing upward mobility of the couple's economic status. As much to the point, given the nonlinear structure of the film, the different styles work as signposts, making it easier for viewers to know where they are in story time at any given point. In contrast to how Givenchy functions for her in her films, including the first two she made with Donen, Hepburn's costumes in *Two for the Road* lay out an ensemble of temporal movement. That is to say, in signaling different moments in time, the clothes imagine movement for Hepburn somewhat differently than when she wears Givenchy. For in *Two for the Road*, the movement in time traced back and forth by the changes in her costumes functions as a trope (symbolizing the couple's economic and social upward mobility), as the representation of the temporal phenomena that her character experiences (the couple's traveling on the road in and through time), and as textual cues (to the narrative's jumbling of that time in its own formal structure).

Years later, after her return to acting, Givenchy reunited with Hepburn on film. He designed two smashing evening gowns for her television movie, *Love Among Thieves*, which gave Hepburn her final leading role. Additionally, a few years before then, he provided a wardrobe for her in *Bloodline*, although he is not given a credit in the film or on the IMDb. (Enrico Sabbatini is the credited costumer designer.) In *Bloodline*, Hepburn's wardrobe is pretty but undistinguished. She wears daywear for the most part—open-collared business dresses with a pearl necklace or a turtleneck sweater, trousers, and shawl, and these outfits enable her to chair a board meeting or to run, fall, and stumble. Imitating what Cary Grant got to do in *Charade*, when someone tries to kill her she even jumps from one balcony to another when her villa is burning down. She has a few evening dresses, too, one of which Givenchy claimed was his favorite (Buck 1989: 8). If I am right, it is the gown Hepburn wears at Maxim's, and in my opinion this is the least flattering of Givenchy's creations for the star. It has a full-length, black sheath skirt and a top of the same material cut diagonally across from one breast to her lower torso; the visible part of her torso and both arms are draped in flesh-colored or transparent material, studded with sparkling rhinestones. One exposed shoulder has a velvet flower sewn onto the see-through fabric, and the same flowery shape covers what would otherwise be Hepburn's exposed breast and nipple, though at the same time it draws the eye to that very spot.

Of course, Hepburn did not wear Givenchy couture or even clothes bought off the rack by trendy designers in all of her films. In *Wait Until Dark*, she reportedly bought her character's several simple outfits in French stores before traveling to Hollywood for the shoot. In *The Nun's Story* and *Robin and Marian* she wore a nun's habit; in *Green Mansions*, a plain, shapeless shift; in *War and Peace* and *The Unforgiven*, clothes appropriate for the period and the Russian and frontier settings; and in *The Children's Hour*, costumes such as sweaters, skirts and blouses, and dresses suitable for a schoolteacher. Indeed, before her first retirement from acting in 1967, Givenchy had only supplied costumes for seven of Hepburn's films; yet the influence of those seven films in establishing the star's iconic association with high fashion, charm, and elegance was at the time unmistakable and, apparently from how fans remember her, is still unforgettable. Because those memories have frozen her in Givenchy outfits, it is important to appreciate that on-screen Hepburn freely moved in his clothes; enhancing her performances and often expressing her characters' liminality, her movement in Givenchy couture contributed to the vivid impression she made in many of her films during the height of her career.

5
Thrillers

"Why should I be in any danger?" Regina Lampert, Audrey Hepburn's character in *Charade*, asks the bogus Hamilton Bartholomew (Walter Matthau) at the American Embassy. Why indeed? She has already learned from the French police a day or two before this meeting that her late husband Charles, who led a very mysterious life with multiple aliases, was murdered, his body thrown from a train like a sack of potatoes. Adding to her confusion, upon returning from a skiing holiday in Megève, she has also discovered that, before he left Paris, Charles had sold at auction the entire contents of their apartment for a quarter of a million dollars. Now Bartholomew is telling Regina that Charles was wanted by the US government for stealing that sum from the Feds. He shows Regina a wartime photo of Charles and his cronies. The other men in the photo—Tex (James Coburn), Gideon (Ned Glass), and Scobie (George Kennedy)— want that money, which Charles recovered from the auction, and they believe that Regina has it. Bartholomew warns her she must find that money, for until she does her life will be in danger because those three men will stop at nothing to get the fortune they believe is theirs.

It is worth adding to that account before going further. For in a subsequent scene of *Charade*, Regina will learn from this same Bartholomew that the stolen quarter of a million dollars was originally in the form of gold bars meant for the French underground. Charles and his cronies had buried the gold, intending to retrieve it after the war's end—only to have a German troop attack them. Moreover, one of the Americans not in the photo Bartholomew had shown her at their first meeting, a man named Carson Dyle, was also involved in the theft but was left to die on the field while the others escaped the Germans. Charles then dug up the gold for himself before the war ended, leaving his co-conspirators empty-handed.

Following her husband's funeral, and with the $250,000 hidden in plain sight in the form of three priceless stamps on the envelope of a banal letter from Charles addressed to her, the three surviving men threaten Regina's life; furthermore, they reveal the lies Peter Joshua (Cary Grant) keeps telling her—like her late husband, he too has many aliases—until she no longer knows whom to believe. Of course, *we* know that Cary Grant can never really play a bad guy. Still, in the climax of *Charade*, after Peter (or whoever he really is) chases her in the Paris Metro because, with the stamps in her possession, she flees from him, thinking he is the killer, Regina cannot decide whether to trust him or Bartholomew (in actuality, the very much alive Carson Dyle, who during the course of *Charade* has killed his four former cronies for vengeance and because he wants the fortune for himself). "I don't know who anybody is!" she exclaims in frustration. Peter tells her, "Just trust me once more." Regina gestures toward him and Bartholomew, acknowledging that he *is* Carson Dyle, tries to kill her to get the stamps.[1]

It also turns out from *Charade* that, as she got older, Audrey Hepburn adjusted her Cinderella persona by playing a woman in danger. Unlike *My Fair Lady*, *Wait Until Dark* and *Charade*, her two other popular and critically acclaimed films of the 1960s, cast her in this light. (It is interesting to note, too, that both films cast her as an American.) Two films when she returned to acting after almost a decade off-screen, *Bloodline* and *Love Among Thieves*, also had her play a character placed in dangerous situations. To be sure, in a few of her films from the 1960s—*The Children's Hour* and *Two for the Road*—she played a mature woman in dramas. And even before then, while still playing girlishness, some of her characters found themselves in dangerous predicaments. In *Green Mansions*, Runi (Sessue Hayakawa), believing that Rima murdered his son, orders Abel (Anthony Perkins) to kill her, which he refuses to do;

and in the climax she is pursued and burned to death by Kua-Ko (Henry Silva), Runi's other son, who has publicly blamed Rima for the murder of his brother that he himself committed. Likewise, in *The Unforgiven*, as the crazed Abe Kelsey (Joseph Wiseman) spreads the truth about Rachel Zachery's origin as a Kiowa, the other whites shun her for being Native American; and having failed to buy her back from the Zacherys, the Kiowas lay siege upon the family and their homestead, with Rachel's adopted brothers determined to keep her from being taken from them. The four thrillers, in comparison, place the Hepburn character in a sticky situation that demonstrates her strength, cleverness, and agency because for the most part she deals with the danger and threats on her own and foils her antagonist's efforts to harm her.

All of this is to say that *Charade*, a well-reviewed box-office hit, was a critical film in Hepburn's career because it crystalized how she could adjust her Audrey screen persona to achieve a better match with her real age of thirty-three years without sacrificing what made that persona so attractive to audiences: by playing a woman in danger who, unlike Rima or Rachel, takes matters into her own hands. Early in *Charade*, Regina tells Peter that the police suspect her of involvement in her husband's murder, that "Charles was mixed up in something terrible," and that she does not know what she is going to do. Peter, essentially still a charming stranger whom she has only recently met, replies, "I wish you'd let me help you. It doesn't sound like something a young woman can handle by herself." Yet Regina does try to handle it on her own since the man she believes is Bartholomew has warned her not to tell anyone about the missing fortune or their lives will be in danger too. Resisting Peter's effort to find out what she knows and why she is in danger, Regina orders him to stop bullying her when he insists that her reluctance to explain is "nonsense." "Everyone is bullying me," she complains. He replies, "I'm not bullying you," but she insists he is: "Yes, you are. You said it was nonsense. Being murdered in cold blood is not nonsense. Why don't you try it sometime?" Peter nonetheless scolds her when she won't tell him anything but keeps trying to romance him. "Stop acting like a child," he reproaches her. "How would you like a spanking?" "How would you like a punch in the nose?" Regina responds angrily. "Stop treating me like a child!"

To be sure, in the climax Peter prevents Carson Dyle from killing Regina, just as earlier in the film Peter has the big fight scene with Scobie on the roof of the American Express building; both sequences serve to make him appear more conventionally virile and heroic. But although she finds herself caught in a maze of misleading turns, some caused by Peter's charades, Regina does pretty much handle things by herself, or at least tries to when she keeps to herself the information given by the man who says he is Bartholomew; when she cannot decide whom to trust; when she aggressively romances Peter or, worse, suspects he may be the killer; when she looks for the fortune in order to keep from being murdered; and when she insists that the money is not hers to keep. As she tells the fake Bartholomew after easily giving the slip to Peter—now known to her as "the late" Carson Dyle's brother—when he tries to follow her, "I'm beginning to think that women make the best spies." Like Tex and Peter, Regina ultimately realizes that the $250,000 is hidden in those three priceless stamps, but *she* is the one who has the stamps, not either of those two men. The one genuinely honest character in *Charade*, Regina returns the stamps to the US Treasury Department—and the department's head in the American Embassy in Paris is none other than Peter Joshua, whose real name is Brian Cruikshank.

On the Criterion Blu-ray, director Stanley Donen says he chose the Peter Stone script after it was previously rejected by all the studios because he wanted "a film with a strong female lead." He adds, "I just wanted to make a movie where the lady rather than the man is being chased." He elaborates, "Cary Grant has been in jeopardy, but not Audrey Hepburn." Furthermore, Donen claims that *Charade* "set the mood for the humorous thriller." Peter Stone then points out that "there hadn't been anything like it in some time."

Actually, there *had* been a humorous thriller rather like *Charade* just four years previously in 1959: Alfred Hitchcock's *North by Northwest*, which starred Cary Grant as a man in danger who is mistaken for a nonexistent American spy, wanted for a murder he did not commit, and chased from New York to Chicago to South Dakota. When *Charade* opened, many reviewers, remembering *North by Northwest*, called Donen's thriller the best Hitchcock film that Hitch never made. For that matter, another year-end release in many American cities during Christmas 1963, competing for holiday viewers with *Charade* (and following it into Radio City Music Hall in late January) was *The Prize*, also a humorous thriller starring Paul Newman as an alcoholic writer and new Nobel Prize winner who is chased around Stockholm by East German Communists, and with a screenplay by Ernest Lehman, who as it happened also wrote *North by Northwest*. *Charade* therefore may not have been as singular as its director and screenwriter claimed after the fact, but due to its great popularity, it *was* influential in establishing for the 1960s and 1970s the genre of the suspenseful thriller that was laced with a good deal of wit and humor. Moreover, unlike *North by Northwest* and *The Prize*, *Charade* featured a strong female protagonist and more sustained repartee between the two leads.

On the Blu-ray, Donen and Stone mention *North by Northwest* in passing along with several other Hitchcock thrillers that they watched in preparation before starting *Charade*, but without acknowledging how that particular film may have served as their template. However, as Donen implies when he mentions that Cary Grant had been chased whereas Audrey Hepburn hadn't, *Charade* is essentially a gender reversal of *North by Northwest*, with Hepburn's Regina the female equivalent of Roger Thornhill, Cary Grant's character in the Hitchcock film. Like Roger, Regina is pursued by dangerous men who refuse to believe in her innocence and place her life in jeopardy, while Grant's character in *Charade* is more like Eve Kendall, the femme fatale played by Eva Marie Saint in *North by Northwest*. For like Peter Joshua (aka Alexander Dyle, aka Adam

Canfield, aka Brian Cruikshank), Eve's intentions regarding Roger Thornhill seem to change from scene to scene. Thus in *Charade*, Regina has to wonder, much as Roger cannot decide about Eve, if Peter is with the bad guys or on her side. Like Eve Kendall's situation, too, the big reveal in *Charade* is that all along Peter has been working undercover for the federal government, in his case to recover the fortune stolen from the United States by Lampert and company during the war.

My brief comparison with *North by Northwest* means to highlight how Cary Grant's masculine figure in *Charade*, while charming and attractive as ever, is, despite his debonair appearance and heroic acts, unstable and unpredictable. For much like Eve Kendall, Peter Joshua is devious, duplicitous, deceptive, and dishonest. His various aliases trace his deceit: "Peter" is the mysterious tall, dark, and handsome stranger Regina first meets in Megève who subsequently offers her help; "Alex Dyle" tells Regina he seeks to vindicate his late brother by working with Tex, Gideon, and Scobie, but he also assures those men that he has been working to gain her trust because she knows where the money is; and "Adam Canfield" is a common thief who wants the fortune for himself. In the final scene, the word *crook* is still embedded in the man's genuine surname ("Cruikshank") despite his turning out to be a loyal federal agent whose sense of professional duty prevented him from being honest with Regina.

Peter Joshua, then, is another male reactive figure in the plot of a Hepburn film, needing to give Regina a new backstory along with a new name as one after another of his aliases is exposed as a fake. Since along with Regina we never know his true motives until the final scene, and one of the few times we see him outside her point of view surprisingly indicates he may be allied with Tex, Gideon, and Scobie to get the fortune from her, he is hardly a figure of identification but remains untrustworthy and at a distance from viewers throughout *Charade*. On the other hand, rather than being along for the ride, the typical role of a female star in most thrillers, Regina drives events. Despite being in danger (or in plot terms, *because* she is in danger), Regina moves things along; she not only has agency in *Charade*, but she also supplies its central point of view on what is happening, which is why Audrey Hepburn, and not Cary Grant, offers viewers an accessible path of identification.

After all, Regina is transparent about her feelings, honest in her intentions, law-abiding, fearless even when terrified, smart and quick-witted, and, most of all, sympathetic. If one cannot pin Peter down, Regina is firmly grounded; in other words, this Hepburn character is no longer the liminal figure of the Audrey films I discussed in chapter 3. Being in danger gives Regina surer footing and a strong sense of who she is even if she has no idea who anyone else really is. But unsure of the identities and motives of others, especially Peter, makes her a different sort of liminal figure nonetheless, a mature version of the younger Audrey persona, so to speak, one that reverses its terms, moving Hepburn from Holly's "I don't know who I am" to Regina's "I don't know who anybody is." This will be a commonality shared with Hepburn's other thrillers as well.

Charade, moreover, is an old-school star vehicle that relies heavily on the performances of Hepburn and Grant, as supported by expert actors in the villainous roles (Matthau, Coburn, and Kennedy, who would each go on in their careers to win an Oscar in the supporting category). This is what Donen means, I think, when he wryly comments on the Blu-ray, "It's not a bad movie when you just look at their faces." The witty dialogue and banter between the two stars as well as their faces in close-ups reinforce their charismatic presence. The romance plot, which has Regina and Peter falling for each other, with her sometimes making the moves on him while at other times being uncertain of his motives and wary of him, crisscrosses the thriller plot. As Peter complains to Regina, "One minute you're chasing me around the shower room, the next minute you're accusing me of murder." Humor connects these two narrative strands, and the two stars performing *as* stars supply the glue for this connection. Similarly, the trio terrorizing Regina is menacing and creepy, yes, but they also are potentially comic types: a nebbishy New Yorker with allergies (Gideon); a thin, nattily suited cowboy who calls her "Mrs. Lampert, ma'am" (Tex); and a growling, groaning hulk with a metal claw in place of his missing hand (Scobie).

The long sequence that commences in the Parisian nightclub and concludes with Regina tailing Peter illustrates how *Charade* seesaws between humor and suspense, between romance and menace, and how Hepburn's nuanced performance anchors this hybrid tone. Her many emotional shifts, as registered on her face and by her eyes and shown in her subtle handling of props, along with her crisp delivery of witty dialogue and non sequiturs, create the necessary continuity for what might otherwise seem generically inconsistent or incoherent. I want to describe the sequence in detail to show the tonal shifts that supply the terms of Hepburn's performance, which I shall then examine.

The sequence begins when Peter takes Regina to a nightclub to cheer her up after she has met with the police detective and Bartholomew. The MC makes the customers his floor show, instructing them to form two lines to start a game: players have an orange placed under their chin that they have to pass along to the next player without using their hands, and so on down the line of people. Laughing, Regina leads Peter to the dance floor to play the game. The sight of Cary Grant trying to retrieve the orange from an expressionless, bosomy woman is funny, to be sure; and from the faces he makes—as the orange slips, as he catches it, as it slips inside his jacket, as he retrieves it without using his hands, as it falls down the woman's chest, and as he catches it with his chin before it drops to the floor—it seems that Grant himself is having fun in this scene, too. When he passes it on to Hepburn—and laughing again, she mutters, "whoops"—the tight close-ups show the two stars chin to chin, face to face, as they struggle with the orange. The background music fades slightly. Still in tight close-ups, Hepburn looks up at Grant, fluttering her eyelids; Grant smiles warmly back at her with obvious interest; she stares at him intently and moves in closer. Because of their mutual attraction, for a moment the orange and the game's humor seem forgotten as these two highly paid heads (as William Holden says in *Paris When It Sizzles*) look like they are about to kiss but, alas, that doesn't happen as they remember the orange.

When Regina gets the orange from Peter and starts to pass it on to the next person in line, the romantic mood abruptly turns sinister for the next man in line is Gideon, who warns her, "Any morning you can wake up dead." During this exchange Hepburn is in another tight close-up as her face shows her initial surprise at being addressed by a stranger, her clenched teeth as Gideon says the money doesn't belong to her, and her growing terror as he threatens her life. Her eyes open wide as she tells Gideon to leave her alone, and she screams "Stop!" as she kicks him in the ankle. Explaining to Peter, "He stepped on my foot," she says she will be right back and leaves the dance floor.

Regina rushes downstairs to call Bartholomew on the pay phone there; she dials but is momentarily flustered because she needs to put in coins for the call to go through. Suddenly Tex opens the door of the booth, and she hangs up the phone. Looking at him directly, she asks what he wants. "You must be kidding," he responds. Telling her she needs to find the money or he might kill her, he throws lit matches on her lap while she puts them out with her hands and screams, "You're insane. You're absolutely insane!" After he departs, from her purse she takes out a stick of candy and sucks it to calm down. The door of the phone booth opens again and she jumps up and screams. But it is Peter, who coolly asks her, "What's the matter? What are you doing in here?" "I'm having a nervous breakdown," she replies tensely. Speaking each word slowly, Hepburn punctuates the line by raising her eyebrows and smiling grimly.

Back in the hotel, the two have the conversation already quoted, in which he asks what happened in the nightclub, she says she is not sure she is supposed to tell him, and he bullies her, telling her to stop the nonsense. Yet in the middle of that conversation in which they parry about her secrets, at odd points Regina changes the topic. They quarrel in the hotel lobby, but she then demurely asks Peter if he will see her to her door. As they enter the close confines of the narrow elevator, she murmurs, "It's a good place for making friends." In a two-shot as they travel to the upper floors, he still tries to get her to talk, she tries to get personal, and when he asks her what her husband was mixed up in, she points to his cleft chin and asks how he shaves in there.

Her question at first may seem like an off-the-wall comment, but her abruptly changing the topic may well be Regina's sly way of evading his interrogation. While Peter persists in questioning her in the elevator, she still tries to romance him, but he remarks, "I could already be arrested for transporting a minor above the first floor." Leaving the elevator, she invites him to her room, but he declines. "I don't bite, you know," she responds, "unless it is called for." When she then asks if he would like a punch in the nose, it is because of his patronizing attitude. But this is also the much-quoted moment when, after he says he is tired and wants to leave, she asks, "Do you know what's wrong with you?" He replies, "No, what?" Then, in a line that some people take to be about Cary Grant even more than his character, she leans forward and says with a smile, "*Nothing.*"

Almost immediately after that, however, the mood turns sinister again, for Regina finds Scobie in her room, tearing it apart in his search for the money. He rushes at her, waving his scary metal claw. Shutting the door on him, she manages to get out of the room in time, but as she slams the door behind her, Scobie's metal claw crashes through the wood. Peter goes into the room and appears to tussle with Scobie. The scene deviates from Regina's viewpoint as Peter follows Scobie to another room in the hotel, with Cary Grant showing he is still a nimble performer as he jumps from one balcony to another. Now it seems that Peter is apparently working with the three men to find the money, they are all convinced that Regina knows where it is, and what is more, he is not Peter Joshua but is

Alexander Dyle, Carson's supposed brother. Peter tells Tex to give him his room, which is next to Regina's, so he can have better surveillance of her.

When Peter returns to Regina, she finally confides in him about the three men and the money. Hugging him for comfort, she asks for his help because he is "the only one I can trust," but she also asks him to promise that he will never lie to her as her husband did. The phone then buzzes and it is Scobie calling; she learns from him that Peter's name is Dyle and Scobie warns her not to trust him because he is just after the money. Abruptly, Regina loses confidence in Peter's honesty. As he embraces her and, with a Cheshire Cat's grin, mentions that he has arranged to take the room next door, her eyes open wide to indicate her apprehension. Her uneasiness is doubled as she peers through the keyhole of the door separating their rooms and sees that he has a gun. Regina phones Bartholomew to arrange a meeting and craftily eludes Peter so he cannot trail her.

Bartholomew's classed, Lower East Side accent, and domesticated, schlemiel-like persona belie how he is really the dangerous Carson Dyle, the murderer of Charles Lampert. His ordinariness, awkwardness, and placid demeanor are disarming and, unlike the ominous air of the just-ended scene with Peter in Regina's hotel room and before that her encounter there with Scobie, the street market at Les Halles, where Regina meets Bartholomew, seems benign and safe. They sit down at a cafe and in a long two-shot Bartholomew tells Regina about Carson Dyle's role in the gold heist and his apparent fatality at the hands of the Germans. She asks him for a cigarette. Ripping off the filter, she explains, "I can't stand these things. It's like drinking coffee with a veil." Putting the cigarette in an ashtray, she appears to forget it, lost in the story about the stolen gold that Bartholomew is telling her, and she takes another cigarette, ripping off its filter. He asks what's wrong with the one she has, and doesn't she know how expensive they are? She shrugs, returns the torn cigarette to the package, and resumes smoking the first one. A waiter brings him a coffee and her a bowl of French onion soup, which, though hungry as always, she doesn't eat, continuing to smoke. Regina announces she intends to leave Paris that night, but Bartholomew dissuades her, reminding her of what happened to her husband when he tried to leave the city.

Ending the meeting, Bartholomew instructs her to find out all she can about this mysterious man "Dyle." "Why me?" she asks. "He trusts you," Bartholomew replies, "and besides, you yourself said women made the best spies." The next morning, Regina dutifully follows "Dyle" to the American Express office. With her attempt not to be noticed, this scene turns from menace to broad visual comedy. Whenever "Dyle" stops or looks back, which happens several times, Regina pretends she knows a German tourist sitting at an outdoor cafe, only to repel the man, who thinks she is picking him up, when "Dyle" continues on his way. Given her costume (a white trench coat over a white dress, a white scarf on her head, white gloves, a black umbrella, black boots, and dark sunglasses), which is unlike how Hepburn dresses at any other time in *Charade*, Regina stands out on the street too. Amplifying the costume, Hepburn walks furtively as if pretending to be invisible while knowing that she is being sneaky. The punch line to this scene is that Peter is completely unaware of Regina's tailing him, though she nearly collides with him once or twice.

I have devoted so much space to describing this long sequence, which occurs with an hour of *Charade* still to come, in order, as I said, to illustrate how the film repeatedly shifts between humor and suspense, which is the context for Hepburn's performance: for *she* controls the shifting tones through her acting, which is subtle in multiple ways. Regina at many times seems like a character from screwball comedy; her emotions, in contrast with Peter's, fluctuate and often seem unpredictable, though not without cause. Regina's thinking strays from a linear path, which results in dialogue that shifts back and forth between witty repartee, shock and terror, unexpected non sequiturs, and attempts to romance Peter.

Hepburn's face registers her character's multiple, fluctuating feelings, signaling each of the script's changes in tone. In particular, she uses her eyes to show Regina's surprise, calm, suspicion, fear, joy, mischief, or desire. Reinforcing her facial expressions, moreover, Hepburn's eyes often indicate a direction, establishing the boundaries of diegetic space within the film frame; from her gaze we know who speaks to her or threatens her and where they are before we see them in a subsequent shot. For instance, when Regina finds Scobie in her hotel room, she enters in darkness. Hepburn's eyes shift immediately from the pleasure Regina feels in finding Peter attractive—despite her irritation at his patronizing attitude moments before—to wide-eyed terror when, turning on the light, she discovers the brutish Scobie pulling apart her bed. Reinforcing the terror shown by her face, the direction of her eyes announces his presence before the next shot discloses him.

By contrast, except for the scene when, to Regina's amusement, he showers in his clothes, plays the game with the orange, or makes a clown face at her in the last scene when she learns he is really Brian Cruikshank, T-man, Grant's face in close-ups or medium shots tends to be more unchanging, befitting his unknowable identity and motives. His eyes rarely show his emotion, nor do they define diegetic space in the way that Hepburn's do. Just as his face hides his feelings—which is to say that Grant's facial reactions are subtle in a different way than Hepburn's, evident in a slight change of expression, a turn of his head, a close-mouthed smile, an insincere grin—he tends to look more squarely at the camera, as if he is unafraid and confident, which gives him a misleading air of transparency.

The two stars come alive as a couple in the precise delivery of their perfectly timed dialogue, where the emotional complexity of both their characters is more apparent as sparks fly between them in their banter. In these exchanges, Grant plays the straight man, remaining aloof in his wooing, while Hepburn plays the often illogical comedian, shifting from the question of the missing money and the men terrorizing her to those funny, off-the-wall, non sequitur comments or questions, like her asking how he shaves in his cleft chin. Likewise, Regina is the one who repeatedly makes clear she is falling for him, acting as the aggressor through her dialogue and body language, whereas Peter refrains from disclosing his feeling for her, repeatedly backing away and calling attention to her youth.

Finally, this sequence illustrates Hepburn's use of seemingly trivial props throughout *Charade*. Regina smokes when thinking or if her nerves are jarred. She eats when unhappy, anxious, or afraid, and in several scenes she either has food on a table in front of her or talks about being hungry. She loses her appetite when she is happy (as when Peter finally confesses on the dinner boat that he has been having trouble keeping his hands off her). In addition to the cigarettes and onion soup in the cafe with Bartholomew, after Tex throws the last lit match at her and leaves the phone booth, Regina fumbles in her purse for that stick of candy, which she unwraps and then sucks on to settle her frayed nerves. Earlier in the police detective's office, Regina similarly takes a bag of candies from her purse and munches on them nervously as she learns of her late husband's dishonesty; with each question that the detective asks about her late spouse, she can only answer softly and without changing the cadence, "I don't know." In Bartholomew's supposed office in the American Embassy, after initially refusing a sandwich, she asks for one as he begins to tell her about the stolen gold, and she eats it; when he hands her a magnifying glass to scrutinize the wartime photo of the men, Regina first brushes sandwich crumbs from her lap before taking the glass from him—a gesture that later rhymes with Tex's tossing lit matches in her lap and her putting out the flames with her hands.

Hepburn's use of cigarettes, candy, and food may seem inconsequential, but they indicate Regina's state of mind and enable the actress to show, without stealing the scene from her costar, that she is listening closely to what the other performer is telling her. In the cafe scene at Les Halles, although Matthau's character will turn out to be the most dangerous villain in *Charade*, the actor has to be convincing here as an unthreatening, somewhat humorous bureaucrat, one worried about the cost of American cigarettes in France, as he tells Regina about his own supposed death, concealing his greed and rage at being left behind by his cronies. Except when she turns her head to exhale smoke, during the two-shot Hepburn sits still, staring at Matthau in astonishment at what he says; but without calling undue attention to it, she continuously moves her hand as she smokes: flicking the ash at one point, at another point removing a piece of tobacco from her mouth; at times clenching three fingers while holding the cigarette, at other times extending her palm while holding it; occasionally gesturing with her arm. Even though Hepburn was herself a heavy smoker in real life (so I have to assume she is really smoking in this scene), given Regina's hefty appetite, when she orders the soup in the cafe with Bartholomew but doesn't taste it, instead continuing to smoke while he finishes his story, the cigarette, functioning as her prop, signals the intensity and interest with which she listens to him.

Listening becomes an even more crucial activity in Hepburn's second thriller, *Wait Until Dark*, for her character, Susy Hendrix, has recently lost her vision in an auto accident. Hearing gives Susy the sensory means through which she slowly realizes that she is being misled by the various men who enter her apartment in her husband's absence. Whereas Tex, Gideon, and Scobie in *Charade* assume that Regina knows where the fortune is hidden, Roat (Alan Arkin), Mike (Richard Crenna), and Carlino (Jack Weston) in *Wait Until Dark* remain convinced that Susy knows the whereabouts of a missing doll her husband, Sam (Efrem Zimbalist Jr.), had received for safekeeping from Lisa, a woman he accidentally met at the Montreal airport, after their plane arrives in New York. The doll is stuffed with heroin, which is why Roat wants it so badly. *Wait Until Dark* differs from *Charade* in consistently building suspense without the humor characterizing the earlier thriller; its tension is unyielding as Susy's dangerous situation intensifies, leading up to her violent confrontation with Roat in the dark. Furthermore,

Susy ultimately has no allies, no Peter Joshua figure to come to her rescue in the climax, but must deal with Roat on her own if she is to survive the night.

In the scene immediately following the opening credits, Roat tricks Mike and Carlino into entering the Hendrixes' apartment in the couple's absence by making the two men think that Lisa, their former accomplice in crime, has invited them there to join her in some sort of new confidence game. The two men have a history (and a police record) of blackmailing married men whom Lisa has bedded. The invitation, however, is a ruse. Lisa betrayed Roat by intending to use the doll to go into business for herself, so he killed her, presumably in the Hendrixes' basement flat shortly before Mike and Carlino arrive. When Mike discovers her body hanging in the bedroom closet, he tells Carlino they should leave, but it is too late: they have left their fingerprints throughout the apartment, incriminating themselves. As for Roat, he informs them he has left no fingerprints, has no police record, and "no known association with Lisa." Because of their carelessness, Roat now compels the men into working with him, first, to move Lisa's body, wrapped in a carpet, which they will deposit on a nearby street, and then to find the doll, which Sam told Lisa he cannot find but which Roat believes is somewhere in the apartment.

At this point Susy, returning from "blind school" (as she calls it), enters the apartment; the men freeze and hold their breath as, unable to see them, she goes to the bedroom closet to fetch a scarf after phoning Sam and arranging to meet him at the coffee shop downstairs in the building where his main photographic studio is located. Without discovering the body hanging inside on the closet door, she leaves. After her departure, Roat orders the two men to move the body so they can clear out since they only have a short time before the Hendrixes return.

Roat's plan exploits Mike's and Carlino's talents to "lie and cheat and playact," as he says, in order "to talk your way into that locked safe" covered by a tablecloth in the apartment, where he assumes the doll is hidden. Since Susy cannot see them, the men will be free to search the entire apartment while their talking distracts her. And to motivate Susy herself to look for the doll, they enact a script whose purpose is to make her believe that Sam not only had an affair with the woman whose corpse was recently found but was her killer as well; the only thing connecting him to the dead woman is the doll, which must be kept from the police so Sam will not be arrested. In this little drama, Mike playacts a friendly military pal of Sam's who offers Susy sympathy and assistance; Carlino playacts a brusque, aggressive cop who believes Sam is guilty and accuses Susy of hiding the doll; and Roat playacts an old man and the man's son who both claim that Sam had the affair with the son's wife, "Luciana," the supposed woman whose corpse was left "in a parking lot practically next door," as Susy has described to Sam the location where Lisa's body was found.

Of the three men, Roat is the most dangerous and mercurial adversary that Susy faces in *Wait Until Dark*. For in contrast with other two, Roat is clever, vicious, and sadistic. As this early scene ends, Mike and Carlino mutter to each other, "Trouble," for they have seen a sampling of the violence Roat is capable of. Although Mike carries a small switchblade and Carlino brass knuckles, their own weapon of choice is persuasive but deceptive talk; the two men are confidence men, after all, who don't plan on killing their marks, just scaring them into forking over cash. Roat's chosen weapon, on the other hand, is "Geraldine," a razor-sharp dagger sheathed in a case sculpted to look like an ancient female goddess. Like the dagger enclosed in an innocent-looking cover, Roat's cool demeanor conceals his unpredictable rage and pleasure in inflicting pain.

Alan Arkin performs Roat as a psychopath, able to switch on a dime from being calm to being monstrous, as, for example, when he suddenly and without warning crouches in a fighting position and flashes his knife at the two men when Mike asks for the key to the locked closet. Roat's steady, controlled, singsong diction conceals his lack of empathy, his enjoyment of playacting and trickery, and his sadism and deep satisfaction from killing. Late in the film, when Mike makes one final but unsuccessful effort to compel Susy to hand over the doll after she does find it, he says, "This is the big bad world where nasty things happen." "It's different with Mr. Roat," Susy replies. "He wants to do evil things." And how right she is! In their final confrontation, Roat not only plans to kill Susy after getting the doll, but he relishes torturing her beforehand.

Roat's dangerous instability measures Susy's heroic strength in comparison. Her kind, stolid husband Sam, who appears only in the opening and final scenes of *Wait Until Dark*, does not protect her; in fact, he is no match for Roat's trickery. Roat has no trouble circumstantially setting up the unsuspecting Sam to appear credible as "Luciana's" lover and murderer or sidetracking him to Asbury Park on a supposed photo shoot so Susy will be alone in the apartment. For his part, Sam is not only Roat's unsuspecting mark but also a bit of a bully, insisting on Susy's independence and her learning "total self-sufficiency," as she tells a neighbor departing for a short holiday. "Do I have to be the world's champion blind lady?" she asks her husband. He retorts, "Yes!" so she responds softly, "Then I will." "I'll be whatever you want me to be," she also says; and while Sam calmly replies that he just wants her "to be Susy," one has to wonder what he means by that comment, given his authoritative air and her deference to him. Setting up the climax, Sam orders Susy to defrost their ancient refrigerator the old-fashioned way, "my way," he calls it, "with plenty of boiling water." She asks what to do if she burns herself, and he reminds her where they keep the ointment for burns. "Where does the icebox plug in?" she asks, and Sam tells her, "You'll find it." The refrigerator and its plug, of course, will be important in Susy's climactic encounter with Roat.

As Roat's script plays out in the apartment, Susy begins to suspect things are not what they seem, but it takes a while for her to figure out what it all means. She first smells smoke from Roat's cigarettes when she returns from school but assumes the culprit was Gloria (Julie Herrod), the adolescent who lives upstairs and helps her out at times. As the film progresses, Susy wonders why both the old and young Mr. Roat wear new shoes that make the same, barely noticeable, squeaking noise (because one man is playing both roles); why Carlino keeps dusting furniture and banisters in the apartment while interrogating her (because he is still nervous about his fingerprints incriminating him); and why everyone keeps playing around with the kitchen blinds (they are signaling cues to the other players who are outside, waiting to re-enter or make a telephone call to the apartment). With Gloria's help as a lookout, Susy ultimately learns that a van and not a police car (as Mike has told her) is parked outside, and that calls have gone to and from the pay phone across the street and not to the police department or the apartment where Mike was supposedly staying.

Once Susy figures out that Carlino and Roat are not police and that Mike is in on the game, too, she sends the latter two men on a fool's errand to Sam's studio for the doll, which she has actually hidden in the kitchen; while they are gone, she evens the playing field. After sending Gloria to wait for Sam at the Port Authority bus terminal because Carlino is on watch outside, Susy breaks all the light bulbs in the apartment and hallway. When Mike comes back for the doll, she refuses to give it to him, and he compliments her before departing: "You're a good, strong lady, Susy Hendrix." Although he thinks Carlino has taken care of Roat as planned, the latter has turned the tables and killed Carlino; and as Mike starts to leave the apartment without the doll, Roat stabs him in the back, and his body falls to the floor. "Now all the children have all gone to bed, and we can talk," Roat will tell Susy minutes later.

The final confrontation dramatizes Susy's courage and smarts in dealing with and ultimately defeating Roat by herself. He enters the apartment, chains the door so it cannot be opened, and spills gasoline on the floor; lighting a newspaper, he frightens Susy with it, and then teases her with a scarf that he flutters against her head and neck. Though terrified and sobbing, and still pretending she does not have the doll, soon Susy is able to get the upper hand, at least for the moment. "Are you looking at me, Mr. Roat?" she asks, and when he says yes, she throws in his face the Hypo photographic fluid she had poured into a vase when darkening the apartment; taking advantage of Roat's temporary blindness, and breaking the one remaining light in Sam's photo lab, in the dark she finds Roat's knife and the gasoline can; as he approaches her, she douses him with the flammable liquid. Getting the matches from him as well, she lights one after another as she orders him to tap with her cane to identify his location. Susy unsuccessfully tries to get out of the apartment and is unaware that Roat is moving toward the refrigerator, which he opens for light and fixes the door with a dish towel so it will not close. Able to see again, Roat uses the cane to draw Susy toward him, hooking the handle around her neck, and he regains control.

Defeated, Susy says she will give Roat the doll if he promises to leave and not hurt her. He agrees but forces her to say, "Please, may I give you the doll." After she takes the doll from where she has hidden it in the trash can beneath the kitchen sink and offers it to Roat, her fingers touch a chef's knife sticking up from the dish drainer, and she grabs it. Once he retrieves all the heroin packets from the doll and stuffs them in his coat pockets, Roat orders Susy to go with him to the bedroom, where he plans to kill her. She reminds him he had promised not to hurt her, but he cruelly says his fingers must have been crossed. Then, as he grabs her close to him to stop her resisting, she stabs him in the stomach with the sharp knife, and he falls toward the floor.

Susy opens the chained door as far as she can and screams for help, her voice hoarse by now. Running back to the kitchen, she mutters to herself, "Windows." Then, in an unexpected move that caused audiences at the time to jump in their seats (and I suspect still startles first-time viewers), the seriously injured Roat leaps out at Susy from the dark and grabs her foot. She is able to escape his grasp and runs to the refrigerator as he crawls after her, using the knife as a crutch to propel him as he slowly slides on the floor toward her. Hiding behind the refrigerator door, Susy frantically searches for the plug—and as she screams horrifically, the screen goes black. After a few tense, silent moments, a police siren can be heard on the soundtrack. Sam, Gloria, and cops arrive. Breaking through the chained door, and replacing some of the bulbs so they can see, they find Mike's and Roat's bodies, and Susy, splattered with Roat's blood, protected by the open refrigerator door and a wooden hutch that had fallen in front as the dying Roat vainly tried to reach her.

Though her character is blind and victimized at first by the three men, *Wait Until Dark* gave Hepburn an unusually powerful female role for her era. When the old Production Code was in force, if actresses were not cast for eye candy or as victims, strong females in thrillers were either femme fatales or worked as B-girls (short for "bar girls"), whose source of income was, to be polite, hazy. When the ratings system replaced the Code after *Wait Until Dark*, strong female figures in the genre tended to work as prostitutes, like Jane Fonda in *Klute* (1971). For that matter, doesn't Susy predict the so-called Final Girl in the cycle of teen horror movies that would begin just a few years after *Wait Until Dark*?

Susy Hendrix, moreover, posed an obvious acting challenge for Hepburn. Unable to take advantage of her trademark wide smile or to suggest a sense of fun and mischief except once, when Susy sticks out her tongue at Sam after he reminds her where the burn ointment is kept, Hepburn uses her face and voice in ways different from her other performances.

While Hepburn screams and sobs in the final act, the cadence of her speech before then tends to be deliberate and unvarying in volume, as if she were measuring her words because of her uncertainty with regard to where she is spatially due to her blindness. Until the terror intensifies, and except for the occasions when she is angry at Sam or Gloria in early scenes or is panicked by the smoke coming from a burning cigarette butt in an ashtray right before Mike arrives, Hepburn's face tends to match her speech pattern, with a nondescript expression, as if blindness has drained excitement from her. As the terror mounts, she opens her mouth, although not widely, to shriek, wail, and moan in panic, as when she has told Mike that she has the doll only to realize shortly afterward that he is one of the bad guys, too; but the sounds Hepburn makes then are not full-throated—that doesn't happen until the final scene with Roat—for she makes it seem as if she is unsuccessfully trying to stifle the sounds, to hold them inside her, as she clutches the doll to her chest.

Forbidden from showing feeling through her eyes or using them to indicate direction for establishing the boundaries of space or for anticipating the next shot, Hepburn adapts a blank stare for the entire film, and her stare rarely if ever wavers. In two-shots or shot/reverse shot sequences with another actor, when speaking, Hepburn never looks directly at the person but arranges her body to be to the right or left of him, indicating that she hears and engages but cannot see who is speaking to her so she does not face him directly—unless she asks where he is. Before sticking out her tongue at Sam, she first asks if he is looking at her, and she does the same with Roat before dousing him with Hypo liquid.

Hepburn also has a different kind of physical business to do as an actress. She stumbles several times when a chair or table has been moved out of place. Look carefully, and you will notice a small, round band-aid on the back of her wrist, which may be in character or due to a mishap that befell the actress while filming, rehearsing, or preparing the role. And she has to make more use of her hands to orient herself spatially, as when, after she realizes that all three men are plotting against her, she feels for the pipes on the wall next to the refrigerator in order to signal Gloria to come downstairs so she can send the girl to wait for Sam's return at the bus station. In the tense moment as Roat crawls toward her, Hepburn first stands by the refrigerator not knowing what to do or where to go; then she frantically tries to shut the appliance door, thinking it is blocked by the cabinet door from beneath the kitchen sink because she cannot see the towel Roat stuffed there to keep it ajar; finally she crouches on the floor by the refrigerator, its bright bulb supplying the only source light for the scene, as she feels around for the plug with her hands, moaning, "Where is it?" In the very last scene, when she stumbles out of her hiding place, first moving to Gloria, who says her name, then to Sam when he calls to her, Hepburn has absolutely no expression whatsoever on her face but looks shell-shocked, and she must use her hands to negotiate her way slowly around the fallen furniture and Roat's body.

The heavy-handed exposition in the opening scenes, along with how the screenplay establishes key elements that will be important subsequently in Susy's big scene with Roat—her fear of fire, the chef's knife, the Hypo fluid in Sam's makeshift photo lab between the bedroom and living room, the refrigerator light and uncertain location of the plug—betray the origins of *Wait Until Dark* in Frederick Knott's Broadway play, a conventional, single-set, well-made if over-oiled thriller. Nonetheless, Terence Young has a firm command of the material, he knows how to keep viewers glued to the screen as he builds the suspense, and he gets fine performances from all the actors in addition to Hepburn. Arkin in particular is extraordinarily effective as Roat, a fitting counterpoint to Susy's virtue; his compelling figure calls to my mind Joseph Conrad's phrase from *Heart of Darkness*: "the fascination of the abomination."

Twelve years later and three years after returning to the screen in *Robin and Marian*, her last film of any distinction, Hepburn agreed to do *Bloodline*, drawn from a potboiler bestseller by Sidney Sheldon. She may have joined the project as a favor to Young, who was directing; that her marriage to Andrea Dotti was crumbling probably factored into her decision to do the film, too, as did the million-dollar salary, since she had not worked in nine years. *Bloodline* came out as the era of successful melodramas with all-star casts based on novels from writers like Harold Robbins, Jacqueline Susann, and Sheldon was finishing. One might say that *Bloodline*, which flopped at the box office and was panned by reviewers, hammered the nail in the coffin of that cycle, though I am sure there were other films also trying to milk it as and even after it died.

Unlike *Wait Until Dark*, Young appears to have had little investment in making a good film with *Bloodline*, for it is sloppily edited at times, with much location footage and as much inserted studio work that does not always match; many scenes lack a proper rhythm, appearing to stop short rather than conclude; some major events happen off-screen; and a longish sequence has voice-over narration that tries clumsily to suture a flashback to the present. The soundtrack reprises a brief yet banal musical theme repeatedly, and I mean *repeatedly*. Worse, there is a subplot about making snuff porn films that makes absolutely no sense whatsoever; it could have been excised without harming the main narrative but was probably included for its sensational value. Incredibly, the snuff film sequences supplied the film's advertising image, the torso of a woman apparently strangled by a red ribbon; this image also appears in the very strange opening credits, which feature all the names of the main cast and other personnel superimposed over those of the producers.

The main storyline of *Bloodline* is even more incomprehensible and preposterous than the snuff subplot. I suppose no one went to this film expecting it to be realistic, but still . . . The IMDb reports that forty minutes of film were added when *Bloodline* aired on NBC. I haven't seen it, but I have trouble imagining that the extra footage could help make the plot more logical or coherent. The assembled and talented international cast tries valiantly to make diamonds from the coal they have been given: in support of Hepburn, *Bloodline* costars James Mason, Ben Gazzara, Michelle Phillips, Omar Sharif, Irene Papas, Romy Schneider, Maurice Ronet, Beatrice Straight, Claudia Mori, and Gert Fröbe. The cast is game, yet there is only so much they can do with this crazy concoction. Hepburn's own disinterest in the project shows in her flat performance. Her voice sounds harsh and lacks the lyric flexibility of her youth; it may be an acting choice, though I suspect it is more likely due to her many years of heavy smoking. At a few times she is also photographed in unflattering lighting that shows the fifty years etched into her face, although her character is supposed to be thirty-something.

Hepburn plays Elizabeth Roffe, apparently a paleontologist; her first scene has her working on a dinosaur exhibit in a Manhattan museum, but her professional training is quickly forgotten and never mentioned again, for she is immediately thrust into heading a pharmaceutical megacorporation in Europe when her father, the CEO, president, and founder of the company, dies in a climbing accident in Switzerland. Her international cousins, all members of the board and eager for the anticipated cash payout, implore her to take the company public, but she refuses because her father had been the single vote against doing so some months before his passing. Leaving behind the kind of boardroom drama and backroom financial shenanigans that the nighttime soaps *Dynasty* and *Dallas* had popularized on television at this time and that might have given the plot more juice, *Bloodline* becomes a mystery once the father's death is determined to have been a murder and, what is more, his demise happened shortly after he learned the identity of a board member trying to sabotage the company. Elizabeth has one ace in the hole for keeping the company private—an anti-aging pill just a year away from production, which gives her some breathing space from the Swiss banks to whom $650 million in short-term loans are soon due—but the scientist working on the pill is also murdered, and the plant where his lab is located is burned down.

A series of attempts on Elizabeth's life follows the disclosure that her father was murdered. She is nearly run over by a man on a snowmobile; the brakes on her Jeep are tampered with; the cable on her private elevator is snapped, sending a trusted assistant to her death in place of Elizabeth, who had forgotten her earrings and gone to fetch them; and finally, at her villa in Sardinia a policeman, whom she assumes is there to protect her, drugs the tea he gives her to settle her nerves, and then he disappears while she is asleep. At this point, *Bloodline* cribs from *Wait Until Dark*. When a groggy Elizabeth realizes she has been drugged, she tries to telephone for help, but the lines are dead; the electricity goes out and she hears someone moving inside the house. Elizabeth trashes her bedroom so that her death cannot be made to look like an accident, but then she sees smoke wafting into the room from underneath her locked door. Her only recourse is to escape to the roof from a window. During this scene, Hepburn repeats what she had previously done when Susy was terrorized in *Wait Until Dark*, but her performance here is nowhere near as nuanced or convincing and seems a pale imitation.

Hepburn had an affair with Ben Gazzara while making *Bloodline*, but they must have kept their passion off-screen because their pairing on-screen has no heat or chemistry; and if Hepburn often looks somewhat bored through parts of the film, as when she goes through the motions of her character's running the company or traveling to Kraków to see firsthand her father's origin as a healer in the Jewish ghetto there, Gazzara seems gruff and sullen, as if he would rather be anywhere else than in this picture. To be sure, their characters' marriage begins as a business arrangement required by the consortium of banks if they are to delay repayment of the huge loans. Rhys Williams (Gazzara), her late father's right-hand man who is a nonvoting board member, has the experience that Elizabeth lacks, but only a family member can head the company. So while he will run things, she will still control the stock and have the authority to decide whether or not to take the company public in the future. All the same, their relationship does warm up at one point. Jealous of the attentions paid to him at Maxim's by several of his former mistresses, Elizabeth rushes outside, and he follows; when she confesses that she loves him, Rhys does not reply but kisses her, and they check into the nearest hotel to have sex.

As for the mystery, Inspector Max Hornung (Gert Fröbe) of the Zurich police force and Interpol suspects all the cousins and Rhys. The curmudgeonly detective spends most of his time checking their alibis and finances on one of those early-generation and ginormous computing machines once called data processors that eats cards and spits out information; this computer also speaks in a primitive digitally manufactured voice. Avuncular Sir Alec Nichols (James Mason), a member of the British Parliament, turns out to be the killer and saboteur; he needs the company to go public to pay off the gambling debts of his wife, Vivian (Michelle Phillips). But since midway through the film and off-screen, the casino people nail Vivan's knees to the floor of the Nichols mansion because her debt is way overdue, it seems like his motive for killing Elizabeth should have lost its purpose. Though maybe he is just greedy, I don't know. Possibly those extra forty minutes would explain it all? Or possibly not.

Anyway, Sir Alec frames Rhys for the crimes so that Elizabeth thinks her new husband is the culprit trying to kill her and destroy the company. Like Regina in *Charade*, she thus runs away from the man to whom she has recently confessed her love. And as in *Charade*, the climax requires Elizabeth to decide which man to trust, as each wants to help her out of her burning chateau in Sardinia. Of course, Sir Alec set the fire; and when Elizabeth mistakenly goes to him, he tries to strangle her with a red ribbon—the same kind of ribbon we have seen around the necks of the women killed by a baldheaded man in the snuff films, which is the only tie (pardon the pun) of the subplot to the main storyline (that, and the revelation in passing that the celluloid was manufactured by the drug company, but we never know for certain who sold it to the snuff film people, or why it matters). Inspector Max shoots Sir Alec, and Elizabeth then jumps from one balcony to another one nearby, where Rhys awaits her with loving arms.

What I find minimally interesting about *Bloodline* is what it shares in outline with *Charade*: a strong female protagonist role for Hepburn and a romantic consort who seems duplicitous, scheming, untrustworthy, and menacing—who could be like Roat but turns out to be more like Peter Joshua (though Ben Gazzara is no Cary

Grant in my eyes). Unfortunately, there is not much else to recommend about *Bloodline*. Some eight years later, Hepburn's final film as a leading lady, the TV movie *Love Among Thieves*, follows this template too. This film is more fun, though—that is, if you like those madcap screwball road movies from the 1930s in which two bona fide movie stars meet cute but have to travel together, and I do have a fondness for that type of film. Truth to tell, though, many sequences in *Love Among Thieves* don't make much sense logically when tied together, so to find pleasure in the film one has to enjoy the ride with Hepburn and Robert Wagner, regardless of the many twists, turns, bumps, and detours along the way.

Hepburn plays the widowed Baroness Caroline DuLac, who steals three priceless Fabergé eggs shortly before performing a piano recital at a gala benefit inside the San Francisco art museum where the eggs were on exhibit. It seems that Caroline's new fiancé, Alan Channing (Patrick Bauchau), has been kidnapped, held in Ledera, a tiny town probably somewhere in Mexico, and the stolen eggs are his ransom. A brutal man in a trench coat and fedora, Spicer (Jerry Orbach), arranges a false pickup in which he tries to grab the eggs from Caroline, but her sister-in-law, Solange (Samantha Eggars), foils his plot. To get to Ledera, Caroline has to take a commuter prop plane to another location first, and her seat mate is Mike Chambers (Robert Wagner), who instantly annoys her with his chatter, cigar smoking, and beer drinking. To make matters worse, there is no immediate flight to Ledera in that second rural airport, and Mike has rented the only available automobile. The two end up traveling together on the mountainous journey; they quarrel, the car stalls, they are captured by Mexican bandits, the leader plans to marry Caroline until Mike trades two boxes of Cuban cigars for her, Spicer shows up, shooting at them, and Caroline sets his car on fire. During all of this, Caroline first hates, then warms to Mike, then dislikes him again; not knowing why he is going to Ledera, she mistrusts, trusts, mistrusts, trusts him. When they arrive in Ledera, he confesses he saw the eggs in her travel bag, and she hides from him. He watches her being driven away by one of the kidnappers yet cannot follow because he has to pay his bill at the cantina but lost his wallet.

Taken to a villa in the country where she can ransom Alan, Caroline soon learns not to trust him either, for he and his supposed kidnapper have partnered to get the eggs. They also plan to kill Caroline in the morning. She is able to grab the eggs and escape, climbing out the second-floor window and across the uneven adobe brick wall until she drops down and flees through the vast wine cellar—where she encounters Mike, who has come to find her. (How he discovered the whereabouts of the house is left unexplained.) At this point, he tells her he works for Interpol and has been chasing Alan for several years. Reaching the town, they find themselves in the middle of a shootout between Spicer and Alan and his men. Spicer is wounded and the police corral all the shooters, which allows the couple to board a train, though they do not stay on it for long; eventually, they reach another town, steal a car that Spicer has just rented, and drive back to San Francisco. (Please don't ask me about the film's sense of geography.)

Back in the city, since Caroline is wanted for a shooting (though I have no clear idea who her supposed victim is), and since they cannot return to her home, Mike drives her to Solange's. Alan sees them in the street and shoots at the couple, so instead they hide at a flophouse. While Mike dozes in the hotel room, Caroline calls Interpol and learns they have no idea who he is. She calls Solange, who tells her to bring the eggs to the Opera House—where Alan awaits her, because he and Solange, as it turns out, are lovers and have been in cahoots the entire time. Alan also has sent his goon to kill Mike at the flophouse. In the Opera House Alan threatens to push Caroline down an elevator shaft to fake her suicide, but she turns the tables on him and pushes him there instead, where he hangs from a cable. She throws the eggs to Solange, who reveals her perfidy, but Mike shows up with the goon's weapon and a bruised face. Anyway, Caroline, Mike, Solange, Alan, Spicer, and an assortment of miscellaneous other characters who apparently were caught up in the adventure end up in a police station, where Spicer identifies himself as an Interpol agent who has been pursuing Alan, and Caroline learns that Mike is a wealthy art collector to whom Alan had sold fake art a few years before. In the closing scene, at another gala Caroline is gorgeously dressed in a vivid red Givenchy gown, and Mike finishes the Cinderella motif established at the movie's beginning in an homage to Hepburn's Audrey films. Leaving the museum in a rush with Solange as the theft of the Fabergé eggs was discovered, Caroline had caught her shoe in a street grate and left it there; a stranger, whose face at the time we could not see, picks up the shoe. In the final moments, Mike returns it to Caroline, and they depart together.

Yes, the plot of *Love Among Thieves* is terribly silly, and, with its switches upon switches upon switches, one has to wonder if the script was written by Richard Benson of *Paris When It Sizzles*. The film also seems self-consciously imitative of *Charade*, and the detours and stops on the road seem present in order to fill out a two-hour time slot. But in comparison with *Bloodline*, there is real chemistry between Hepburn and Robert Wagner; movie stars both, they know how to spin Hollywood straw into gossamer, and they both seem to be having fun with this old chestnut of a storyline. Hepburn, moreover, looks radiant and gets to do her usual bag of tricks as an actress, moving back and forth between comedy, romance, and suspense. And again, she plays a strong, determined, and feisty female character who shows initiative and takes her dangerous situation in stride, even though she is tricked and deceived.

Bloodline and *Love Among Thieves* both record how middle age had caught up with Hepburn as far as Hollywood was concerned. To be sure, at this point in her life, she seemed less interested in her acting career; she still showed up at many tributes and galas dressed by Givenchy (and she also wore Ralph Lauren, another friend), but after the TV movie aired she would begin her humanitarian work for UNICEF, which, until the end of her life, would have much more meaning for her and offer more gratification. Yet one also cannot forget the lack of good leading roles for women in their fifties during this period, or the effect Hepburn's frequent absences from the screen since *Wait Until Dark* probably had in diminishing her box-office appeal and clout with producers. Furthermore, a new crop of younger actresses associated with what was called "the New Hollywood" had succeeded those stars who had been groomed by the old studio system. I am thinking of Diane Keaton, Jane Fonda, Faye Dunaway, Barbra Streisand, and Goldie Hawn, among others. *Bloodline* and *Love Among Thieves* thus turned out to be a bittersweet ending to Hepburn's film career. The best thing to say about *Love Among Thieves* is that it is a pleasant timewaster. The best thing to say about *Bloodline* is that it is not widely available in any home video format, though you can stream it on Amazon.

6
The Actress

Audrey Hepburn was not an actor like Robert De Niro, Meryl Streep, and Christian Bale, known, praised, and awarded for disappearing into their parts. Nor am I going to claim that Hepburn was one of the greatest actresses of her time, but I do think she was a very good one; she had charm and elegance, yes, but she did not simply skate on those qualities. She was, after all is said and done, an actress who gave many fine performances as well as a major movie star. Hepburn made many romantic comedies, and comedy seldom wins awards—yet she *did* win an Oscar for starring in one. What about her acting in dramatic films? This chapter will look at some of those.

Hepburn arrived at Paramount as the old studio system was still in force, albeit its demise was in the cards, and where production of star vehicles was still the order of the day. The major actors of the studio era became stars because they attracted audiences, who responded to their physical appearance, their film roles, and their screen personalities. Along with her unusual beauty, Hepburn's big, wide smile, which illuminated her face, and her lyrical voice were central to her appeal. This is also why her critics thought Hepburn was just a personality—that she simply projected her own sparkling and delightful self on-screen—and not a genuine actress, but that is far from the truth, as evident already in my discussions of *Charade* and *Wait Until Dark* in the previous chapter. Similarly, when talking about the Audrey films in chapter 3, what I did not always point out explicitly, but which nonetheless motivated what I wrote there, is that the desiring, willfulness, intellect, and playfulness of her characters are apparent *because* of Hepburn's nuanced acting. Furthermore, in the fourth chapter, on fashion, when I discussed how Hepburn moved in Givenchy's haute couture, I was responding to the importance of her physical movement as a basis for seeing how fashion is a transformative event for her characters.

Now, in this chapter I look at a few films I have not yet spent much time on—*The Nun's Story*, *Robin and Marian*, *The Children's Hour*, and *Two for the Road*, as well as *Roman Holiday* and *How to Steal a Million*—and I focus my comments explicitly on Hepburn's acting. I shall be looking at examples of her acting alone, with another actor, and in an ensemble. As in previous chapters, when discussing her acting, moreover, since it is so bound to the narrative worlds of her films, I will sometimes refer to what her character does with others in the story, while being fully aware that Hepburn is the one doing the doing.

Movie-star acting during the studio era when Hepburn was most popular was made to appear as if it were *not* acting, but that isn't to say it lacked training or craft. In an oral history collected at the Herrick Library of the Motion Picture Academy, writer-director Richard Brooks described the process by which studios created and perpetuated the personas of stars in their films. He stated, "The roles are often tailored for who the public has decided you are because the studio told them that's who you were, and that's *not* who you are. It's a very hard kind of acting, and people are quick to dismiss it as not acting at all" (Basinger and Wasson 2022: 255). But acting it is. As James Naremore once observed about Cary Grant, "A vivid star personality is itself a theatrical construction" (1988: 235), and this comment applies equally well to Audrey Hepburn.

Even before much attention was given by the popular press in the 1950s to the serious training of new young actors from New York—Marlon Brando, Montgomery Clift, Geraldine Page, Julie Harris, and Paul Newman—in schools with their own distinct methodologies like the (in)famous "Method" for creating characters, it had already been customary for actors, even big-name stars, to take classes or private tutorials, whether their teachers or coaches were regularly employed by their studios or at off-site acting schools. In addition to instruction in diction, line-reading, and movement, actors were taught how to prepare for scenes before filming began by studying the script as a blueprint for characterization and to provide backstory for their roles and subtext for their acting (Baron 1999, 2016: 171–87). Hepburn herself may have stated repeatedly when she started out in Hollywood that she had received no professional training as an actress, had not been taught how to manufacture responses that she had hitherto never felt personally and therefore performed intuitively, but I have to assume that she received instruction from her directors and others at Paramount as well as relying on "instinct rather than knowing" (Jones 1956: 105), as she described her early performances. For that matter, before going Hollywood, in addition to classes in London with the renowned ballet teacher Marie Rambert, Hepburn had taken lessons in movement, dance, and speech early in her professional career while working as a chorus girl in stage musicals and doing bit parts in British films. In New York, her costar in *Gigi*, Cathleen Nesbitt, had coached her in private during rehearsals of the play, and Hepburn had continued to take dance classes while in the city.

As an actress, Hepburn had an excellent sense of timing in her line readings and interaction with other actors. Timing for an actor is difficult to teach, so it *is* intuitive in that sense. In Hepburn's case those classes in movement and dance probably heightened her innate sense of physical timing when it came to acting. About timing, Mitchell Leisen, a major director at Paramount during the 1930s and 1940s, commented in his oral history at the Herrick:

> Timing is so vitally important to stardom. It's a kind of instinct. If you have a sense of timing, it's wonderful. . . . Timing is knowing exactly when to come in, to keep the rhythm flowing, cut into another line. When they had no sense of timing you couldn't help them out. It's just impossible. So in addition to the predictable

things of looks and personality, sometimes it's timing that can make a star. (Basinger and Wasson 2022: 372–73)

Cary Grant was known for his spot-on timing, which is why he and Hepburn worked so well together in *Charade*. They each knew where and when to land a joke or how to punch a line of dialogue for comic or dramatic or even ambivalent effect; they knew when to interrupt the other actor or to wait a beat or two before speaking. Hepburn can switch her train of thought for humorous effect in *Charade*, as in the scene when she and Grant walk along the Seine, because of her sense of timing. Timing, furthermore, makes the interaction of Hepburn and Grant sparkle with sexual heat and tension in *Charade* even when their characters are not talking about their mutual attraction but trying to solve the mystery.

Timing is more than engaging in clever banter. You can see Hepburn's sense of timing at work beyond repartee in the nightclub scene of *Charade* as she modulates Regina's emotions, from her laughing with Peter Joshua, as she leads him to the floor to play the game with the orange, to her terror when first Gideon and then Tex threaten her. Similarly, Hepburn's timing is apparent when she smokes or eats, seemingly "unacterly" gestures on her part. Recall, as I noted in the last chapter, how Hepburn paces in front of the police inspector while eating candies as he questions her; her slight action here, as she removes a small sack from her purse and takes out one candy at a time to chew, may seem casual and impromptu, but, along with showing Regina's nervousness, what she does with the candies is in sync with her somberly replying, "I don't know" to each question about her late husband.

Hepburn's performance in *Wait Until Dark* relies on her acute sense of timing, too. She had to adjust the rhythm and tempo of her speech and reactions to other actors in order to show her character's slow realization that she is being fooled by dangerous men; and she had to move around the apartment clumsily while using her hands to find her way so as to make Susy's blindness credible. Along with line delivery, then, timing enables a performer to move around a set for maximum effect, whether to stroll casually or take a pratfall, do a double-take, an eye roll, or a slow burn, or stumble or catch oneself, often while speaking dialogue but as often just listening to another actor, or doing something quietly in the background.

Hepburn's sense of timing was already apparent in *Roman Holiday*. Watch closely what she does in her scene at the outdoor cafe with Gregory Peck. As she and Peck get to know each other, with both concealing who they really are, Hepburn casually chews on a roll and sips champagne; she leans back in her chair, looking relaxed as she enjoys the impromptu alias she is creating in order to conceal her royal identity. Opening a straw, she blows the paper cover in the air; she smiles and laughs slightly. Hepburn's gestures here, which enact her character's youthful sense of fun and relaxation, seem spontaneous and natural because of her timing. Hepburn knows "instinctively" how fast or how slowly to pick apart the roll and chew it while speaking; she knows "instinctively" just when in the exchange with Peck to lean back and then play with the straw; she knows "instinctively" just when to giggle to suggest the princess's relative immaturity, her inexperience in being alone with an attractive man. These small, well-timed gestures together show that Princess Ann has dropped her usual royal composure and feels comfortable with the reporter, whom she has just met under unconventional circumstances. And all of this happens as the two stars engage in conversation.

Some reports indicate that Hepburn had to be manipulated into giving her Oscar-winning performance in *Roman Holiday*. Because it was her first major role in a motion picture, it is true that this film was a sort of training ground for her, in which she was learning from her experienced and renowned director, William Wyler, how to build upon what she had done in her few brief previous performances so far. Her sense of timing was nonetheless crucial to her performance as Princess Ann. Apparently one thing Hepburn couldn't do on her own, though, however much she tried, was to cry convincingly with real tears during her farewell scene with Gregory Peck in the car outside the embassy. After numerous takes, Wyler had to scold Hepburn to get real tears from her.

Or consider the famous "Mouth of Truth" scene in *Roman Holiday*. Entering a cave, Peck tells Hepburn about the legend that, if someone is given to lying and puts his hand in the open mouth of the sculpted stone lion's head, it will be bitten off. Apparently, and I presume this repeated account is factual, Peck told William Wyler that he wanted to hide his hand in the cuff of his jacket sleeve as he pulled out of the lion's mouth, pretending that he has really lost his hand. Wyler told him not to tell Hepburn in order to get an authentic response of shock from her, so her surprise when this happens in the film was evidently not due to her acting but to her reacting.

However, before that trick happens, Hepburn *does* act. Peck challenges her to put her hand in the lion's mouth. In shot/reverse shot close-ups of the stars intercut with one of the lion's head, Hepburn looks uncertain; Peck returns a challenging look with a smile; she looks determined in response. In a medium shot that rapidly closes in on her, she approaches the sculpted lion's head. She slowly places her hand in the outer rim of the lion's mouth, barely touching it, then quickly pulls back with a silly giggle that indicates her nervousness. She then challenges Peck to try it. In a close-up Hepburn watches; her eyes slowly follow his arm as he places it in the opening. In a medium shot, when Peck shouts and cries out as if in serious pain and seems unable to move, Hepburn screams and grabs him by the back as if trying to pull him away. When he pretends his hand has been bitten off, she shrieks and covers her face; popping his hand out of his coat sleeve, he says, "Hel-lo." "You fiend!" Hepburn cries and hits Peck. Muttering so softly that one can barely hear, she says, "You beast! It was perfectly all right!" Peck embraces her and the two laugh at his joke. "You're okay?" he asks and she says, "Yes." They leave the cave, with Hepburn racing ahead, as if she cannot get out of there fast enough.

Hepburn's frightened response to Peck's trick may well have been spontaneous and unrehearsed—and there is a moment when it looks like Peck is seeking assurance that Hepburn herself, not her character, *is* okay after his practical joke—but whether acting, as in the beginning of the scene before the joke occurs or reacting to it, this effective scene illustrates Hepburn's already evident sense of timing as an actress. For even though some lines here may be impromptu and her acting extemporaneous at some point because she had not expected Peck to pull his stunt, if her timing had been off in her reactions, the scene would not have worked as it does so well in the release print. If that had been the case, as in the farewell scene when she couldn't cry, Wyler would have had to do at least one additional take, possibly more.

Hepburn would further hone her timing in her next comedy, Billy Wilder's *Sabrina*, where timing was even more crucial, not only in her dialogue and rapport with Humphrey Bogart and William Holden, but also, as discussed already, in how she moved in Givenchy's clothes, as when her character arrives from Paris at the train station or she is waiting for Holden to meet her in the indoor tennis court before Bogart enters in his place. Over a dozen years later, Hepburn's expert comic timing was still evident when she made another romantic comedy for William Wyler, *How to Steal a Million*. Just watch, for example, her physical byplay with Peter O'Toole and her delivery of their bantering dialogue in their meet cute moment, that is, the early sequence when, reading in bed and alerted by a noise somewhere in the otherwise empty mansion, she catches him holding her father's fake Van Gogh painting in a darkened room on the first floor.

Thinking he is a thief, Nicole (Hepburn) aims an antique gun at Simon (O'Toole), while stating she will telephone the police. As she looks down toward the painting, which he has dropped flat on the floor when she turned on the light and startled him, she notices what he is stealing and hesitates, grimaces, mutters a sound, thinks, closes her mouth, and decides she must protect her father's forgeries from being discovered. He pleads with her not to call the police but to let him go. With her eyes still looking down toward the painting, she asks him, "Why did you choose that particular painting?" As he replaces the painting on the wall, she still has the phone close to her ear, but the gun gets entangled in the wire, and without letting go of either the telephone or the gun, she tries to untangle the weapon by shaking it loose. Once the gun is freed, she aims it more directly at him. The pair go back and forth around a marble pillar in the room; he moves to one side of the column and she follows, but he scurries away to the other side, and she goes there too, still aiming the gun at him. They do this dance for several turns.

Simon then challenges Nicole, saying he is sure the gun is not loaded. Assuring him it is, though her face says she is uncertain, she cocks the trigger. After he convinces her that he is unarmed, she says she will let him leave this one time and puts down the gun. It goes off and accidentally nicks him, knocking him to the floor, while she races upstairs, hands covering her ears. Slowly she walks back downstairs, her face expressing concern and even some guilt. He shows her the blood from his wound and she leans against the pillar, hand clutching her stomach; he falls face down to the floor and she faints as well, sliding down against the pillar. Regaining consciousness, he slaps her cheek and fans the flap of his tuxedo jacket to her face to awaken her; touching his own arm, he informs her, "*I'm* the one that's bleeding." She looks at his wound and, wide-eyed, she rises. The next scene shows her ministering to him, cleaning his wound, which is no more than a bad scratch, and bandaging it. He then convinces her to drive him in his car to his residence at the Ritz Hotel. During this exchange Hepburn's face shows Nicole's befuddlement not only at his request but at how he has gained the upper hand, which she nonetheless allows in order to keep her father's secret safe.

In their meet cute scene, both actors play to the screwball tone of their unexpected and unorthodox encounter, so the timing of their speech and movement matters if they are to achieve the right comic note for the scene. The sequence, moreover, comprises a lot of shot/reverse shot editing of the two stars, with Hepburn receiving more close-ups than O'Toole, who is shown in medium or three-quarter shots (one exception is his tight close-up, meant to show off his vibrant blue eyes, when Hepburn catches him holding the painting). This not only establishes Hepburn's viewpoint but also, in another glimpse of her timing, enables Wyler to focus on her subtle facial reactions in support of her movement, as in her business with the phone and the gun, and her expressions, as when she mentally weighs calling the police against the need to safeguard the forged painting.

Earlier I also mentioned Hepburn's close-ups in the "Mouth of Truth" scene of *Roman Holiday*. While for the popular imagination during the studio era, stage and screen work signified differently in terms of training, expertise, preparation, talent, and status and prestige, as far as the film industry was concerned, the two differed from each other only by degree; a close-up on film required more restraint than a performer needed when acting on stage and playing to the last row of the balcony (Baron 1999). The close-up, with a larger-than-life face looking at the viewer, was a crucial tool of film acting during Hepburn's time (as it still is today, obviously). The actor's face implies a heightened subjectivity, often anchored by dialogue but just as often without the addition of words. A viewer's response to and understanding of what that face expresses is also subjective, and this intersubjectivity motivates audience engagement with the emotions shown in the face. The close-ups of a movie star like Hepburn, in short, rely on spectators like you and me *interpreting* her face based on the cues supplied by her expressions and usually, but not always, by her voice. This is the subtle work of a star's acting that often goes unnoticed as craft.

Additionally, a central difference between acting on stage and acting for the camera involves the kind of labor film actors undertake when building their characters. Richard Brooks succinctly differentiated acting for the camera from acting on the stage:

It's the toughest kind of acting there is in the world, much more difficult than on the stage, because on the stage you have a chance to build a character from beginning to end. . . . But in film, you shoot for twenty seconds, thirty seconds, maybe a minute, two minutes. You have no audience to respond. The crews are busy doing their jobs. You perform your story out of sequence, with no continuity, and you do it perfectly, impeccably, but the take is spoiled by some technical things and you have to do it over, maybe twenty times, finding the right tone and emotion time after time. (Basinger and Wasson 2022: 354–55)

This difference is especially important when considering the work of stars who have to carry the entire movie. Individual scenes are typically constructed from numerous shots and often require multiple takes, and for economic reasons a movie is rarely filmed to follow the story's sequencing. For certain dialogue scenes filmed in close-up for a shot/reverse shot sequence, sometimes the other actor might even be absent from the set, with a stand-in feeding lines to the person being filmed. Usually, too, close-ups are filmed after a master shot of the scene has been recorded, so, as Brooks observed, the movie actor had to find the same emotion and tone in the scene for each camera setup. In the "Mouth of Truth" scene, for instance, the close-ups of Hepburn and Peck before he pulls his stunt may have been filmed after the master shot with the stunt was done; if this was the case, then in her uncertain and determined looks in the close-ups prior to the stunt, as well as the shot that quickly moves in on her to focus on her tentatively placing her hand in the mouth and giggling, Hepburn is acting the scene with knowledge of the trick that Peck has played on her.

All of this is to say that Hepburn's acting "intuitively," as she often referred to her craft, did not mean that she simply learned her lines, showed up on set to find her marks, and then acted unconsciously from her gut and without premeditation, for she had to build her character beforehand and perform consistently in scenes filmed out of order and in small sections at a time. As Hepburn herself said early in her Hollywood career, "That's what's so difficult. You must keep the same thread of inspiration for months on end with all the normal and necessary interruptions of lunch breaks and rehearsals.... Believe me, to keep the continuity of emotions through months of production is a task. It permits no diversions" (Jones 1956: 105).

Nor did this arduous method of making a film require her director to build a performance for her through judicious editing, as Sam Wasson believes happens in *The Nun's Story*. "Strategically placed point of view and reaction shots did the trick. It was a triumph of implication, of cinematic finesse," he writes (2010: 153–54). Elsewhere, Wasson refers to Hepburn's acting in the film as "a magic trick" (103). He alludes here, I am guessing, to the famous Kuleshov effect proven in the early twentieth century, which showed that two different shots in a row had more meaning for a viewer than a single shot, and that a shot of an actor's face could mean very differently depending on the one that followed—though as Naremore comments in his recent book on Cary Grant, "Kuleshov oversimplified the task of film acting" (2022: 107).

Nonetheless, Wasson thinks *Breakfast at Tiffany's* gave Hepburn something more challenging to do as an actress than did *The Nun's Story*, requiring more of her than she had yet shown on the screen. Holly Golightly is without question a superb piece of work on Hepburn's part. *The Nun's Story*, on the other hand, required something as nuanced but in a very different register, since as a nun Hepburn had to convey interiority silently or with just a few words. While Wasson acknowledges that in *The Nun's Story* Hepburn provided "the material," his comment about her "blank look of integrity" makes her seem like a passive clay figure molded one way, then another, by her director and his editor (103). However, that is not what Fred Zinnemann himself said about working with Hepburn on that film.

When interviewed by Arthur Nolletti Jr., Zinnemann recalled how he and Hepburn prepared for *The Nun's Story* in advance of shooting:

> We got together and talked about the character, how it develops, and how it reacts to the other characters. It took many hours of going into lots of details. I always work that way with almost all actors. Then when we are rehearsing, I always want to see what the actor brings to the part, without telling him what to do. And invariably, if the actor is a talented person with imagination, he has already a well-developed idea about how to bring the part to life. (Nolletti 1994: 22–23)

After Nolletti commented about Hepburn's expressive face, Zinnemann explained it was because they had "talked in great detail" about what her character was thinking, "but not on the set. We talked about it months before. So she gradually started to live with that and she gradually started to find it in concrete form in the convent when she saw the nuns." (Hepburn had stayed a short time in a convent for research and close observation.) The director concluded his remarks about Hepburn by noting how all that preparation enabled him to work "very fast" with her once they had started filming (1994: 22–23). It is also worth pointing out that wearing a nun's habit for most of the film, which hid her entire body in shapeless clothing and confined her movement, Hepburn *had* to craft her "expressive" performance with her face and mainly through her eyes, which is no doubt why Zinnemann relies on so many close-ups of her, depending on Hepburn "to bring the part to life."

In *The Nun's Story*, after arriving at the convent to become a nun, the postulant Gabrielle van der Mal (Hepburn), who will become Sister Luke, receives a first lesson from Sister William (Patricia Collinge): "Your hands must learn to stay still and stay out of sight, except when they are needed for nursing or prayer." Gabrielle must also learn to speak softly and with little expression; she must practice humility by walking slowly and close to the wall; she must forsake mirrors to dispel vanity; she must forget and never think about her discarded secular life. In other words, the future nun must drain all emotion from herself. She must respect the rule of interior and exterior silence, to free her mind of everything but her spiritual communion with the Holy Father. Perfection is sought and achieved, she is repeatedly told, through obedience, penance, and humiliation, which demands the conquest of her pride and will.

Sister Luke is forever troubled by her imperfections. She remains proud of her scientific accomplishments and her medical training as a nurse, she is ambitious in her desire to practice in the Congo, and she has difficulty leaving a patient each night as required once the Grand Silence begins. In the Congo, she ably assists and impresses the nonbeliever Dr. Fortunati (Peter Finch), but she refutes or denies to herself his observation that the tension he witnesses in her "is the sign of an exhausting inner struggle." Similarly, she won't accept his belief that she is too willful and proud ever to be a perfect nun. When Sister Luke must leave the Congo and return to the motherhouse in Bruges, the doctor worries that she will not have the strength to survive the cloistered life there, for it will amplify her failings. Finally, with the Nazi occupation of Belgium and despite the church's official stance of neutrality during World War II, Sister Luke cannot let go of her hatred of the Germans after they murder her father, which causes her to renounce her vows and reenter secular life, where she will join the resistance as a nurse.

In a change from her customary performances up to this point in the late 1950s, Hepburn rarely smiles in *The Nun's Story*. There are a few instances, which are indirectly telling of Sister Luke's repressed emotions at most other times. As her term as a postulant concludes and she becomes a novice, her patients in the hospital give her a bouquet of flowers and clap in unison when she enters the ward. She blushes and smiles but has to retreat outside the room to compose herself and suppress the feelings evoked by the gift. In the Congo, Sister Luke explains to Emile, an orderly from this African region, why the sisters in white all have the same husband since the church forbids polygamy. She smiles widely when he says that, unlike the older and less pretty nuns, she would of course have a husband, though he is now in heaven, a thought that saddens Emile since he thinks Sister Luke is an ordinary widow. A relaxed Sister Luke also smiles—and laughs—during her convalescence from tuberculosis under Dr. Fortunati's care. When she leaves the Congo, Sister Luke discovers that the native orderlies in the hospital have filled her carriage on the train with flowers as a tribute to her service. Her slight smile shows how she tries to hold back her emotions to avoid displaying her pride in having earned the affection of her staff. Aside from such moments of pride or gratitude Hepburn seldom shows other emotions openly, only covertly. One instance of Sister Luke openly indulging her feelings happens in the Congo, albeit she does this in private, when she breaks down and sobs in the operating room after being assigned to the hospital for white colonists instead of the one for the native population, which has been her hope. Then, looking at her reflection in the glass door of a medicine cabinet, she adjusts her veil to restore her sisterly poise, a sign of her still-present pride and vanity.

Although she does not have recourse to her usual repertoire of joyous, exuberant, playful, and energetic gestures as an actress, Hepburn nonetheless uses her face to show her character's struggle to achieve perfection as a nun. Given the constraints of the nun's habit and the restrictions of the Order regarding the concealment of her hands and body, Hepburn's face is practically the only instrument of her craft that she *can* use in playing Sister Luke, as I have said. And her face is not, as Wasson complained, "a blank look of integrity" filled in by the following shot.

For instance, on Gabrielle's first day as a postulate before she is renamed "Sister Luke," Sister Margharita (Mildred Dunnock), the mistress of postulants, leads the young women to the upper floor of the chapel for evening prayers. Zinnemann cuts to a close-up of

Hepburn alone after an initial shot of the young women (including Hepburn)—their heads bowed, their hands clasped together near their faces—praying in silence along with the congregation of nuns assembled below. In the close-up, Hepburn's face is still except for her eyes as she raises her head slightly to watch the ceremony below, shown in a reverse shot. At one point a nun arrives late, throws herself prostrate on the floor, arms outstretched, in front of Reverend Mother Emmanuel (Edith Evans), and then takes her empty seat. A cut back to Hepburn's close-up shows her raising her head to see more clearly, then another shot of the chapel floor with nuns praying, followed by a two-shot of Gabrielle and Sister Margharita, whose eyes look toward the younger woman to admonish her silently for straying with her gaze. After meeting Sister Margharita's eyes, in a close-up Gabrielle resumes her prayers.

The stillness of Hepburn's face in this sequence, the direction of her eyes, how she holds up her head as she gazes intently below, these slight gestures indicate her curiosity about religious life, which distracts her from prayer. It is also a means by which *she* establishes the film's viewpoint through her face, since her gaze directs us to look *with* her—at the convent, at the chapel's space, at the other nuns, as well as *at* her—so she encourages our identification with what she sees and hears. Moreover, the close-up of a silent face always uses "implication" and "cinematic finesse" to suggest interiority, what the character is thinking or feeling, which requires the actor herself to provide the clues in her face as to what is going on internally; that work is not done solely by the second shot. Rather, as here, Hepburn's gaze prepares us for that reverse shot.

In another scene, when the novices say their *culpa*, confessing their imperfections from that day, and as other novices inform on them "in charity," Sister Luke must enact the penance for hers: she and her friend who together broke the Great Silence by talking with each other are ordered to kiss the feet of all the nuns during the dinner hour and to beg for their bread. In the next scene, as she kisses the shoes of Reverend Mother Emmanuel, Sister Luke looks up at her superior, who smiles back. Hepburn's face subtly shows Sister Luke's response to this small kindness: she looks straight at the Reverend Mother with a slight smile; then her face gets serious again and she looks down and continues performing her penance. After a shot of the novices scrubbing the floor, Sister Luke is by herself in the chapel. With her hands clasped, her face tilted upward in thought, Hepburn is first shown in a medium shot, but a cut to a close-up has her praying, her voice speaking as if in casual conversation with God to indicate her sincerity and earnestness: "Dear Lord, the more I try, the more imperfect I become. I seem to fail in charity, humility, and obedience. Pride has not been burned out of me. When I succeed in obeying the rules I fail at the same time because I have pride in succeeding." Zinnemann holds this shot for the length of the prayer, which lasts for half a minute. Then there is a cut to the reverse shot of the ornate altar.

Such relatively long close-ups of Hepburn occur frequently in *The Nun's Story*, whether in a single shot like that one of her praying or in a shot/reverse shot sequence. A notable illustration of the latter occurs in a scene after Sister Luke returns from a day of classes at the School for Tropical Medicine.

She enters the office of Mother Marcella (Ruth White) to discuss her fraught relation with another nun in the class, Sister Pauline, who is older, slower to catch on, and afraid she will fail the course and be unable to return to the Congo. Every effort at helping her or offering friendship has been rebuffed, Sister Luke says. Mother Marcella explains that Sister Pauline "thinks you are full of pride. She doesn't think you will achieve humility." What is left unsaid is that Sister Pauline is competitive and worried that Sister Luke will outperform her in the final examination. For in class, the instructor has several times praised and singled out Sister Luke not as a nun but as the daughter of her father, the famous surgeon who already had taught her much in his laboratory; because of her prior learning, this teacher encourages Sister Luke to help her fellow sisters when they cannot identify a specimen.

Mother Marcella gives Sister Luke her advice, which is to offer "a sacrifice for God" by intentionally failing the final examination in humility. In this lengthy shot/reverse shot sequence, Hepburn is in a somewhat tighter close-up than the other woman. The shot of Hepburn staring at the camera, momentarily deviating from the required stance of submission, shows her shock at Mother Marcella's proposal; to enhance Hepburn's facial expression, violins soar ominously on a soundtrack that, up to now in this scene, has been without musical underscoring. Just as quickly, Hepburn lowers her face again in submission as the music quiets down. Sister Luke asks if the motherhouse is to be informed of her willful failure in order to give their approval. Mother Marcella rationalizes that seeking approval would not be true humility. As they go back and forth, Sister Luke wrestles with the proposal, asking about the difference between courage and humility and how to recognize the latter.

In her many close-ups here, Hepburn registers her character's internal struggle by adjusting the position of her face as she looks directly at Mother Marcella, looks down again in the required subordinate stance, then glances up or to the side; her face initially tries to remain emotionless, but during the conversation Hepburn fleetingly shows Sister Luke's conflicted feelings as pride and ambition battle internally with humility and obedience. Finally, Hepburn looks up at the camera. At first silent, she vocalizes the anguish she feels at the prospect of this terrible choice: her face tilts and she asks desperately, "How can I know God wants this from me?" Told to go ask him and warned that such an opportunity may never happen for her again, Hepburn expresses her character's distress by closing her eyes halfway and frowning slightly. Regaining her composure, she turns her head and lowers it once more in submission. During this sequence, Hepburn's speech remains soft and low, with the steady, unemotional cadence required of her by the rules of the convent. She does not raise her voice or utter a sob to show her inner turmoil, so one has to ponder Hepburn's face as she asks her resistant questions of Mother Marcella in order to see what is going on in Sister Luke's mind and heart.

The very next scene dramatizes the consequence of the conversation with Mother Marcella. Will Sister Luke sacrifice her training, not to say her pride, and purposefully fail the examination? The exam begins with her instructor announcing he has promised to telephone her father with the results as soon as the test is over. Sister Luke does not reply but sits down; her body looks heavy, as if she is carrying a great weight inside her formless nun's habit. This sequence first shows us the three examiners, then their viewpoint of Sister Luke in a medium shot looking down at her. As they ask the first question, Sister Luke is silent: her mouth looks like she is trying to speak but cannot form words. A medium shot shows Hepburn's face registering indecision about what to do, as she looks up and around the room, again without speaking; she tries to force her mouth open and utters a few words hesitantly and pauses. After a close-up of her instructor asking if she would like the question repeated, and one of another examiner silently waiting for her answer, a cut to Hepburn in close-up follows.

This close-up is a long, single shot. Hepburn shuts her eyes and twists her face, again struggling to find words; her conflicted expression registers her contemplation of the answer, her indecisiveness about what to do, her sense of guilt and imperfection should she answer correctly. With sweat on her brow externalizing this inner struggle, she looks like she wants to cry but, after a moment or two of silence, she finally replies to the question. Looking down, her eyelids fluttering, she speaks the answer quickly in a monotone, as if she has learned it by rote. The examination continues with a second question that she again answers rapidly, but as she speaks, she looks like she is struggling to hold back tears. Back at the convent in the next scene, we learn Sister Luke passed fourth in a class of eighty; however, unlike the three other nuns who took the class with her and did not score as highly, Sister Luke is not yet ready to go to the Congo according to the motherhouse, although she will eventually be sent there.

These two sequences work together to illuminate Sister Luke's struggle to obey and overcome her pride. In the sequence with Mother Marcella, the many close-ups afford Hepburn generous opportunities to act with her face, to externalize and register—albeit subtly with shifts in her expression, in the direction of her eyes, in the position of her head—Sister Luke's distress resulting from Mother Marcella's discomforting proposition (and Sister Luke will learn from another superior in a subsequent scene that the proposal was not justified). We see the same drama occurring on Hepburn's face as Sister Luke begins the examination, which climaxes with close-ups of her as she refuses "the Sacrifice for God" and passes near the very top of her class. Moreover, Hepburn's face moves and changes expression in these close-ups; whether in the shot/reverse shot sequence in Mother Marcella's office or the cuts from overhead to medium shot to close-up in the examination, the editing enhances rather than creates her performance, by instructing us what to look for in Hepburn's face and by charting the growing conflict of emotions in Sister Luke's consciousness. As Zinnemann stated, he and Hepburn talked about her character at length beforehand, and he wanted to see what the actress herself would creatively do "to bring the part to life." A viewer like Nolletti could thus report that he understood what Sister Luke is thinking and feeling because of Hepburn's expressive face. At no time is her face "blank," as Wasson remarked, for Hepburn's face is what creates the drama in *The Nun's Story*, and it is no magic trick.

Hepburn played a nun a second time when, after nearly a decade off-screen, she returned to acting in *Robin and Marian*, which would prove to be her last decent film. Despite its several battle and combat scenes, this is a relatively quiet, elegiac movie about being old yet living in the shadows of one's youthful adventures and romances. The main focus is on Sean Connery's Robin Hood, who returns to Sherwood Forest from the Crusades disillusioned, estranged from and disgusted by the late Richard the Lionheart, and with a battle-scarred, aged body whose physical limitations he refuses to acknowledge. Robin thinks he can recapture his adventurous life in Sherwood Forest and rekindle the romance with Maid Marian, whom he had left behind when he went to fight in a long, bloody, futile war in a far-off land.

During Robin's absence of twenty years, Hepburn's Maid Marian became a nun, Sister Janet, the Mother Abbess of Kirkley Abbey. Unlike Sister Luke, whose inner turmoil is readable on Hepburn's face, her Sister Janet / Maid Marian is given a more sedate performance, though the character is feisty—and she even skins a rabbit! The older Marian, having forsaken fleshly pleasures, is wary of Robin's heroics and conscious of their middle-aged bodies; it takes a while for her to revive her passion for him. Thus, for a good deal of the film, Hepburn's face and voice belie much emotional unevenness. Until she removes her veil and wimple, which does not happen immediately, her face is framed by the nun's headdress, which forces one to pay close attention to her few expressions. In her several intimate scenes with Connery, director Richard Lester films the two stars in shot/reverse shot close-ups but also relies on many two-shots of them together in the same frame. In each successive one of these scenes, Hepburn shows Marian opening up to Robin again emotionally and remembering what it was like to have desired him in the past.

Having returned to Sherwood Forest from his two decades serving his king in the Crusades, Robin goes to the abbey to see Marian, but she resists him and tells him to go away. She is waiting for the Sheriff of Nottingham (Robert Shaw) to arrest her because King John (Ian Holm) has ordered all the high clergy out of England, but she will not leave. Robin exclaims, "I'm saving you!" Since Marian refuses to be saved when the Sheriff and his men arrive, Robin has to knock her unconscious in order to carry her away to the forest. In Sherwood, she confesses to him, "It's odd. I know I loved you, but I can't remember how it felt. . . . It's a blur, but I think I thought that of all men you'd mind most if I married Jesus." During this conversation, Connery is building a bed of branches for sleeping while Hepburn sits in front of him, hands in her lap, as she speaks softly in a controlled voice. "I don't dream about you anymore, Robin," she adds; then, rubbing her cheek and moving her jaw, she states, delivering a well-timed jibe to him for socking her in the face, "I think one of my teeth is loose." As the couple continue their conversation, Hepburn remains seated; she turns to Connery, her profile concealed by the black veil of her nun's habit. Then she turns to face the camera in a dissolve to the next morning, when the two awaken, their reunion unconsummated.

The next intimate scene occurs after Marian, along with Friar Tuck and Will Scarlett, has helped Robin and Little John (Nicol Williamson) escape from the fortress where they have gone to rescue the three nuns from the abbey, who have been imprisoned in Sister Janet's absence, and where they have fought with and escaped safely from the Sheriff's men. Marian drives the nuns back to the forest in a wagon, with Robin and the others on horseback, but when they cross the stream, the wagon gets sucked in by the muddy water and topples over. Robin carries Marian to the shore, where they collapse on the ground. "Let me take a look at you," she says, and he exposes his bare shoulder and upper chest. In a shot/reverse sequence, Hepburn feels the scars. "Oh, so many," she utters. In a close-up, she continues, saying tenderly, "You had the sweetest body when you left. Hard, not a mark. And you were mine." She then reveals that after he was gone, "I thought I'd die." She cut her wrists, but someone found her and took her to the abbey for healing, and she stayed there. "No more scars, Robin. Too much to lose you twice." He wants to kiss her. Hepburn smiles, then closes her lips. Slowly and carefully, she removes her nun's veil and wimple, for the first time exposing her head and hair, which is short and curly. They move in for the kiss, but a horn signal from Will Scarlett alerts Robin to the presence of strangers in the forest, so the kiss does not happen. Before Robin leaves to see who is there, Marian begs him not to kill anyone.

The third intimate scene occurs after Robin returns from threatening Sir Ranulf (Kenneth Haigh), King John's emissary, who was the cause of Will's warning. Robin tells Marian that he warned Ranulf that Sherwood is *his* forest, and that he wants to live there with her. Hepburn's face shows Marian's quiet satisfaction at the thought. She returns to the stream, where she peers at her reflection in the water. Robin asks, "What are you looking for?" In a close-up, she replies, "Some trace of Marian. Or Mother Janet. Either one." Hepburn chews on a reed. A cut to a medium shot shows her with Connery. "A good woman, Janet," she says, now with the familiar Hepburn cadence, though the voice sounds older and deeper. "Years of religion to leave the flesh behind, but she achieved it. She could look at men and feel nothing. See, she looks at you." In another medium shot, Marian says, "Touch her hand." Looking at Connery, she adds, "Hold it." But she pulls her hand from him. "Just as well." Now she looks down and away. "She wouldn't feel anything. I think of what I did, and it makes no sense." Hepburn looks at the reed, and a quick cut to a tight close-up of her wrist shows the scars there. "To want to die from wanting you. Some other girl it must have been." Connery wants to hold her, but Hepburn pulls away. She asks about the women he had while fighting in the crusade, then quickly takes back her question. He replies evasively that they all looked like her. Hepburn looks down, gestures with her hand on her hair and cheek, takes her hand away from her face. She asks if she is old and ugly, and if he still wants her. In a long shot, the couple wander into tall grass, where they sink down, renewing their love there.

In the final scene of the film, Robin is wounded from his confrontation with the Sheriff, who is stronger but whom he kills; and though John kills Sir Ranulf, many of Robin's men are slain, captured, or scattered. John takes Robin, his torso and a leg covered in blood, to the abbey. Marian realizes that her lover is seriously injured, possibly dying, though he is boasting what a day this has been and that there will be many more like it, with "great battles. We'll have a life to sing about." Mixing poison in a goblet of wine, she drinks some and has Robin do the same, telling him it is medicine that will dull his pain. Marian sinks back along the wall of the room, her body slowing down from the poison as it takes effect on her, while her face reveals her sorrow. "I love you more than God," she whispers, as Robin realizes he will never have another day like this again, and that she is saving him from a crippled life if he should live. Robin shoots an arrow through the window and asks Little John to bury him and Marian together in the spot where the arrow lands.

I have described these four scenes in some detail because, with the exception of a few additional moments, they recount all of Hepburn's presence in *Robin and Marian*. Hers is an interesting performance in these scenes because it is so understated, which dramatizes the age and solitary life of her character after twenty years in the abbey. Her mature character is unlike her youthful characters in the Audrey films, whose faces and voices are expressive and vital, or the proud and conflicted Sister Luke, whose face and eyes make evident her suppressed feelings, pride, and will. As the slowly thawing Marian, Hepburn keeps strong emotions out of her voice and relies on the few glimpses of feeling in her face, or she implies their displacement onto external gestures such as her playing with the reed, to indicate what emotions may be submerged in her steady voice as she quietly speaks with Robin.

Though she has fewer scenes than Connery's Robin Hood, Hepburn's Maid Marian is nonetheless a crucial figure in the film because, having accepted middle age and a quiet life, she offers a counterweight to Robin's anxiety about growing old and having an aged and battered body. Her figure implies a critique of the reliance on fighting, brutality, and homosocial bonding (with Little John) and blind loyalty (to King Richard) that underwrites the heroic masculinity of the legendary Robin Hood. Indeed, my takeaways from Hepburn's performance are that Marian is sick and tired of the old men's boyish exploits, that her two decades in the abbey have offered her a satisfying respite from that masculinist secular world in Nottingham and Sherwood Forest, and that if she is to leave the religious life and rejoin Robin, she wants domesticity and tranquility, not heroic battles and corpses. As she asks Robin once they renew their romance, when they rebuild their house in the trees, can they have a second floor?

With the exception of a few emotional scenes, Hepburn also gives an understated performance in *The Children's Hour*. Her second film with William Wyler was an interesting choice for Hepburn in 1961, coming immediately after *Breakfast at Tiffany's*. Hepburn's Karen Wright is the polar opposite of Holly Golightly. Stalwart, honest, college educated, and unpretentious, she is a dedicated teacher, best friend since college to Martha Dobie (Shirley MacLaine), who co-owns a girls' boarding school with her, and in love with her fiancé, Dr. Joe Cardin (James Garner). Yet while she shares top billing with Shirley MacLaine, Hepburn's restraint as Karen serves to support her costar's Martha, the more histrionic and emotionally volatile character of the pair. Hepburn's careful timing of her dialogue, gestures, and movement thus work in concert with her costar's, with whom she shares most of her scenes. Hepburn's restraint, moreover, does not fully prepare us for her shocked and horrified reaction in the devastating climax, which makes that reaction all the more powerful. *The Children's Hour* is more of an ensemble piece, too, with juicy parts for all the main actors—in addition to MacLaine and Hepburn, James Garner, Miriam Hopkins (as Martha's aunt, Lily Mortar), Fay Bainter (as Mrs. Tilford), and the two children, Karen Balkin (as the lying Mary Tilton) and Veronica Cartwright (as Rosalie), all acquit themselves well with exceptionally strong performances.

The major ensemble scene occurs when Karen, Martha, and Joe confront his aunt, Mrs. Tilford, who has spread to all the students' parents the story about the two teachers being lesbians that her granddaughter, Mary, has told her in order not to have to return to the school after running away. Mrs. Tilford has called Joe to her house to tell him he must not marry Karen, and the two women arrive, angry yet confused because all the students have been removed from the boarding school by their parents, effectively shutting it down. Fay Bainter's Mrs. Tilford is a proud, aristocratic woman; she claims that she felt compelled to get all the girls out of the school because they were just children and needed to be protected from the teachers' "unnatural" relationship. She is trying to be fair but is disgusted by the two women. When Martha exposes a false detail in the fabric of the lie, the older woman is momentarily shaken by uncertainty, but her resolve returns as the scene forcefully ends when an alleged witness confirms the lie. Bainter, who well deserved her Oscar nomination for this role, determines the beats of this scene; in the composition of almost every shot except close-ups, as well as through the sequence's editing, she is the focus, the dramatic center point, around which the other actors move and to whom they respond.

During this scene, Hepburn and MacLaine each have their own dramatic moments, of course. "What are you doing to us?" Martha shrieks as she bursts into the Tilford mansion with Karen. Rubbing her face in frustration and controlling her anger, Karen tells Joe what has happened, that there is no longer a school because the students have all been taken away, and that she was finally told why by one of the uncomfortable fathers who had come to fetch his daughter. "Told you what?" Joe demands. MacLaine turns away before Hepburn answers, and then a cut to an overhead medium shot shows Hepburn with James Garner. Hepburn looks down, then raises her head to stare directly at him, as she says, her voice indicating disbelief, "that Martha and I have been lovers." She is quiet for a second, then looks in the direction of the older woman, stating, "Mrs. Tilford told them." A medium long shot shows the four actors again. When Tilford answers her nephew's question why she did it—"because it's true," she defiantly states—a tight close-up shows his surprised reaction, while a two-shot then shows the two younger women together, their faces expressing disbelief and shock. MacLaine calls Tilford a "crazy old woman," and Hepburn now raises her voice, but without shouting: "You mean, you *did* say it? You *knew* what you are saying?" Whereas MacLaine is furious at the start of this scene and never lets up, Hepburn is more self-possessed, letting the expression of her anger build in its intensity.

In some shots, Hepburn stands still with her back to the camera, while MacLaine moves in the frame more often, at times showing her profile. As the women force Mrs. Tilford to explain, the older woman and MacLaine stay in the foreground while Hepburn and Garner remain silently in the background. With her lips pursed, her expression indicating that she is trying to process what is happening along with her frustration and tightly controlled anger, Hepburn shakes her head and folds her arms in front of her chest as she watches. MacLaine confronts Mrs. Tilford, shouting, "It's not true, it just isn't true," while in the background Hepburn places a hand to her chin, still trying to take in what is happening; then she lowers her hand as she stares at her friend confronting the older woman. As the scene continues, MacLaine frantically states they are here, defending themselves against "what? Against nothing. Against a lie, a great awful lie." When Mrs. Tilford repeats that she believes the story to be true, Hepburn approaches her friend but stops, lowering her head again, as MacLaine turns away from the camera. A medium shot of the two women shows a pensive Hepburn, while MacLaine turns, moving closer toward the camera to threaten Mrs. Tilford with a libel suit. When the older woman warns MacLaine not to do it because the public arena will only bring them more shame, Hepburn advances toward her, saying, "It frightens you, doesn't it." She has realized that Mary is the source of the lie and asks to see her. "She's a bad girl, your Mary," Hepburn informs the grandmother, speaking plainly. "She always has been."

In the final part of this scene, Joe forces his aunt to let them interrogate Mary, which is when Martha angrily points out the inaccuracy in the child's story. An agitated Mary finally claims that her friend Rosalie was the real witness to the two women kissing, and the child is called downstairs to be queried. First Karen and then Martha each speak to the child gently, asking her to tell the truth. But Mary has been blackmailing Rosalie; after being pressed by the adults, she finally and hysterically screams that everything Mary said is true. As the child shrieks and sobs, there is a close-up of a shocked Hepburn, then one of an equally shocked MacLaine.

Even more telling of Hepburn's understated acting in *The Children's Hour* are scenes in which she basically watches on the sidelines without having many lines of her own or much business to do, as other actors take center stage. Sometime after their unsuccessful libel suit, Martha's silly, selfish Aunt Lily unexpectedly returns after having avoided the summons to testify on the two women's behalf at the trial. At first, with Martha, Karen, and Lily seated together in a medium long shot, the niece feigns sympathetic interest in her aunt's account of performing in a theatrical tour during her absence. Hepburn looks on without saying anything; with her tightly closed mouth and tilted head, her expression suggests that she watches as an interested bystander, waiting to see what will happen next. MacLaine sits down next to her aunt, still feigning interest as Lily prattles on about the sad state of the contemporary theater, while Hepburn leans forward to follow the conversation, again saying nothing.

When MacLaine finally lets out her anger, asking why her aunt did not answer any of their telegrams, Hepburn looks down, then rises from her chair, saying, "What difference does it make anyway?" She goes to the fireplace, cradling her head in her arms on the mantel, as she stands with her back to the camera. Aunt Lily tries to ingratiate herself, saying she is here now, but Hepburn, turning to face her, her arms crossed above her waist as if she were hugging herself for security or to stiffen her body defensively, replies, "Things have changed."

Karen continues to watch as Martha yells at her aunt, informing her in detail what happened in their failed libel suit, which they lost because their primary witness, one Lily Mortar, failed to show up "to confirm, explain, or deny" her remarks about her niece's "unnatural" devotion to Karen, which Mary's roommates overheard and had told her, and which Lily herself had repeated to Mrs. Tilford. Lily's absence worked in favor of Mrs. Tilford in the suit Karen and Martha had brought against her for slandering them, confirming to the judge that the lie was truthful and that the two women had engaged in "sinful relations." Lily replies that there was no reason for everyone "to get mixed up in this unpleasant notoriety," but now that she is here, she will stand "shoulder to shoulder" with them. Facing the camera but still by the fireplace, Hepburn closes her eyes as a furious MacLaine orders her aunt to leave on the eight o'clock train. When Lily looks shocked at the command, MacLaine complains that all her life she has hated her aunt, who has "treated me as something for you to pick dry." In the background, Hepburn moves away from the fireplace and crosses her arms again.

Joe enters, makes a sarcastic remark about Lily's now showing up after the trial, and Karen smiles, leaving the fireplace, her hands clasped together. The direction of her gaze in a close-up indicates that she is looking at him. After Martha goes in the kitchen to prepare dinner for the three of them, we see the tension in Karen's relationship with Joe. Though he plans to move with her and Martha to a rural area as a country doctor to escape the gossip and start their lives over, Karen knows that, due to the trial and her notoriety, she has taken away everything that matters to him, for he has been well established as a family physician in their town. Furthermore, she reads rejection into everything he says or does, like his turning away from her to toss his cigarette into the fireplace when she goes to embrace him, or his saying they will need to wait to begin a family, whereas before he had been anxious to get started. "Every word has a new meaning," Karen says quietly. "Child. Love. Friend. Woman. There aren't many safe words anymore. Even marriage doesn't have the same meaning anymore." Tenderly informing him, "It won't work . . . the two of us together," she orders him to ask the question that she knows has been on his mind: Was there any truth to Mrs. Tilford's accusation? Holding back tears and not letting him ask that question, Karen shakes her head and mouths "No" before uttering that simple denial. But she still has to say, "Martha and I never touched each other." Nonetheless, because of his doubt, which she knows will linger even after their marriage, and her own questioning of his honesty when he says he believes her, she sends him away.

After Joe's departure, Karen returns to the background in the scene that moves *The Children's Hour* toward its wrenching climax. With Joe gone, Karen—sitting in the window seat, looking stunned—is in the foreground of the frame as Martha returns from the kitchen. In close-ups of the two women as Martha goes to her friend, Karen tells her why Joe isn't coming back: "because he thought it was true." In the conversation that follows, Martha begs Karen to take Joe back, but Karen says they should pack and leave on the morrow, though neither has any idea where to go. Their exchange will lead to Martha's heartbreaking speech in which she will articulate to herself for the first time that her strong feelings for her best friend *were* sexual, an erotic attachment that now makes her "feel so sick and dirty, I can't stand it anymore."

This is a powerfully acted scene. At first, after Hepburn points out that others in situations like theirs haven't had their lives turned upside down and ruined, MacLaine chatters on, replying that newspapers around the country have made them infamous and that they have not chosen that way of life as those others have done. Starting to cry, she acknowledges they *have* been close to each other, and that she *has* loved Karen as a friend, the way thousands of women have felt about other women. Hepburn, meanwhile, hasn't moved but listens in the foreground in the left side of the frame. At one point, she mutters softly, "I'm cold." MacLaine continues trying to rationalize the normality of their friendship, but the realization of her inchoate lesbianism hits her.

Closing her eyes, Hepburn asks, almost under her breath, "Why are you saying all of this?" In a close-up, MacLaine confesses, "Because I *do* love you." In a matching close-up, Hepburn mutters that she loves her friend too. But with a return to the scene's master wide shot of Hepburn in front and seated in the window seat on the left, and MacLaine seated in a rocker in the background, staring in space to the right, the latter finally declares that what they were saying was true, that she does love Karen in *that* way. In more matching close-ups, MacLaine shrieks at Hepburn, "*Listen to me!*" Hepburn, in turn, faces her with an expression of shock and concern. In another wide shot of the room, with each actress positioned now at opposite sides of the frame, MacLaine continues, sobbing and talking about the feelings she had not known, and Hepburn listens in disbelief, telling her at one point, "Stop it." Finally, she rises, goes to MacLaine, and grabbing her, tells her to stop the crazy talk. Hepburn starts to walk away, again telling Martha to stop, but the latter pulls her back, shouting, "*I'm guilty!*"

Hepburn moves out of the frame as the camera focuses on MacLaine, who delivers her speech about the bewilderment and guilt she has felt ever since hearing the child utter the lie. "I never felt that way about anybody but you," she states, as Hepburn, returning to the frame, tries to reassure MacLaine, her own tearful expression showing concern, fear, and sadness. Rejecting Hepburn's compassion, MacLaine sobs, "Don't you see? I can't stand to have you touch me. I can't stand to have you look at me." Hysterical now, she states that she has ruined both of their lives. "It's all my fault." A close-up shows Hepburn's sorrow for what MacLaine is going through, as someone knocks on the front door. It is Mrs. Tilford, who has her own guilt to announce. She informs the women that the two children have confessed their lie, that the judge will reverse his decision, that an apology will appear in the newspapers, and that she will pay the damages and anything else the two victims want.

After they send the older woman away, wanting nothing from her that will her assuage her conscience, Martha retreats to her room while Karen takes a walk. Silently—and the only phrase she will utter in the remainder of the film will be Martha's name—she strolls away from the house. The expression on Hepburn's face, as she stares ahead, indicates that she is trying not to think about what has just transpired, though when she closes her eyes and looks down, it is clear that she cannot do so. She glances around her, whether to try to enjoy the autumn day or to watch for curious onlookers, who have been harassing the two women, is unclear. As she reaches the outer boundary of the school's property, she leans against a tall lattice fence, and smiles enigmatically.

Lily comes outside and calls out, asking if she has seen Martha. Shaking her head to say no, Hepburn looks back at the house and stands there for several moments, then decides to return. As she walks, lost in thought, she begins to worry, and, with anxiety written on her face, she races to the house; to dramatize her trepidation, Wyler cuts back and forth between medium and tighter close-ups of Hepburn running. Inside, a puzzled Lily tells Hepburn that her niece's door is locked. Calling Martha's name several times, Hepburn tries to push open the door, then she breaks the lock with a heavy candlestick. From extreme close-ups of Hepburn we see her discovering Martha's body, her distraught gaze indicating what the camera discreetly will not yet show. Tearfully, Hepburn first looks down, implicitly at the fallen chair, then looks up, wide-eyed, her mouth open in shock, implicitly staring at the hanging body. With a moan, her face drawn and pinched in horror at what she sees, she sobs, "Oh, Martha!'" With tears trickling down her cheeks, she shuts her eyes tightly in disbelief. A medium long shot finally reveals the fallen chair and, on the wall, the shadow of legs hanging in the air as Hepburn sinks to the floor, crying.

Admittedly, I find this melodrama of "the lie with the ounce of truth," as Martha calls it when confessing her guilt for having lesbian thoughts about Karen, to be hard to watch, despite—or maybe because of—its fidelity to the period's homophobia. That drives the lie's power in causing everyone to shun the two women as if they were diseased or to look at them as if they were a sideshow attraction, just as it causes the heartbreaking self-disgust that makes Martha kill herself *after* the lie is exposed as a pernicious falsehood. To be sure, *The Children's Hour* was groundbreaking at the time; it helped to break the taboo about overtly mentioning homosexuality in Hollywood film. And for all its overwrought melodrama, this film still interests me for showing how Hepburn supports other actors in strong emotional scenes in which she is not always the main figure, pulling back on her emotions as an actress for the most part until the climax in a fine, understated performance.

Before I close this chapter, I want to look at the performance that I consider to be Hepburn's best. In *Two for the Road*, her third film with Stanley Donen, Joanna Wallace is the most multifaceted and complex character Hepburn has played. This is due to the narrative of *Two for the Road*, which recounts Joanna's five trips in France with her husband, Mark (Albert Finney). These trips occur over a period of a dozen years or so. Hepburn is on-screen for almost the entirety of this film, and the script gives her the opportunity to develop her most fully rounded character; in varying stages of her marriage Joanna is innocent, romantic, joyful, mischievous, passionate, drunk, maternal, unhappy, angry, jealous, unfaithful, disappointed, bored, regretful, bitter, and always sexual.

Each of the five journeys reveals a different stage in the Wallaces' tumultuous relationship as their marriage rocks and threatens to break but, as Joanna states to Mark in the final moments, "We're a fixture." Neither spouse is solely to blame for their friction. Mark has always been arrogant, egocentric, pompous, argumentative, yet also sexy, charming, and funny. Though they both were deeply and passionately in love, Joanna forced his hand to get married when she threatened never to see him again, just as she wanted a child more than he did, and, while she appreciates the income and status, she resents how much and how often his work preoccupies him. He is also more doubting of their love for each other than she is, or perhaps it is the case that she believes in romance more than he does, while for him their love is more about the sex. She is also more insightful and self-reflective than he. In the end, the couple recommits and acknowledges that the spark has not gone out of their relationship as Joanna initiates a lovemaking session in their automobile.

Frederic Raphael's screenplay complicates this story of how a deeply rooted love bends and buckles over time by recounting it through a nonlinear structure; his script cuts up and rearranges the five trips so that, in the reshuffling of moments from each, one trip comments on another one, often connected by a comparable line of dialogue. Additionally, by cutting between comparable moments or images, director Stanley Donen eases the transitions back and forth in time. For instance, their young daughter doesn't want to finish a cup of ice cream, and Joanna asks Mark if he wants it, but he declines. Cut to their first trip together as hitchhiking young lovers, when Joanna puts in Mark's mouth a spoon of ice cream, which gives him brain freeze; he moans through a closed mouth and she kisses his forehead, as thunder can be heard overhead. With a return immediately to the family trip, it starts to rain heavily, but the top on their convertible is down, as Joanna reaches back to see if she can pull it up. Cut back again to the first trip as Mark and Joanna, sopping wet in pouring rain, laugh heartily and smile lovingly at each other. To be sure, while most of these transitional edits are subtle, a few are too obvious. At one point, for example, Donen cuts from a server at a ritzy beach club carrying a tray with boiled lobsters in the present day to the young lovers lying asleep on the beach during their first trip, their bodies badly burned by the sun. Donen also cues viewers as to where they are in story time, as already stated in an earlier chapter, through Hepburn's hairstyles and costumes, which change as the couple's fortunes increase, and by virtue of the different cars that the couple drive. Taken together, these road trips, which each follow the same route in southern France, sketch a palimpsest of the couple's marriage—their love and desire for each other but also their tensions, their frustrations, their doubts, their arguments, their infidelities.

Framing the film is a trip in the present day (circa 1966) as the couple leaves England, crossing the channel by air ferry, and drives to France in a Mercedes to meet Mark's wealthy client Maurice (Claude Dauphin). This trip establishes the married couple's estrangement as they snipe at each other and wonder why they are still together. With voice-overs from both actors, the film flashes back to their accidental meeting a dozen or so years earlier, to around 1953 or 1954, when Mark was an architectural student hitchhiking to take photographs of French buildings and Joanna was traveling with a girls' choir in a Volkswagen bus on a holiday tour while enroute to a music festival. The choir's tour gets sidelined when everyone but Joanna comes down with chickenpox, so she and Mark end up spending the week hitchhiking together in the South of France. She falls in love with him and they begin a romantic affair as they travel to the Mediterranean, after which they decide to marry.

Three other trips happen in between those two. Mark and Joanna, married just a couple of years by now, ride in a Ford station wagon during a 1957 trip with Mark's annoying American friends, Howard (William Daniels) and Cathy (Eleanor Bron) Maxwell Manchester and their irritating, spoiled young daughter, Ruthie. Howard's obsessive efforts to control every aspect of the trip and Ruthie's awful behavior eventually cause Mark and Joanna to depart and continue on their own. The last we see of this trip, the couple are checking into a hotel in the early afternoon to make love.

A few years later, in 1959 or 1960, the couple takes another road trip, driving a very used 1950 MG. During this trip Joanna announces to Mark her pregnancy. They are at first happy and lighthearted, camping out, teasing each other, playing on the beach, and just enjoying being together on holiday—until their MG catches fire and is totaled. They have to take refuge in an expensive hotel, which, along with the fees and taxes to have the blaze put out, blows their travel budget. As they leave the next day, they meet Claude and his wife, Françoise (Nadia Gray), who are also departing the hotel and who give them a ride. Claude is looking for an architect to solve a problem with a building project. Joanna mentions Mark's profession, and the meeting jump-starts his career, but it quickly causes her to feel like a parasite, feeding off Claude's beneficence as he works out a deal with her husband during the next several days. This is the first glimpse of tension in the marriage, as she cannot wait to leave and is impatient with Mark for spending all his time with Claude discussing the latter's project. Nonetheless, the couple is still very much in love, their desire for each other still evident.

Finally, in 1963 the couple takes a road trip in a red Triumph with their young daughter, Caroline; by this point, the marriage is in trouble, as Mark and Joanna quarrel nonstop or remain silent, and neither seems happy. He is preoccupied with work, and she is resentful and tired from caring for their daughter by herself. The Triumph signals a wider swath of time, too. Sometime before his daughter is born, Mark drives in this car by himself to a job site and has a one-nighter along the way. At some point after this trip, Joanna meets, falls in love and sleeps with, and plans to go away with Françoise's brother David, but she decides to return to Mark and asks for his forgiveness.

I want to concentrate my remarks primarily on the road trip with the family in the Triumph and the parallel scenes from the first trip edited into it. What is especially telling to me in this section, in contrast with the comic and romantic underpinning of Hepburn's performance in the first trip, is the care with which she uses her face and relies on a steady, controlled voice to show Joanna's growing agitation and sorrow at the cracks that have appeared in her marriage.

The section begins, as I indirectly noted already, with the couple driving with their daughter in the Triumph, with Mark refusing the ice cream, and then they get caught in the rain; but the drama in this sequence occurs after they have checked into a hotel for the night. Joanna orders in flawless French a boiled egg for her daughter's supper while Mark is on the floor poring over a blueprint. In an unemotional voice and rolling up the sleeves of her blouse, she asks him to watch Caroline while she washes out a few things. She picks up a few items from a suitcase, goes into the bathroom, and looks out through the doorway as he mutters, "Okay." An overhead shot shows Hepburn turning on the faucets and washing her daughter's things. As she wrings them out, a cut returns to the young Hepburn wringing out her wool cap in the first, much happier trip, when she and Finney were caught in the rain. The two are together in a medium shot, but she suddenly runs out of the frame. At first puzzled, he realizes she has found shelter inside an empty culvert lying in a pile on the side of the road. "Come on in," Hepburn says, smiling, laughing, and happy, as he enters; they cuddle together. With her hearty laughter and wide, mischievous grin, this very young Joanna evokes Hepburn's early roles, Princess Ann and Sabrina. A cut back to the hotel returns to a more emotionally distant Hepburn as she asks Finney if the boiled egg has arrived. He does not seem to know what she is asking about, so she adds, "Caro's supper." Leaving the bathroom and rolling down her sleeves, she discovers that, while he remained distracted by his work, the toddler has squeezed toothpaste all over the carpet. Her irritation with his negligence begins to show in Hepburn's voice. "I thought you were watching *Caroline*," she says, angrily stressing the child's name. About the boiled egg that never arrived, she states firmly, giving him a dirty look, "Never mind, *I'll go.*"

The two argue over who will go downstairs to check on Caroline's supper. Though Hepburn snipes back at him, "Don't bother," Finney insists he will go. Hepburn gives him a look, then silently turns away, staring down toward the floor. She returns to cleaning up her daughter's mess as Finney leaves, slamming the door behind him. Downstairs in the lobby, he yells and berates the hotel manager, while upstairs, Hepburn turns her head, indicating that she hears the ruckus her husband is causing. Finney returns and declares, "We're leaving." Still on the floor cleaning up the child's mess, she looks surprised. "Leaving?" Hepburn gets up and sits on the bed. In a close-up, she says, speaking quickly and clipping each word to emphasize her irritation, "I asked you for a boiled egg and you come back with an eviction notice."

With a cut, they are driving in the rain, trying to keep the child entertained, and with a second cut, we return to the first trip, with the young couple asleep in each other's arms in the culvert. A third cut returns us to the older couple, as Hepburn puts Caroline to bed in a new hotel room. She walks over to the bed, pulls down the bedspread, and, letting out a sigh, lies down, exhausted. Finney sits on the opposite edge of the bed; he admits it was all his fault. Hepburn pulls one of the pillows away, tosses it, and lies back down. In a low, tired voice, she mutters, "I've been telling Caroline bedtime stories for an hour and it would be nice if you can avoid fortissimo for a while." They now quarrel in loud whispers. He claims that he didn't want the boiled egg, she did. "I suppose Caroline has nothing to do with you," she replies. "*You* were the one who wanted a child," he retorts. Angry at that response, she asks why he doesn't wake Caroline to tell her that. He replies he is telling *her*, because he loves Caroline.

During this heated exchange, Hepburn's face shows little emotion, instead expressing her fury through her voice, through what she says, and in her whispered speech. But when Finney states, "I love Caroline," Hepburn sits up in the bed, and her face now reveals her pain. "You don't know what love is," she yells. He shushes her, and she repeats what she has said in a whisper. "That's tough on me," he replies with a note of sarcasm. Annoyed at his self-centeredness, she calls him on it: "All you can do is take the salute at an endless march past of yourself." In matching close-ups, Finney laughs, while Hepburn looks forlorn, her face half in shadow. A motion of her head shows that she hears his laughter. In a return to his close-up, we can see Hepburn from the back, sitting hunched and defeated by the quarreling. Finney pulls her to him. In her close-up, Hepburn looks like she wants to cry, her face twisted in sorrow.

In a medium shot, Finney pulls her down on the bed. She looks away and he pulls her face toward him. A close-up shows the two looking at each other; she still lies flat on the bed and he has perched himself above her. He kisses her; her eyes are closed but she slowly opens them. "I have an appetite," he whispers. "Do you?" Bitterly, she answers, "It wouldn't matter who I was, would it?" A close-up reveals Hepburn still lying on the bed, her face showing no expression. He says matter-of-factly that he is willing to call it a day and asks if she is. "You never wanted to call it anything else," she retorts, and he snidely agrees with her. "You're damn right there." Another close-up shows Hepburn with her eyes and lips closed, and her face now exhibits a sadness that hurts. She gets up, burying her face in a pillow, muttering, "Oh." He reaches over, touches her shoulder tenderly, mutters her name. Caroline makes a noise that breaks the mood as Hepburn goes to tend to her. "We can't even have a fight in peace," he snarls. With her back to the camera, Hepburn pleads, "Oh, leave me!" Now off the bed, he slams the wall, and she turns, yelling in a whisper, "Selfish!"

The next shot reveals the couple in bed; both appear to have removed all their clothes, intimating that they may have had makeup sex. Finney is asleep, but Hepburn is awake, staring at the ceiling. In a close-up of the couple, her facial expression suggests that she is thinking about her troubled marriage, which pains her. She turns to look at her sleeping husband as if she wants to say something, or perhaps she is reflecting how soundly he sleeps while she cannot. Then she closes her eyes in resignation.

A cut again to the young couple shows them waking in each other's arms in the culvert, which is being transported to the Mediterranean. The young lovers climb out and rush to the water. With another cut, Hepburn, Finney, and the child arrive in the Triumph at the same beach; it is presumably the next day after their quarreling over the boiled egg. "I don't understand sex," Finney announces. "Seriously, why is it we enjoy it more, and it means less." With a pained look, Hepburn replies, "Because it isn't personal anymore." A cut back to the young lovers at the seashore shows them embracing at sunset, as the film's romantic theme music swells on the soundtrack. "I'm so happy! I'm so happy!" Hepburn exclaims, adding that she loves Finney. They race to find a hotel as she shouts, "Last one undressed turns out the lights."

In the hotel room Finney is in his underwear while Hepburn lies in bed, the covers pulled up to her neck. He reflects a moment, pulls the blankets off her, and discovers that she is still fully dressed. She laughingly says that it was worth a try, and he tickles her relentlessly. They giggle raucously as she falls off the bed and he follows her to the floor. At some point, they cease their playfulness and stare at each other with longing. The next morning, Hepburn mentions in bed that she dreamed of a train, and they joke about Dr. Freud and the dream's sexual content. But it turns out there are tracks right outside their bedroom window, which they discover after she opens the curtains. After a train roars by, Hepburn laughs and says, "Sexy, wasn't it?" Finney mutters, "Okay, you're not frustrated," and motions for her to return to bed. She dives in and they embrace under the covers.

This carefree Hepburn—her body loose and without tension, her expressive face showing her joy in being with her lover, her desire for him—contrasts with the older, more bitter Hepburn in the Triumph trip. The contrast makes a thematic point for the film, consistent with Raphael's and Donen's dissection of a marriage in *Two for the Road*, but this intent on their part requires Hepburn to play both versions of Joanna very differently, just as she plays her character differently in the other road trips. For instance, there are many scenes in the MG trip where Hepburn gets to play physical comedy with Finney and jokes with him, until she turns sullen when she tires of staying at Claude's. Similarly, Hepburn's brittle sniping at Finney in the Mercedes trip expresses her remoteness from him, just as her repeated wide-eyed look in the Ford trip with the American family implies her bewilderment at their obnoxious, self-congratulatory behavior in indulging their daughter's many tantrums. Finney remarks that he thought she wanted a child, to which Hepburn replies, "I do. Just not *that* one."

To be sure, the changes in her hairstyles and clothing styles visually identify each Joanna in the various stages of her marriage. And some lesser actresses might have stopped there. What impresses me about Hepburn's performance in *Two for the Road* is how she adjusts her voice and body as well as her face to indicate the different ages and moods of her character. Tonally, her voice shows the progressive sophistication, cynicism, and weariness as Joanna grows older. Similarly, Hepburn moves and carries her body differently in each trip, from the loose-limbed and physically enthusiastic Joanna in 1953 to the defeated wife in the Triumph trip to the more elegant, more diffident and ironic, if still honest, wealthy woman in the present day. Each trip, in short, marks a stage in Joanna's maturation, and Hepburn's performance expertly identifies the differences in Joanna's personality and bearing as she ages. Yet throughout, as she readjusts the emotional notes of her face, body, and voice, one still senses the core Joanna, despite the erosion of her youthful exuberance for life and love.

Conclusion

Audrey Hepburn was an actress as well as a movie star. Although she was an international cover girl for nearly all of her adult life even when not making films, as Scott Brizel lavishly illustrates in his book, she was not simply a fashion model, as her detractors grumbled. Nor did she lack "bite," as Emma Thompson complained. And to see how she could even act with "a blank look," as Sam Wasson wrongly described her Sister Luke, just watch *Wait Until Dark*, where her character is blind. As an actress, Hepburn gave her directors substantial characterizations to work with in post-production. For although the various shots comprising a scene were put together in the editing room after filming completed, Hepburn was the one who made her character's interior life seem real in the finished product, as manifested through her facial expressions, the register of her voice and cadence of her speech, the direction of her gaze, a gesture or turn of her body, her physical movement, the subtle use of a prop, her timing, even her costumes. These are the tools of a film actor.

Looking over her relatively small filmography, one can see her growth as an actress, too, which reached its zenith in the 1960s with *Breakfast at Tiffany's*, *Charade*, *Two for the Road*, and *Wait Until Dark*. To be sure, there were a few misfires in Hepburn's career when the scripts did not give her much to build on: *Green Mansions*, *The Unforgiven*, *Paris When It Sizzles* (for all its quite interesting failings), and later on in her middle-aged years, *Bloodline*, *They All Laughed*, and *Love Among Thieves*. Then there were pictures that were flawed in one way or another, yet in which she stood out (for me at least) as the main point of interest, a testament to her acting as well as her charisma: *War and Peace*, *Love in the Afternoon*, *Breakfast at Tiffany's*, and *My Fair Lady*. On the other side of the ledger were three films in which her performance centered pictures that were excellent all the way around: *The Nun's Story*, *Two for the Road*, and *Wait Until Dark*. Adding to this latter tally were those wonderful films in which she sparkled with her costars, demonstrating that she was not a solo player: watch her rapport with Gregory Peck in *Roman Holiday*, Humphrey Bogart and William Holden in *Sabrina*, Fred Astaire in *Funny Face*, Cary Grant in *Charade*, and Peter O'Toole in *How to Steal a Million*. Hepburn clearly had a flair for romantic comedy, but she could be as fine a dramatic actress: witness *The Children's Hour* and *Robin and Marian*, as well as *The Nun's Story*, *Two for the Road*, and *Wait Until Dark*.

Aside from considering her skill as an actress, it is as important to appreciate her stature as a major movie star in the final years of the studio era. Why did Hepburn stand out so vividly and singularly from those other young actresses emerging in films at the same time? Hepburn's success in her first two films, *Roman Holiday* in 1953 and *Sabrina* in 1954, was so immediate, with movie reviewers everywhere writing rapturously about her, and her face was so omnipresent in magazines of all kinds thereafter, that her stardom did not pale when she was then absent from the screen for the next two years, since *War and Peace*, her third Hollywood film, did not open until the fall of 1956. Certainly, her agent, Kurt Frings, and she chose her projects carefully and wisely, for she had a string of hits in the 1950s and 1960s, despite those few misfires; and by her third film Hepburn had become the highest paid actress in the world, culminating in her later record-breaking contract for a million-dollar-salary plus incidentals for *My Fair Lady* (although reportedly Elizabeth Taylor's million-dollar-plus salary for *Cleopatra* [1963] topped hers, but not by much; Frings also represented Taylor). What did Hepburn mean for the postwar era that contributed to her rapid rise to major stardom and a mega-salary?

Hepburn represented an alternative to the ideology of conservative femininity that women of this period were receiving from all sides: from movies, radio, and television, from advice columns and women's magazines, from parents and teachers, from multiple social, governmental, and legal institutions. They were told proper women did not work but were wives, mothers, and homemakers, and that they should be virgins before marriage and faithful afterward to their husbands, to whose authority they were expected to defer. That was one of the messages of the Audrey films if one viewed them solely as stories of how virginal Audrey found true love with an older man, confirming the patriarchy. To be sure, not unlike Sister Luke, teenage girls and women did not all conform to that ideology by any means but buckled under it, resisting, openly rebelling, or dulling their unhappiness with alcohol or the prescription drug Miltown. I think even in the Audrey films, Hepburn offered those people a refreshingly different role model, despite or maybe because of the contradictions her liminal persona held together. For those teens and women were themselves inhabiting ideological contradiction and unconsciously feeling it weighing heavily on their own lives. This may be a source of the deep affection fans continue to have for Holly Golightly. Not every viewer responded to Hepburn in the same way, obviously; remember my friend's mother, who dismissed Hepburn for being "painfully thin." But for those women who became fans, she offered, I think, a means of their identifying with her on-screen empowerment and self-realization.

It is therefore worth looking past the narrative arc of the Audrey films with their closures on the asymmetrical couple, and instead appreciate, as I argued in chapter 3, how Hepburn's energetic, determined, ambitious, desiring, feisty, troublesome, mischievous, and intelligent characters drive the narratives with the potential always to derail the conventional endings. This is the pleasure of watching Princess Ann's holiday from royal protocols in *Roman Holiday*; of Sabrina's reinvention of herself in Paris and determination to win

David when she returns home, as well as her thawing of Linus, in *Sabrina*; of Jo's intellectualism and double characterization as a beatnik and model in *Funny Face*; and of Ariane's vicariously living out her sexual fantasies through the stories she tells Flanagan in *Love in the Afternoon*. From this perspective, too, Holly Golightly was no outlier role for Hepburn but the inevitable development arising from those vaguely rebellious virginal Audrey figures.

Furthermore, despite her inclusion in Sheilah Graham's 1954 account as just another member of the new cohort of slim, young, gamine actresses challenging the dumb, bosomy blonds and sexy, seductive brunettes in movies, Hepburn's body was not like any of those others. She was much thinner and more flat-chested than the other gamines, for one thing, and more androgynous. Additionally, Hepburn's body was unlike the other Hollywood gamines because her ultra-thin figure was more like those of the French fashion models on display in the pages of *Vogue* and *Harper's Bazaar*, where she herself also appeared at times. Hepburn's association with Givenchy and couture worked to diminish her androgyny but never concealed it entirely; while they never came to pass, the few projects that would have cast her as a boy responded to the ambiguity suggested by her slender frame, short hair, and flat chest in 1954.

That Hepburn's uncommon female body connoted something subversive or disturbing of the status quo was evident in rumors after her Oscar win that she was "seriously ill with anemia" and "suffering," as if picturing her body as diseased was the only way to process it (Battelle 1954). But as I emphasized in chapter 4, more than concealing her androgynous body, fashion was a transformative event for Hepburn's characters. On-screen she moved freely in Givenchy's couture, and her characters' fashionable makeovers represented the emergence of a fuller, more complete realization of an autonomous selfhood. In the films, haute couture enabled Hepburn's characters to be the energetic and libidinal heroine of an Audrey film. Hepburn, in this sense, was an appealing and unorthodox oxymoron for her time period: a glamorous gamine.

French couture condensed a range of additional meanings for Hepburn's star image that further accounted for her great appeal during the fifties, complicating what I have just been saying. We should not forget that couture signified expensive tastes of a moneyed class, the economic recovery of Europe after the war, and America's postwar boom, which sent travelers across the pond to buy dresses from French designers; furthermore, couture's origins in France evoked Hepburn's own European background, her traumatic experience of the war as a youth, and her triumphant escape from privation as an adult. As I mentioned early on in this book, Hepburn represented the war-torn Europe rescued by America and recovered through American commerce—and I suppose that was another message to be found when the wealthy older American male carried her off in the closure of an Audrey film like *Love in the Afternoon*.

Still, Hepburn's impact as a fashion trendsetter served to democratize designer clothing, as I also noted in chapter 4, since knockoffs of her outfits were available in department stores nationally, just as beauty salons imitated her trendsetting haircuts. Young women everywhere could be like Audrey Hepburn, and all that she signified about willful womanhood, because they could dress and look like her, and a pleasure to be gotten from her films, while ignoring the conventional endings and possibly shrugging at the older costars, was in finding inspiration for ways to look and act, whether as an elegant sophisticate or a beatnik intellectual. For the same reason, Hepburn's flat-chested figure was probably a relief to similarly built teens and young woman in an era of big breasts, falsies, pointed bosoms, and bullet bras. Hepburn may have been from the elite, given her aristocratic European background and tony British accent, but she was accessible to an average female who could identify with her unconventional body and association with fashion.

So again, Hepburn's films, like her stardom, were never without contradictions but required viewers to negotiate their way through the disparate meanings to be found there. Her popularity indicated that many, many viewers did, often, I suspect—and as Rachel Mosley's interviewees in the UK confirmed—reading against the grain of the conservative narratives to find pleasure in watching Hepburn as a source of identification through her affiliation with fashion as a means of transformation; in conjunction with her strong female characters and unconventional body, this is why she was so beloved by so many.

All of this is to say that Audrey Hepburn represented differences from the norm for viewers at mid-century in ways that no other actress of the moment did, which explains her impact when she appeared in *Roman Holiday* and then again the following year in *Sabrina*. Yet why should we still care about Hepburn today? After all, she only starred in twenty Hollywood films, and her reign as a major star ceased after *Wait Until Dark* completed its theatrical run in 1968—well over half a century ago. Though she remained in and out of the public eye until her death in 1993 at age sixty-three, the more youthful Audrey is the surviving image. What accounts for her enduring fame? Even if people today have never seen any of her films, Hepburn is still known to many as the epitome of charm, poise, and elegance, and her image, particularly as Holly or Eliza, has commodified that meaning for her name. A better question to ask, though, is, Why should we continue to care about her films? Are they now simply antiquated relics of the postwar years?

One reason for Hepburn's iconic stature today is surely nostalgia for an older, "classic" style of apparel and deportment, which she personified on-screen and off at public events and in magazines. On the other hand, her stardom is important today for historical reasons, for its revelatory connection to mid-century cultural tastes and values. Can one talk about movies of the 1950s or the 1960s without bringing some of hers into the conversation? But looking more closely at her films, I can imagine other, more complex responses to Hepburn that suggest, not her universality or even her historicity per se, but how contemporary times may yield new twists on what she formerly signified. Here, I have to speculate, though in doing so I hope I do not fall too wide of the mark.

Hepburn's thin body does not appear as radical or disturbing today as it did when she was a star, that is clear. But in her films, fashion, when viewed as an instrument of transformation for her characters, signifies that femininity is not innate or an essence but a masquerade, a point made overtly at times in *Funny Face* and more indirectly by Sabrina's and Holly's makeovers. In my opinion, Hepburn on-screen now speaks to those contemporary viewers like me, who understand the artifice of genders, how "masculinity" and "femininity" are neither monolithic nor organic but are cultural constructs and performances. Similarly, the implications of androgyny in Hepburn's body no longer seems as unorthodox or radical, but her liminality in being perceivable simultaneously as girlish and boyish exposes the fluidity of one's experience of being gendered in our culture. This may have been as true in the fifties as it is today, but then it was barely legible. Now we have a better, more precise vocabulary for articulating and perceiving this experience instead of being fearful of it, as would have happened to most people in Hepburn's own lifetime.

While her private life, star image, and almost all of her characters were undeniably heterosexual, her liminality may account for why Hepburn has acquired a queer following over the years, too. Just as her strong association with fashion calls attention to the basis of genders in masquerades, it may also encourage a queer viewer engagement with the style, excess, and artifice that fashion builds upon, exploits, and celebrates. It strikes me today that in *Breakfast at Tiffany's* Hepburn brings out those senses in her performance, which is why the romance with Paul always seems so arbitrary to me, simply a narrative device for getting Holly to conform before the film ends. But Holly can easily incite a queer fascination with her difference, though gay men, lesbians, bisexuals, transmen, and transwomen would not respond to her in the same way nor find the same pleasures in her liminality, her feminine masquerades, or her excessive, campy sense of style, as when she first appears at her wild cocktail party wrapped in a bedspread and polishing her fingernails.

Or consider *The Nun's Story* as it pivots around the regulation of Sister Luke's body because her human imperfections need endless correction. Today, one can perform an interesting queer reading of Sister Luke and the motherhouse, which itself can be understood as confining for its repression or as liberating for its homosocial female community. The real-life Sister Luke, Hepburn's friend Marie Louise ("Lou") Habets, came out as a lesbian after renouncing her vows, so the potential for a queer reading is there in the genesis of *The Nun's Story*, I think.

A queer engagement with *The Nun's Story* might begin for viewers who identify with Sister Luke's disinterest in heterosexual relations—even with Dr. Fortunati, despite his obvious sexual attraction to her—whether or not they attribute her asexuality solely to her following her vow of chastity as a nun or see it as something more personal and deep-rooted. I can imagine queer viewers taking vicarious satisfaction from convent life for its repudiation of ordinary heterosexual concerns; its relief from the pressures of dating, sex, marriage, and motherhood; its disinterest in assimilation. Remember that in the opening, Sister Luke has bidden farewell to her fiancé, Jean, and returned his ring; years later when her father visits her in the convent, he remarks that the man has never married, as if he still carries a torch, while she replies that it has been years since she has ceased to think of him. Or viewers might identify with Sister Luke's inability to conform fully to the enforced repression of her pride, her ambition, her feelings, and her body, not to say her willful character and strong sense of independence, all of which brings out her difference from the other nuns and which causes her inability to obey fully the rules set by the convent for everyone to follow in their community. Two sides of the same queer coin, I think.

Actually, I would not be surprised if *The Nun's Story* had already found a responsive queer audience among some people in the mainstream crowds who saw the film in 1959, especially given the decade's homophobia and sexual repressiveness. Obviously I cannot speak for lesbian viewers of that era, but I can imagine that the female-centric world that Sister Luke inhabits and the rigorous self-denial demanded by her Order to overcome her imperfections may have connected to their own experiences of being problematically different and unable to conform to societal expectations "perfectly." I know as a queer Jewish boy approaching adolescence, I found *The Nun's Story* strangely compelling when I saw it in a neighborhood movie palace in Chicago after its downtown engagement, though I did not understand why. At the time and for years afterward, I thought it was because of the exotic strangeness of Catholic rituals and the cloistered life in the convent, and because I was already a fan of Audrey Hepburn after seeing *Funny Face*. Today, the queerness of Sister Luke, while only latent in the narrative, may rise to the surface for those viewers who see it or wish to look for it, and I now have a different, if revisionist, understanding of my strong response to the film as a youth.

I realize I have been speculating, while also ignoring matters of race, ethnicity, nationality, age, and class that would further determine the specifics of responses to Hepburn and her films today, as those same issues must have mattered in the past, albeit with different inflections. Audrey Hepburn, after all, was a white, aristocratic, heterosexual, Anglo-European woman, and while she represented difference on-screen, that signification could only go so far. For all of the disturbances one may infer arising from her Audrey persona and her body, Hepburn and her films primarily addressed a hegemonic class of straight, middle-class, white people. And while she could and still can signify being other than the norm, this signification will always rest on her privileged position of being white. Perhaps that privileged status is what made her liminality safe for audiences in postwar America to engage with. I don't know. As I have said many times in this book, the star image of Audrey Hepburn was rife with contradictions, and when all is said and done, that is what has always fascinated me about her stardom and her films.

Notes

Chapter 2

1. The multiple reasons for the project's cancellation have been gleaned from accounts in Paris 1996: 168; Spoto 2006: 197–99; and Brizel 2009: 145–46.

Chapter 5

1. Because Cary Grant's character goes through several aliases in *Charade* and it would be confusing to keep adjusting his moniker, I will mostly refer to him as "Peter Joshua," the first name by which we know him. Likewise, for the most part I will refer to Walter Matthau's character as "Hamilton Bartholomew" even though his real name is Carson Dyle.

Works Cited

Baron, Cynthia. 1999. "Crafting Screen Performances: Acting in the Hollywood Studio Era." In Alan Lovell and Peter Krämer, eds., *Screen Acting*. London: Routledge, 31–43.

Baron, Cynthia. 2016. *Modern Acting: The Lost Chapter of American Film and Theatre*. London: Palgrave Macmillan.

Barthes, Roland. 2012. *Mythologies*. Trans. Richard Howard and Annette Lavers. New York: Hill and Wang.

Basinger, Jeanine, and Sam Wasson. 2022. *Hollywood: The Oral History*. New York: HarperCollins.

Baskette, Kirtley. 1954. "Dutch Treat." *Modern Screen*, April, 28–29, 91–94.

Battelle, Phyllis. 1954. "Audrey Hepburn Is Reported Seriously Ill with Anemia." *Morning Call*, April 7, 1, 3.

Brizel, Scott. 2009. *Audrey Hepburn International Cover Girl*. San Francisco: Chronicle Books.

Buck, Genevieve. 1989. "Givenchy, Hepburn: Well Suited." *Chicago Tribune*, September 10, Section 5: 1, 8.

Chandler, Charlotte. 2002. *Nobody's Perfect: Billy Wilder, a Personal Biography*. New York: Applause Theatre & Cinema Books.

Collins, Amy Fine. 1995. "When Hubert Met Audrey." *Vanity Fair*, December, 278–88, 292–95.

Cronin, Steve. 1955. "It Just Happened." *Modern Screen*, January, 30–31, 70–71.

de la Hoz, Cindy. 2016. *Audrey and Givenchy: A Fashion Love Affair*. Philadelphia: Running Press.

"Early Easter, Late Connery Give N.Y. a $235,000 'Robin Hood'; 'Taxi Driver' $100,000 in Three." 1976. *Variety*, March 17, 10, 18.

Ferrer, Sean Hepburn. 2003. *Audrey Hepburn: An Elegant Spirit*. New York: Atria Books.

Graham, Sheilah. 1954. "Hollywood's New Look in SEX." *Photoplay*, September, 62–65, 80.

Handyside, Fiona. 2003. "'Paris Isn't for Changing Planes; It's for Changing Your Outlook': Audrey Hepburn as European Star in 1950s France." *French Cultural Studies* 14, no. 3, 288–98.

Hepburn, Audrey. 1996. "Introduction" to Stephen M. Silverman, *Dancing on the Ceiling: Stanley Donen and His Movies*, xi–xv. New York: Alfred A. Knopf.

Johnson, Ellen. 1955. "Will Hollywood Ever See Audrey Hepburn Again?" *Modern Screen*, April, 52–55, 79–82.
Jones, Mary Worthington. 1956. "My Husband Doesn't Run Me." *Photoplay*, April, 52–53, 104–6.
Miller, Jacqui. 2014. *Fan Phenomena: Audrey Hepburn*. Chicago: Intellect Books and University of Chicago Press.
Mosley, Rachel. 2002a. *Growing Up with Audrey Hepburn*. Manchester: Manchester University Press.
Mosley, Rachel. 2002b. "Trousers and Tiaras: Audrey Hepburn, a Woman's Star." *Feminist Review* 71, 37–51.
Mosley, Rachel. 2005. "Dress, Class and Audrey Hepburn: The Significance of the Cinderella Story." In Rachel Mosely, ed., *Fashioning Film Stars*, 109–20. London: British Film Institute.
Nadel, Alan. 2018. *Demographic Angst: Cultural Narratives and American Films of the 1950s*. New Brunswick, NJ: Rutgers University Press.
Naremore, James. 1988. *Acting in the Cinema*. Berkeley: University of California Press.
Naremore, James. 2022. *Some Versions of Cary Grant*. New York: Oxford University Press.
Nolletti, Arthur, Jr. 1994. "Conversation with Fred Zinnemann." *Film Criticism*, Spring, 7–29.
Paris, Barry. 1996. *Audrey Hepburn*. New York: Berkley Books.
Parsons, Louella O. 1953. "Audrey Hepburn—Greatest Since Garbo?" *Cosmopolitan*, September, 10–11.
Pasetta, Marty. 1981. *American Film Institute Salute to Fred Astaire*. Broadcast on April 18, CBS Television.
Post Staff Report. 2010. "Audrey Hepburn 'Can't Really Act,' Emma Thompson Says: Report." *New York Post*, August 9.
Remer, Jay. 1954. "Exhibitors Name the Stars of Tomorrow." *Motion Picture Herald*, August 21, 14–15, 19–20.
Saylor, Kate. 1961. "How Does a Girl Become a Woman?" *Photoplay*, November, 68–69.
Sellers, Susan. 1995. "How Long Has This Been Going On? *Harper's Bazaar*, *Funny Face* and the Construction of the Modernist Woman." *Visible Language* 29, no. 1, 13–35.
Sikov, Ed. 1998. *On Sunset Boulevard: The Life and Times of Billy Wilder*. New York: Hyperion.
Silverman, Stephen M. 1996. *Dancing on the Ceiling: Stanley Donen and His Movies*. New York: Alfred A. Knopf.
Spoto, Donald. 2006. *Enchantment: The Life of Audrey Hepburn*. New York: Harmony Books.
Steimatsky, Noa. 2017. *The Face on Film*. New York: Oxford University Press.

Studlar, Gaylyn. 2013. *Precocious Charms: Stars Performing Girlhood in Classical Hollywood Cinema*. Berkeley: University of California Press.

Swanson, Pauline. 1954. "Knee Deep in Stardust." *Photoplay*, April, 58–59, 102–3.

Taylor, Tom. 1954. "What 'Life' Did Not Print about Audrey Hepburn." *Top Secret*, Spring, 6–8, 48.

"Ten Top Money Actresses." 1954. *Independent Film Journal*, November 27, 38–39.

"Top Dramatic Performance." 1954. *Independent Film Journal*, November 27, 45.

Wasson, Sam. 2010. *Fifth Avenue, 5 A.M.: Audrey Hepburn, Breakfast at Tiffany's, and the Dawn of the Modern Woman*. New York: HarperCollins.

Willoughby, Bob. 2008. *Remembering Audrey*. Des Moines, IA: Life Books.

Index

For the benefit of digital users, indexed terms that span two pages (e.g., 52–53) may, on occasion, appear on only one of those pages.

Always, 26, 56
Anderson, Robert, 41
Andrews, Julie, 24–25, 46–47, 49, 64–65, 89
Arkin, Alan, 52–53, 135–36, 141
Astaire, Fred, 11–12, 37–39, 73–74, 86–87, 104, 108, 190–91
"Audrey films," 11, 18–19, 58–89, 91, 125, 150–51, 172, 192–93
Audrey Hepburn's Enchanted Tales, 27
Avedon, Richard, 38–39, 109
Axelrod, George, 83–84, 86–87

Bainter, Fay 44, 173
Ballet Rambert, 21
Barthes, Roland, 6–8, 14
Beaton, Cecil, 114
Bloodline, 17, 25, 54, 55–56, 117, 141–46, 148–49, 190–91
Bogart, Humphrey, 11–12, 33–34, 39–40, 73–75, 99, 190–91
Bogdanovich, Peter, 17, 26, 55
Breakfast at Tiffany's, 3, 11, 15, 16, 17, 18, 23–24, 43–44, 58–59, 78–84, 86–88, 100–3, 111–12, 160, 173, 190–91, 192, 196–97
Brizel, Scott, 93–94, 103, 190
Brooks, Richard, 151, 158–59

Chanel, Coco, 98
Charade, 8, 10–11, 17, 24, 44–46, 56, 58–59, 73–74, 89, 93–94, 102–3, 112–13, 117, 119–34, 145, 148, 150–51, 153, 190–91
The Children's Hour, 17, 24, 43–44, 58–59, 117–18, 121–22, 151, 173–81, 190–91
Cobb, Lee J., 40–41
Colette, 21–22, 29, 76
Connery, Sean, 25, 53–54, 168–69, 171
Cooper, Gary, 4–5, 11–12, 39–40, 73–75, 76–77
Cukor, George, 5, 8–9, 17, 24, 48

de la Hoz, Cindy, 98, 100–1
Dickinson, Thorold, 30–31
Donen, Stanley, 13–14, 17, 23, 24, 25, 37–38, 45–46, 50–51, 62–63, 106–7, 115–17, 122–24, 125–26, 181, 182, 188
Dotti, Andrea, 25, 53, 141–42
Dotti, Luca, 15–16, 25, 28, 53
Dutch in Seven Lessons, 21

Edens, Roger, 37–38, 109
Edwards, Blake, 13–14, 17, 24, 43

fashion-as-transformation, 1, 91–96, 110–11, 150–51, 193, 194–95, 196
Ferrer, Mel, 17, 22, 23, 25, 34–37, 40–41, 50–52, 53, 73–74, 86–87
Ferrer, Sean, 16, 23–24, 25, 28, 44–45, 51–52, 93–94

Finney, Albert, 25, 51–52, 181–88
Fonda, Henry, 11–12, 35–36, 73–74
Frings, Kurt, 36–37, 191
Funny Face, 8, 10, 11, 16, 17, 23, 28–40, 41, 45, 58–59, 61–64, 65–67, 73, 86–87, 89, 90, 102–12, 115, 190–91, 192–93, 196

Garbo, Greta, 6–8
Gardens of the World with Audrey Hepburn, 26–27, 56
Garner, James, 75–76, 173, 174–75
Gazzara, Ben, 25, 55–56, 144, 145–46
Gershe, Leonard, 37–38, 109
Gigi (play), 21–22, 29–30, 36–37, 76, 151–52
de Givenchy, Hubert, 8, 14, 16–17, 87–88, 90–103, 106–14, 115, 116–18, 150–51, 193
Graham, Sheilah, 76, 193
Grant, Cary, 11–12, 24, 39–40, 45–46, 73–74, 113, 117, 120, 122–24, 125–29, 131–32, 145–46, 151, 153, 190–91
Green Mansions, 17, 23, 40, 120–21, 147–48, 190–91

Habets, Marie Louise ("Lou"), 23, 40, 197
Handyside, Fiona, 90
Hanson, James, 21, 22
Harper's Bazaar, 10, 76, 106–7, 110, 193
Harrison, Rex, 11–12, 46–48, 49, 64–65, 73–74
Head, Edith, 8, 93–95, 103
Hepburn, Audrey,
  actress, as, 1, 8, 12, 13–14, 15, 16–17, 33, 35–36, 40–41, 60–61, 62–63, 65, 69–70, 71–73, 74–75, 77–81, 85–86, 88–89, 91–92, 96–97, 101, 108, 115, 117–18, 126, 130–33, 139–41, 142–44, 150–52, 153–58, 159–60, 162–89, 190
  age difference of costars, 70, 73–78
  awards, nominations, and tributes, 17–18, 22, 23–24, 25, 26–27, 34, 46, 53, 87–88, 150, 193
  biography of, 2–3, 10–11, 12, 14, 20–27, 28–29, 33, 59, 194
  body of, 1, 8–12, 16–17, 48, 90–91, 93, 94–95, 96, 101–2, 188–89, 190, 193, 194, 196, 198–99
  face of, 4–8, 12, 16–17, 61, 62–63, 71–72, 74–75, 95–98, 106–7, 108, 130, 139–40, 158, 161, 163–65, 166–68, 169, 171–72, 174–75, 176, 184, 186–89, 190
  fashion, and, 11–12, 16, 18–19, 91, 102, 117–18, 193, 194, 196–97 (*see also* fashion-as-transformation)
  icon, as, 1, 8, 10, 14, 15–16, 18–19, 56–57, 90, 117–18, 195
  liminality of, 11–12, 66–68, 78–79, 91, 117–18, 125, 192, 196–97, 198–99
  movement of, 4, 92, 97–98, 101–2, 108–9, 116–18, 119–20, 150–51, 157–58, 193
  persona and star image of, 1, 5–6, 11–12, 16–17, 33–34, 70–74, 78–79, 87–88, 91, 120–22, 139, 192, 198–99
  queer reading of, 196–98
  voice of, 1–2, 3–6, 16–17, 47–48, 139–40, 142–43, 150–51, 153–54, 157–58, 171, 172, 184–86, 189, 190
Hitchcock, Alfred, 41–42, 122–24
Holden, William, 22, 24, 33–34, 44–45, 73–75, 84, 86–87, 88–89, 99, 126–27, 190–91
How to Steal a Million, 8, 17, 24–25, 49–50, 89, 113–14, 115, 151, 156–58

Huston, John, 17, 42

Jackson, Michael, 106

Kennedy, Jacqueline, 112

Lancaster, Burt, 42, 73–74
Laughter in Paradise, 21, 30
Lavender Hill Mob, 21, 30
Lehman, Ernest, 30–31
Lester Richard, 17, 25, 54, 169
Leisen, Mitchell, 152–53
"little black dress," 98–103
Love Among Thieves, 26, 56, 117, 120–21, 145–49, 190–91
Love in the Afternoon, 5, 17, 23, 39–41, 56, 58–59, 69–71, 73–75, 76–77, 99–100, 102–3, 109, 111–12, 190–91, 192–93

MacDonald, Dwight, 13–14
MacLaine, Shirley, 43–44, 76, 173, 174–80
Matthau, Walter, 132–33
Mayerling, 17, 23, 36–37
Miller, Jacqui, 91
Monroe, Marilyn, 4, 5, 8–9, 15, 31–32, 39–40, 76
Mosley, Rachel, 11–12, 90, 91, 105–6, 111, 194–95
Movie-star acting, 151–52, 190
  timing of, 152–58
  closeups of, 158
  labor of, 158–59
My Fair Lady, 4, 5, 11, 13, 14, 15, 16, 17, 24, 46–50, 53, 58–59, 64–67, 73, 86–87, 89, 114–15, 120–21, 190–91

Nadal, Alan, 76
Naremore, James, 151, 160
Nesbitt, Cathleen, 151–52

Nixon, Marnie, 4, 24, 47–49
No Bail for the Judge, 41–42
Nolletti, Arthur, Jr., 4–5, 7, 161, 168
North by Northwest, 74, 122–24
Nous irons à Monte Carlo/ Monte Carlo Baby, 21–22, 29
Nun's Story, The, 4–5, 7, 13–14, 17, 18, 23–24, 40–41, 58–59, 73–74, 117–18, 151, 160–68, 172, 190–91, 192, 197–98

Ondine (play), 17–18, 22, 34
One Wild Oat, 21, 30
O'Toole, Peter, 49–50, 156, 190–91

Paris When It Sizzles, 8, 17, 24, 44–45, 58–59, 73–74, 83–89, 111–12, 126–27, 148, 190–91
Parsons, Louella, 6
Peck, Gregory, 22, 29–30, 31–32, 73–74, 154–56, 159, 190–91
Peppard, George, 3, 75–76
Perkins, Anthony, 40–41, 75–76
The Prize, 122

Quine, Richard, 17

Radio City Music Hall, 30, 38–39, 40–41, 43–44, 46, 49–50, 51, 52–53, 84–85, 122
Rambert Marie, 2, 20, 151–52
Raphael, Frederic, 182, 188
Robin and Marian, 17, 25, 53–54, 55–56, 117–18, 151, 168–73, 190–91
Roman Holiday, 5–6, 7–9, 17, 18, 21–22, 29–30, 31–33, 34, 35–36, 56–57, 58–59, 67–69, 73–74, 92–93, 111, 151, 154–56, 158, 159, 190–91, 192–93, 195
Rooney, Mickey, 43
Ruston, James, 2, 20, 23, 26

Sabrina, 7–8, 11, 17, 18, 20, 22, 33–34, 39–40, 44–45, 58–61, 64, 65–67, 71–75, 77–78, 85–86, 89, 90, 92–99, 102–3, 111–12, 156, 190–91, 192–93, 195, 196
Secret People, 21–22, 30–31
S1m0ne, 3
Spielberg, Steven, 26, 56–57
Spoto, Donald, 1–2, 41
Steimatsky, Noa, 7–8
Stone, Peter, 45–46, 122–24
Studlar, Gaylyn, 9–10
Swanson, Pauline, 59

Tayler, Elizabeth, 8–9, 15, 191
They All Laughed, 17, 26, 55–56, 190–91
Thompson, Emma, 12, 190
Thompson, Kay, 38, 109–11
Trumbo, Dalton, 32–33
Two for the Road, 17, 25, 50–52, 53, 56–57, 89, 115, 120–21, 151, 181–89, 190–91

Unforgiven, The, 17, 23–24, 42, 58–59, 73–74, 117–18, 120–21, 190–91

van Heemstras, Ella, 2, 20, 21, 26, 34

Vidor, King, 17, 20, 35
Vogue, 9–10, 76, 106–7, 110, 193

Wagner, Robert, 56, 145–46
Wait Until Dark, 17, 18, 25, 52–53, 56–57, 89, 117–18, 120–21, 133–41, 142, 148–49, 150–51, 153–54, 190–91, 195
War and Peace, 8–9, 17, 22–23, 35–37, 39–40, 58–59, 73–74, 94–95, 117–18, 190–91
Wasson, Sam, 13–14, 79–80, 160, 163, 168, 190
Wilder, Billy, 17, 22, 23, 33–34, 39–40, 69, 74–75, 95
Wolders, Robert, 26, 55
Wyler, William, 8–9, 17, 22, 24–25, 29–30, 31–32, 43–44, 49–50, 154–55, 156, 157–58, 173, 180

Young, Roger, 26
Young, Terence, 17, 25, 52–53, 55, 141–42
Young Wive's Tale, 21

Zinnemann, Fred, 4–5, 13–14, 17, 23, 41, 160–61, 164–65, 168